FULL TEXT DATABASES

Recent Titles in
New Directions in Information Management

FULL TEXT DATABASES

CAROL TENOPIR
and
JUNG SOON RO

FOREWORD BY
STEPHEN HARTER

NEW DIRECTIONS IN INFORMATION MANAGEMENT,
NUMBER 21

GREENWOOD PRESS
New York • Westport, Connecticut • London

Library of Congress Cataloging-in-Publication Data

Tenopir, Carol.
    Full text databases / Carol Tenopir and Jung Soon Ro ; foreword by
Stephen Harter.
       p. cm—(New directions in information management, ISSN
0887-3844 ; no. 21)
    Includes bibliographical references.
    ISBN 0-313-26303-5 (lib. bdg. : alk. paper)
    1. Text processing (Computer science) 2. Data base management.
I. Ro, Jung Soon, 1950–   . II. Title. III. Series.
QA76.9.T48T46   1990
025.04—dc20   89-25683

British Library Cataloguing in Publication Data is available.

Library of Congress Catalog Card Number: 89-25683
ISBN: 0-313-26303-5
ISSN: 0887-3844

First published in 1990

Greenwood Press, 88 Post Road West, Westport, Connecticut 06881
An imprint of Greenwood Publishing Group, Inc.

Printed in the United States of America

The paper used in this book complies with the
Permanent Paper Standard issued by the National
Information Standards Organization (Z39.48–1984).

10 9 8 7 6 5 4 3 2 1

Contents

Figures and Tables

TABLES

Foreword

Whether it be a CD-ROM product or a file searchable through a commercial online search system, the full text database is the fastest growing type of publicly available database in machine-readable form. Indeed, largely because of improvements in storage technologies and rapidly dropping storage costs, the number of full text databases will soon exceed those of all other classes. How is this new product different from bibliographic and other reference databases? What special system features have been specifically developed for full text searching? What kinds of strategies are required for success in achieving different search goals? What future developments in system software, such as ranking algorithms, seem warranted? Some might say that full text databases make controlled vocabulary fields obsolete. Is this claim wildly extravagant or cautiously justified?

The authors of this book bring a wealth of practical experience and knowledge as well as an impressive body of research findings to bear on these and related questions. Carol Tenopir and Jung Soon Ro are well qualified to write this book. Tenopir has built an enviable reputation for herself as an expert in online information retrieval, and both authors' doctoral dissertations treated research problems related to full text searching.

The principal thrust of this book is on the findings of research. Most of the studies analyzed were conducted on large databases loaded on operational systems, and often resulted in suggestions for improving searching technique, database production, or system design. The last chapters of the book focus on such recommendations.

Tenopir and Ro have created a much-needed work on full text searching that is at once a state-of-the-art summary of current technology and commercial offerings, a comprehensive review and synthesis of research findings, and a set of practical recommendations for searchers, database producers, and designers of future systems. I am most pleased to have the opportunity to introduce it.

Stephen Harter, Associate Professor
School of Library and Information Science
Indiana University

1

Introduction to Full Text Databases

This book has two purposes: (1) it provides a state-of-the-art look at commercially available full text databases, and (2) it reviews research pertaining to the use and retrieval characteristics of full text. The scope is limited to those full text databases that are available for searching via publicly searchable online information retrieval systems such as BRS, DIALOG, LEXIS, NEXIS, and WESTLAW. (Such online systems may also be referred to as online vendors or online services.) The databases themselves are created by a database producer or a publisher, but only rarely are the online vendors responsible for the intellectual content of the sources they make available. The online vendors simply make the databases searchable on their host computer with the system's interactive retrieval program. Users connect to the host system via telecommunications lines (see Figure 1–1).

CD-ROM (compact disc–read only memory) databases, on the other hand, are purchased or leased for use on a local microcomputer, eliminating the need for a telecommunications link. Compact discs are a high density optical-digital storage medium that allows textual databases of up to 600 million characters or so to be housed and searched locally. CD-ROM products are not featured in this book, but neither are they excluded from our discussion. Many of the products discussed are available in both online and CD-ROM forms, and much of the research is applicable to either.

Even though much of the book is devoted to reporting research projects, the outcome of this research is practical. The discussion of research projects in Chapters 4 to 7 culminates in the advice in Chapters 8 and 9 to help

Figure 1–1
The Online Information Process

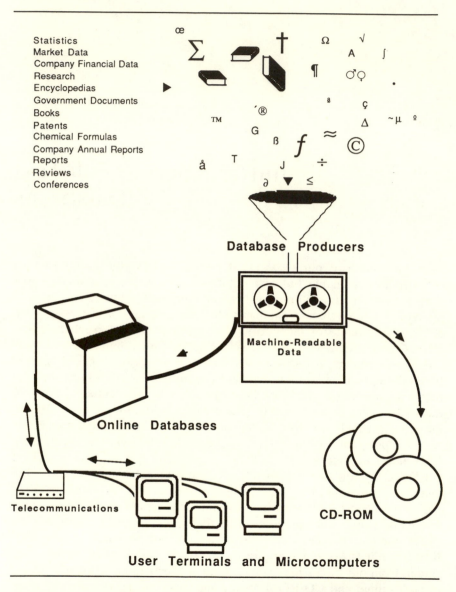

Statistics
Market Data
Company Financial Data
Research
Encyclopedias
Government Documents
Books
Patents
Chemical Formulas
Company Annual Reports
Reports
Reviews
Conferences

Database Producers

Machine-Readable Data

Online Databases

Telecommunications

CD-ROM

User Terminals and Microcomputers

searchers develop better full text search strategies, suggestions to help database producers design better full text products, and information to help online or CD-ROM vendors make system enhancements that facilitate full text searching.

FULL TEXT DEFINED

Our working definition of full text databases follows closely the definition used in the Cuadra/Elsevier *Directory of Online Databases*.[1] Full text databases "contain records of the complete text of an item, e.g., a newspaper article, a specification, a court decision, or a newsletter." They are one type of "source databases: those that contain complete data or the full text of the original source information."[2] Referral sources such as directories are specifically excluded from the definition of full text, as are numeric or textual/numeric sources such as statistical reference books or handbooks of chemical or physical properties. Also excluded are secondary textual publications (bibliographic databases), the traditional type of textual database used online for over twenty years by professional online searchers. Bibliographic and referral databases are called "reference databases" in the Cuadra/Elsevier directory, or those that "refer or point users to another source . . . for additional details or for the complete text."[3]

The full text databases of today have evolved from electronic production of printed books or periodicals, much as the bibliographic databases of the past two decades evolved from electronic production of printed indexing and abstracting publications as shown in Figure 1–1. Nowadays most publishers are producing their primary documents with computer typesetting techniques, ironically making computer-readable texts available as a by-product of more efficient publication techniques for the printed product.[4] Other full text databases are created by converting printed texts into machine-readable form, either through keyboard entry of the text or through scanning texts with optical character recognition scanners that convert printed text into computer characters.

However they are put into machine-readable form, as we enter the 1990s, we are still at what F. Wilfred Lancaster calls the first stage in the evolution of electronic publishing; that is "electronic technology is used either to produce conventional print on paper or to generate new electronic publications that virtually simulate print on paper (i.e., electronic technology is used to display an information source but has little effect on the way information is organized and presented)."[5] Second-stage electronic publications are those designed specifically for electronic distribution and that exploit the full capabilities of an electronic medium. Only at this second stage is there a fundamental change in the way information is packaged and presented.[6] Some of these are now beginning to be developed, but the two stages will likely coexist for at least the next decade. Much of the innovative second-stage development is taking place at the local level, especially with CD-ROM or other optical storage technologies.

Most of the full text databases described in this book are of the first stage. Most have a corresponding print product that is the driving force of the publication's design, but the electronic equivalents are not even exact duplicates of their printed counterparts. With the technology to date usually only the text portions of primary materials are included in the database version. Soon more graphic material will be included with the words in full text databases, but for now, especially in online versions, the complete *textual* portions, not the complete document, are available. Photographs, charts, most tables, maps, and the like typically are excluded. Captions, footnotes, and simple tables may be included, at the discretion of the database producer. Figure 1–2 shows an article from *Sunset* magazine as it is available online in the DIALOG information retrieval service version of the Magazine ASAP database.[7] If you check the library for the print version of this same article, you will find a map of the island of Oahu with beaches marked, several color photographs of smiling people on the beach, and a variety of type sizes and typefaces.

The aesthetic difference between print versions and online versions is, of course, more important for some materials than others. It is also dependent on hardware, which is improving all the time. Aesthetically inferior electronic texts are not a permanent situation as better monitors, printers, storage devices, scanners, and other technologies are beginning to change the way databases look. The research reported in this book was mostly conducted on operational online systems that provide full texts much like that displayed in Figure 1–2. A detailed discussion of physical layout, products under development, and impacts of aesthetic concerns is beyond the scope of this book.

TYPES OF FULL TEXT

Scanning a list of full text databases is like browsing through the catalog of a large library or bookstore, with all the variety of subject matter, writing style, intended audience, length, and structure. Full text databases available on large commercial search systems range from reference books of 500 or more pages to newswire news summaries to articles from popular magazines. It is, therefore, useful to categorize this variety of databases by major characteristics and subjects. The following categories are not always mutually exclusive, but they provide a helpful way of refining the overgeneralized concept "full text database." The intended audience, potential uses, and effective search strategies for each type might be expected to be different.

Categories of full text databases are listed below.[8] Examples of sample databases and online systems that provide access to them are given for each type. Further information on many of these is given in Chapter 2.

Statutes, court decisions, and other primary legal documents. Intended audience is most often legal experts. Materials are decisions from U.S. federal and tax courts, laws and legislation from every state in the United

Figure 1–2
Full Text Database Version of an Article from Sunset Magazine

---

04696686 DIALOG File 647: MAGAZINE ASAP   * Use Format 9 for FULL TEXT*
Oahu's other beaches. (Hawaii)
Sunset Magazine   v178 p72(6) March, 1987
SOURCE FILE: MI File 47
CODEN: SNSTA
illustration; photograph; map
AVAILABILITY: FULL TEXT Online LINE COUNT: 00170
GEOGRAPHIC LOCATION: Hawaii
CAPTIONS: 20 favorite beaches all around Oahu.
DESCRIPTORS: Beaches--Hawaii; Oahu--bathing beaches; Hawaii--description

---

    Oahu's other beaches

    Hawaii means the beach, and for many visitors, "the beach' isstill the
1 3/4-mile crescent of gleaming sand called Waikiki. With good reason:
Waikiki has great places to swim, it's safe, and it's within a Frisbee toss
of Oahu's biggest hotels.

    But within an hour's drive of Waikiki are more than 130
otherbeaches,
each with its own attractions. How do you decide which one to head for?
    There are wave-battered volcanic headlands, sweeps of whitesand that
stretch around distant points, intimate coves secluded behind lacy ironwood
trees. You can find reefs for tidepooling, lagoons for snorkeling, or
sheltered bays for safe ocean swimming. There are beaches where you can
learn to ride a surfboard, maneuver a sailboard, or take a wave on a body
board or on your own belly. Other beaches are just right for shoreline
walking or quiet shorefront picnicking.

    That's not really too surprising when you consider the numbers.Of
Oahu's 60 designated beach parks, 19 have lifeguards, and all but one of
the guarded parks are fully developed with picnic areas, rest rooms,
showers, and drinking water.

    But even in this beach abundance, there are problems. RalphGoto shakes
his head. "Many of our facilities are aging, and we have vandalism in some
picnic areas. At a few parks, there are thefts--mostly from cars while
people are on the beach.'

    In spite of the problems, Goto is quick to point out that Oahustill
has the best-developed and most varied system of beach parks and water
safety programs in the state. And on Oahu, you can enjoy the water just
about any time: when conditions on one side of the island are marginal,
it's likely that they're fine on another.

    How do you find the best beaches, the safest places for newadventures?

Figure 1–2 continued

We polled the experts--lifeguards and ocean recreation specialists--for recommendations on the safest places for swimming, snorkeling, windsurfing, tidepooling, and the various forms of board and body surfing. Their comments are summarized and keyed to the map of our favorite beaches above.

But before you can make a choice, you need to understand howOahu's weather works and what beach conditions result.

Weather and a four-sided island: are the trades blowing?

While the island of Oahu may not be square, it does have fourdistinct beach exposures. The northeast trade winds are a major influence. But combinations of weather, topography, ocean swells, winds, and tides determine beach conditions in specific areas. And a lot depends on the season.

In winter (October into April), storm systems to the northwestgenerate big swells that roll into the north and west shores. They crest as breakers, some up to 30 feet high, colliding against the coast with a fury at once glorious and frightening. While these months are no time for a dip up north, southern shores can be at their best.

In other months, the trade winds are steadier, resulting in alarger break on south shore beaches. Although this surf isn't nearly as imposing as winter's, it has its own dangers.

After ocean swells, trade winds are the single most importantfactor shaping water conditions. They blow most of the time, from east-northeast, usually at 10 to 20 miles per hour. Kona conditions--when the trades aren't blowing--range from calm to southerly storms, creating unpredictable seas everywhere.

Ocean conditions are broadcast daily by most radio stations.Along with playing Hawaiian music, KCCN (1420 AM) reports wind direction and speed, times of high and low tides, and surf conditions around the island about 20 minutes before the hour from 5 to 10 A.M. and from 2 to 7 P.M. Or call the National Weather Service's recorded forecast: (808) 836-0121.

When you go to the beach, leave valuables at your hotel. Neverleave purses or wallets in your car or unattended on the sand. Try to park where your car can be seen from the beach. Remember that alcoholic beverages are not permitted in public parks. And don't feel guilty about sleeping in: rush-hour traffic in Honolulu is a bumper-to-bumper crawl, all too familiar to big-city commuters. Set out after 9 in the morning, and avoid returning between 4 and 6.

North Shore: lion in winter, lamb in summer

Stretching from Kaena Point northeastward to Kahuku Point,the North Shore is Oahu's most changeable coast. In winter, it can be a maelstrom of pounding surf and ripping currents; beaches wash away, highways can be closed by the storms.

Mid-May into September, however, this coast can offer some ofthe

Figure 1–2 continued

island's best family beachgoing.

From Honolulu, the most direct route is via Interstate H2 andState Highway 99 to the old sugar town of Haleiwa. Haleiwa is the spiritual home of "shave ice'--paper cones mounded with shaved, not crushed, ice that's drenched with a flavored syrup-- a treat that has revived more than one sun-crisped surfer.

The North Shore is Oahu's surfing haven, and two beachparks--Haleiwa Alii (see map) and Haleiwa--are good places for beginning surfers and body-boarders. Surf 'N Sea (637-9887) rents boards ($18 per day) and can arrange 2-hour lessons for $35, including board. Hawaii Surf and Sail (637-5373) rents furfboards ($10 per day). Both shops also rent body boards ($13 and $8 per day) and sailboards ($40 and $25 per day). Snorkeling gear is $9.50 per day at Surf 'N Sea only.

Another good North Shore spot for surfing lessons is the smallcove in front of the Turtle Bay Hilton near Kahuku Point. Group lessons (293-8811; call ahead) cost $22 per hour, including use of a board. Aquaventures, the hotel dive shop, can arrange guided skin-diving excursions.

Windward Shore: cloudy (even rainy), spectacular

Round the shoulder of Kahuku Point and the shoreline begins tochange dramatically. The rugged eastern face of the Koolau Range pushes right to the shore in places, climbing abruptly 1/2 mile above the road. These steep, serrated cliffs hold the low clouds, blown ashore by trade winds, that condense as rainfall over the lush tropical forests below.

Windward Oahu can be divided into two parts. The northernportion, from Kahuku Point to Kualoa Point, gets our vote for Oahu's most spectacular coast. Rain forest pushes right down to the beach along this thinly populated strand, creating cool, shady parks ideal for leisurely picnicking--although mosquitoes can be annoying at times. Gather picnic basics in Honolulu, but stop at a roadside stand for home-grown papaya, fat "apple' bananas, juicy pineapples, and crisp mountain apples.

Farther from the mountains, the stretch of coast from KailuaBay to Makapuu Point is more dependably sunny. Kailua, roughly a half-hour's drive from Honolulu over the Pali Highway (State 61), draws windsurfers from around the world because of its large sheltered bay, reliable onshore winds, and sandy bottom and shore. It's one of the best places anywhere to learn the sport.

Three outfits in Kailua offer lessons and rentals. WindsurfingHawaii (261-3539) will get you started with a 2-hour introductory lesson, including board, for $25; rentals are $15 for a half-day, $20 from 9 to 5. Wave-skis cost $15 per day. Others are Naish Hawaii (261-6067; also rents body boards) and Kailua Sailboard Company (262-2555).

Rent surfboards ($15 per day; lessons can be arranged), bodyboards ($12), and adult-size snorkeling gear ($5) at Straight Up surf shop (261-7873).
Onshore winds may blow in more than just rain along this shore.Most

Figure 1–2 continued

worrisome are occasional invasions of the Portuguese man-of-war, whose
sting can cause allergic reactions in some individuals. The worst times are
December through February, mid-April, and the end of August. If you see
purple jellyfishlike bodies washed up on the sand, find another beach.

Waianae Coast: undiscovered, sunny

Sheltered from all but the strongest trades by the WaianaeMountains,
the western edge of the island from Kaena Point south to Barbers Point is
Oahu's desert coast. When the rest of the island is socked in with heavy
clouds, this is the one place you're likely to find sun. Local advice:
bring your own shade. While winter surf here approaches North Shore
conditions and storms occasionally shut down the beaches, summer swells can
also come in from the south, creating treacherous rip currents that make
the surf break close to or on the shore.

Unlike the other three coasts, which can be sampled in a varietyof
day-loop drives, the Waianae Coast is a dead-end trip: the dirt track
around Kaena Point is impassable. From Waikiki, it's about 45 minutes to
Makaha; rent snorkeling gear and body boards in Honolulu. Most weekends,
picnickers will find a huli huli chicken stand on the south edge of
Nanakuli, but the slowbarbecued, marinated birds sell out early.

Until a recent police crackdown, cars parked at these uncrowdedbeach
parks were being broken into on a daily basis. Last summer, the number of
reported thefts was down to about one a month. Still, out here it's best
to park at populated or lifeguarded beaches and to leave--when the guards
do--by 5 P.M.

South Shore: urban, usually good, always crowded

With long white crescents of reef-protected beaches and
dramaticheadlands of tortured lava, South Shore beaches have only one
problem: a chronic lack of parking. One reason is that these beaches are so
near the sprawling neighborhoods of Honolulu. They also happen to be some
of the best on the island.

Under almost any weather conditions, the central Honolulubeaches--Ala
Moana and Waikiki--are going to be among the island's safest bets. The rest
of the coast can be trickier. In summer, swells can generate rip currents
along the southern shore, a condition even experienced beachgoers might
misjudge.
The most potentially treacherous stretch is the 6 1/2 miles fromKoko
Head to Makapuu Point. Here, summer swells crash right into the lava
headlands. This stretch can offer great walking on calm days at low tide,
but when swells are big, waves often break right over the trail. Nearby
Sandy Beach is favored by experienced local bodysurfers who know when (and
how) to turn into a wave. But in summer it gets a wicked shore break that
has pounded many a beginner head-first into the sand. Sandy has the
island's highest rate of serious beach injuries.

Before you go: useful and entertaining reading

Two particularly useful books can expand your beach savvy.The Beaches

Figure 1–2 continued

of Oahu, by John C. Clark (University of Hawaii Press, Honolulu, 1977; $5.95), is the authoritative guide to every beach on the island. Tips on water safety, with a light look at beach etiquette, are wrapped up with maps of the island's most popular beaches in A Guide to Beach Survival, by Ken Buise and Rell Bunn (send $3.95 to Honolulu Water Safety Consultants, Box 1211, Haleiwa, Hawaii 96712).

Free copies of the recently revised Oahu Ocean RecreationGuide, an informative map, are available from the Department of Parks and Recreation, 650 S. King St., Honolulu 96813. For a free 1987 schedule of occean sports events, write to Box 661, Kailua 96734.

Photo: Waimea Bay Lined up on lava rock, jumpers contemplate 30-foot plunge into crystal waters. Swimming and snorkeling are great in summer; winter surf's too big

Photo: Kahana Bay Grassy border of beach-front park makesfine year-round lunch stop. Pick up picnic supplies, local fruit, straw beach mats at shops on road from Honolulu

Photo: Sunset Beach Monster winter surf (inset) dies down bysummer, lapping gently against a graceful arc of sand that leads strollers toward the palm-fringed tip of Sunset Point

Photo: Paddle, catch wave, stand: learn to surf at Waikiki and North Shore beaches "Oahu's beach parks may be one of the best-kept secrets in the Islands,' claims Ralph Goto, director of water safety for the City and County of Honolulu. "Sure, some places are well known--Sunset Beach for surfing, Sandy Beach for bodysurfing --but they're really only for experts. Many of the beaches where inexperienced ocean swimmers can most safely learn water sports are places visitors don't hear about.'
Photo: Windsurfing: novices hoist masts,grab arching booms, and quarter into the wind across Kailua Bay

Photo: Reef-watching: a mask with snorkeland a pair of fins are all you need. At Hanauma Bay, fish rush toward snorkelers for a handout of frozen peas

Photo: Wave-skiing: the latest import from Australia, wave-skis can be paddled in the surf or, as here at Kailua, along quit shoeines
Phoo ufng: in re cini at Halia Ai,beginners learn basic stance on moderate-size plastic or foam boards

States, and various legal materials from many other countries. Length and characteristics of the documents vary widely, but certain key elements are particularly important. These include such things as name of the judge, names of the defendants, the case name and number, cases cited as precedent, date, court, location, and other particulars. The major systems in the United States that provide these materials are LEXIS and WESTLAW.

Other government documents, patents, regulations, and other official publications. Intended audience varies; patents are often accessed by experienced patent searchers. Each publication has its own characteristics, varying from the short requests for proposals in *Commerce Business Daily* to detailed regulations in the *Code of Federal Regulations.* Some cover many different topics; others are more narrowly focused. Important information elements include issuing agency, date, patent or contract numbers, type of document, and subject. LEXIS has patents; NEXIS offers many U.S. documents such as the *Code of Federal Regulations* and the *Federal Register.* DIALOG has *Commerce Business Daily.*

News releases and other unpublished information. Intended for subject experts, other business people, or journalists. Most cover one narrow topic, and the length is rarely more than two pages. Press releases are issued by a government agency or company to announce new products or give new information. They usually include name and phone number of a contact person. Unpublished reports may also be summaries of new developments or information about an organization. Important access points include date, issuing company, contact person, and subjects. These are most often part of another database and are available on systems such as DIALOG, NEXIS, and CompuServe.

Newspapers. Intended audiences include people of all ages who are interested in current events. Frequent users include news professionals and reference librarians. Newspaper databases include articles, columns, and other selected features on a variety of topics. Length varies from several paragraphs to long feature stories. Many of the news stories are written in the "top-down" style, with important information at the beginning (who, what, when, where, and how). Most newspaper databases do not include everything found in the printed equivalent. Typical exclusions include such things as advertisements, classified listings, weather forecasts, sports scores, syndicated columns like "Dear Abby," and stories taken from wire services (see next category below). Major national and international papers such as *Wall Street Journal, Pravda*, and *New York Times* are available, as are local dailies or weeklies such as the *Fresno Bee, Allentown Morning Call*, and others. Major suppliers of newspaper databases are NEXIS, VU/TEXT, DIALOG, Dow Jones News/Retrieval, and InfoGlobe search service.

Newswire services. Intended audiences are the same as those of newspapers. Newswire service stories vary in length, but are often concise summaries of major news events. Timeliness is critical, and they are often updated frequently. Slightly different versions of the same story may therefore occur several times in the same database. Backfiles may not be kept online for long. Even more than other newspaper stories they group important information at the beginning and share a certain consistency of style. Many major newswires from all over the world are available online, including Associated Press, United Press International, Reuters, Tass, and Kyodo English Language News. Major online systems for newswires include DIALOG, NEXIS, NEWSNET, Dow Jones News/Retrieval, and CompuServe.

Newsletters. Intended audiences are subject experts or information professionals, usually within a corporate environment. Each newsletter has its own style and language, and a database may consist of a single newsletter or many. They are subject-specific, often highly technical or of interest only within the target industry. Information may be very time-sensitive. Important access points include date, newsletter title, and subject. Hundreds of newsletters are available online, from many different industries. The two major vendors for newsletters are NEXIS and NEWSNET.

Reference books. Intended audiences range from school children to researchers, depending on the book. There is much variety in terms of style, length, audience level, and useful access points. Many are used primarily for fact retrieval and most are highly structured into short, fairly consistent sections. Encyclopedias are the most widely available type of reference book. Footnotes are important access points in encyclopedias in addition to subjects. Other reference books online range from highly technical standard works such as Kirk-Othmer Encyclopedia of Chemical Technology and the Merck Index, to Internal Revenue Service tax information, to the Bible. Vendors with reference books online include BRS, DIALOG, NEXIS, STN International, Data-Star, Dow Jones News/Retrieval, and others.

Scholarly or technical journals. Primary audience is subject specialists, usually researchers. Most articles are lengthy with many footnotes. Sentences and paragraphs may be long, and language is technical. Printed versions include many tables, figures, and equations which may or may not be in the database version. Abstracts may precede the article. Usually only the major articles are included in the online version. Letters to the editor, book reviews, news stories, and columns from the printed versions may not be in the online version. Subject access is most important, but journal name, authors, cited authors, and dates are useful as well. Many of the journals from the American Chemical Society are online, as are major medical journals such as the *New England Journal of Medicine, Lancet,* and the *British Medical Journal.* STN International, BRS, and DIALOG are major vendors that provide journals.

Nonspecialist or general interest magazines. Most of these are for the

Table 1–1
Online Databases by Type

TYPE OF DATABASE	% OF TOTAL 1980	% OF TOTAL 1989
Bibliographic	38%	27%
Referral	10	15
Numeric, Textual/ Numeric or Properties	47	24
Full Text	5	34

1980 figures as tabulated by Fran Spigai and Peter Sommer, *Guide to Electronic Publishing*. White Plains, N.Y.: Knowledge Industry Publications, Inc., 1982, p. 7.

1989 figures calculated from a random sample of 435 titles from the January 1989 edition of the *Directory of Online Databases*. New York: Cuadra/Elsevier, 1989.

general reader. They are especially useful for students or laypeople for personal or school-related information. The writing style, subjects, and length of articles varies tremendously, but most do not include technical language, footnotes, or abstracts. The printed versions contain many photographs, charts, sidebars, and other graphics, most of which are not included online, though captions may be. By far the most important access point is subject, but magazine title and date are useful as well. Several hundred magazines are available, either as stand-alone titles or within a multititle database such as Magazine ASAP or McGraw-Hill Publications Online. The range of titles includes *Forbes, Time, Newsweek, Science, Sports Illustrated, Popular Photography, Psychology Today, Atlantic, Changing Times, Byte*, and many others. Vendors that provide access to magazines include BRS, DIALOG, and NEXIS.

HOW MANY FULL TEXT DATABASES?

Full text databases are the fastest growing segment of the textual database market. Although they do not yet equal referral or bibliographic databases in numbers, if current trends continue, full text databases will one day soon be the predominant textual form online. In the 1980 edition of the *Directory of Online Databases*, full text databases made up 5 percent of all databases, with bibliographic at 38 percent and referral at 10 percent.[9] (The remaining 47 percent were numeric, textual-numeric, or properties.) By January 1989 full text had grown to an estimated 34 percent of the 4,062 total databases or 44 percent of the textual databases listed in the Cuadra/Elsevier directory.[10] (See Table 1–1). Full text has shown a steady

Figure 1–3
Increase in Full Text in the 1980s

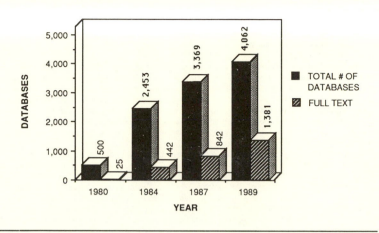

Estimates calculated from random samples of databases in the respective issues
of the Directory of Online Databases. New York: Cuadra/Elsevier.

Source: *Directory of Online Databases,* January 1989. Copyright 1989 by Elsevier Sience
Publishing Co., Inc. Reprinted by permission of the publisher.

and dramatic increase in percentage of the whole and in actual numbers
in the decade of the 1980s as illustrated in Figure 1–3.

The categories in this directory are not mutually exclusive; some databases are categorized by more than one type. To derive the figures shown
in Table 1–1 and Figure 1–3, a database was counted as full text if it had
any full text included, even if the directory indicated it also had bibliographic, numeric, or referral information. A growing trend is to mix types
of information within a database, especially for those databases that do
not correspond exactly to one printed source. Sample records from the
Cuadra/Elsevier database shown in Figure 1–4 illustrate the problem of
assigning type of database categories. The mixing of database types is a
trend that is likely to continue as users look to a database for all types of
information on a topic and as database producers strive to create new
products for the online environment.

The estimate that 34 percent of all databases are full text in whole or in
part means that in absolute numbers as of January 1989 there were over
1,400 full text databases searchable on one or more of several hundred
major online systems. It is difficult to know exactly what a number like
1,400 means, because there is so much variety in how full text databases
are counted. Some, such as *Harvard Business Review* online, the *Academic*

Figure 1–4
Sample Database Entries from the Cuadra/Elsevier *Directory of Online Databases,* **January 1989**

Washington Press Text®
Type: Source (Full Text)
Subject: Government-U.S. Federal
Producer: PressText News Service
Online Service: DIALOG Information Services, Inc. (File 145)
Content: Contains full text of official White House and U.S. Department of State news and policy information documents. Presidential documents cover speeches and statements, news conferences and interviews, broadcasts, messages and letters to Congress, executive orders and proclamations, signed and vetoed legislation, nominations and appointments, state dinner toasts, and arrival and departure remarks of diplomats. State Department documents cover speeches and statements by Department personnel, news conferences and interviews, congressional testimony, appointments, actions on treaties, and arrival and departure remarks of diplomats.
Also includes lists of foreign diplomats in Washington, U.S. diplomats oversees, and foreign consular offices in the U.S., as well as profiles of 170 foreign countries, covering demographics, economy, government, foreign relations, and history. Sources include the White House Office of the Press Secretary and the U.S. Department of State Offices of Press Relations and Public Communication.
Corresponds in part to *Weekly Compilation of Presidential Documents and Public Papers of the Presidents: Ronald Reagan* (for presidential material); *State Department Bulletin, Current Policy,* and "gist" policy summaries (for State Department material); *Key Officers of Foreign Service Posts, Guide for Business Representatives, Washington Diplomatic List,* and *Foreign Consular Offices of the U.S.* (for directory material); and *Background Notes* (for country profiles).
Language: English
Coverage: Primarily U.S., with some international coverage
Time Span: 1981 to date
Updating: About 25 records a day; news items available within 24 hours of release.

WESTLAW® TAX DATA BASE
Type: Reference (bibliographic); Source (Full Text)
Subject: Legal & Regulatory-U.S. Federal; Taxes-U.S.
Producer: West Publishing Company
Online Service: West Publishing Company
Conditions: Subscription to West Publishing Company required
Content: Contains full text of the Internal Revenue Code; full text and headnotes of federal tax cases from the Supreme Court since 1754, the Courts of Appeals since 1891, the Court of Claims since 1932, the Claims Court since 1982, and the District courts since 1789; U.S. Tax court Reported Opinions since 1942; U.S. Tax Court Memorandum decisions since 1954; board of Tax Appeals opinions from 1924 to 1942; U.S. Code Title 26 and Code of Federal Regulations Title 26; Tax Reform Act of 1986, including legislative history and related documents; relevant sections of the Federal Register; Federal Tax Rules; international acts since 1954 containing relevant conventions or agreements entered into between the U.S. and other countries; federal tax administrative materials, including revenue rulings, revenue procedures delegation orders, executive orders, and Treasury Department orders since 1954; General Counsel memoranda since 1967; Internal Revenue Service (IRS) written determinations, including private letter rulings and National Office Technical Advice Memoranda since 1954, Actions on Decisions since 1967, IRS Technical Memoranda since July 1967; IRS Taxpayer Information Publications used for the preparation of federal tax returns; IRS Manual; IRS News Releases; and selected law review articles.
Language: English
Coverage: U.S.
Time Span: Varies by source (see Content)
Updating: Varies, from daily to quarterly

Figure 1–4 continued

CHICAGO TRIBUNE
Type: Source (Full Text)
Subject: News-U.S.
Producer: Chicago Tribune Company
Online Service: DIALOG Information Services, Inc. (File 632). VU/TEXT Information Services. Inc.
Conditions: Subscription to VU/TEXT required
Content: Contains full text of news items and feature articles from the Chicago Tribune (Illinois) newspaper. Regional coverage emphasizes local government and agriculture, energy, financial services, manufacturing, and transportation industries.
Language: English
Coverage: U.S. (primarily Chicago. Illinois area)
Time Span: VU/TEXT. 1985 to date. DIALOG. 1988 to date.
Updating: Daily; items appear within 24 hours of publication

TRADE AND INDUSTRY ASAP®
Type: Reference (Bibliographic). Source (Full Text)
Subject: Business & Industry
Producer: Information Access Co. (IAC)
Online Service: BRS (TSAP). BRS/COLLEAGUE (TSAP). DIALOG Information Services. Inc. (File 648). Mead Data Central Inc. (as a NEXIS database)
Conditions: Subscription to Mead Data Central required
Content: Contains citations, with the full text, to articles from more than 125 business and trade periodicals indexed in TRADE AND INDUSTRY INDEX (see). Also contains press releases from PR NEWSWIRE (see) and Kyodo News International. Inc.
NOTE. On Mead Data Central will not duplicate full-text records already contained in NEXIS (e.g. press releases from PR NEWSWIRE)
Language: English
Coverage: International
Time Span: 1983 to date
Updating: About 8000 records a month

Reproduced with permission.

Source: *Directory of Online Databases*, January 1989. Copyright 1989 by Elsevier Sience Publishing Co., Inc. Reprinted by permission of the publisher.

American Electronic Encyclopedia, or the *Wall Street Journal* online include information from a single source. Others, such as Magazine ASAP, McGraw-Hill Publications Online, or ACS Chemical Journals put together articles from dozens or hundreds of printed sources into one full text database. Several aimed at the home computer user (such as Kaypro Knews and PComm) include a mixture of full texts of magazine articles, unpublished information, directory information for software and hardware, and computer programs.

Is the NEXIS search system *one* full text database because all of its hundreds of sources can be searched simultaneously as the "Omni" file, or is it a collection of hundreds of individual databases because each can be searched separately at the searcher's discretion? Does all of the legislation for the state of California make up one database, or is it a part of a larger U.S. states legislation database?

Perhaps a more meaningful figure would be the number of source materials that are available online in complete text form. That number is not readily available, and is difficult to derive for some categories of text such as monographs, news releases, and laws or legislation. For other materials it is difficult because of the trend to mix full text, bibliographic, and other types of information in a single database.

The Cuadra/Elsevier directory includes books in full text and mixed-type full text databases, as well as the more common periodicals online. In the sample of 435 titles from the January 1989 directory, 148 were full text in whole or in part. Of this 148, seven, or 5 percent were monographs (nondirectory type). Full text databases counted as "other," including legislation, press releases, unpublished materials with no print equivalent, or a mixture made up approximately 27 percent (39 titles) of the sample full text offerings.

Periodicals are the most common type of full text databases (68 percent of the sample), but they are tricky to count because the treatment online varies. The first issue of *Fulltext Sources Online* imposes some consistency by listing magazines, journals, newspapers, newsletters, and newswires individually by title whether they are included in a multititle full text database or are available separately.[11] (Some sources are available both ways, depending on which online vendors make the periodical available. *Fulltext Sources Online* will always list them individually.) Law journals are included, but legal citations, opinions, cases, and codes are not.

Almost 1,700 sources are listed in the 1989 edition of *Fulltext Sources Online*. These are available on sixteen different online systems, names of which are shown in Table 1–2. Many databases are available on more than one system. Chapters 2 and 3 include information about many of the vendors listed in Table 1–2 and their major full text offerings.

The first databases offered on CD-ROM were mostly bibliographic databases with print equivalents, just as early online databases were online equivalents of major printed indexing/abstracting publications. By 1988, the *Optical Publishing Directory* listed 35 (18 percent of the total) full text databases available on CD-ROM.[12] Table 1–3 shows the breakdown by type of all 200 databases in the Directory.

Some of these databases have both print and online equivalents, such as *Kirk-Othmer Encyclopedia of Chemical Technology* and the *Wall Street Journal*. In these cases, CD-ROM is just another convenient distribution medium that has no fundamental impact on the products it carries. Others, such as Microsoft Bookshelf, are combination products that exploit the special advantages of CD-ROM distribution. Bookshelf combines many reference books that each have separate print equivalents (such as the *American Heritage Dictionary, Roget's Thesaurus, Bartlett's Familiar Quotations*, the *Zip Code Directory*, and others) and links it with a user's word processing functions to provide a complete writing reference tool. Still others are beginning to get beyond unaesthetic text. A group of international publishers of scientific journals has put together the trial system called Adonis, which combines ASCII bibliographic information with

Table 1–2
Full Text Vendors Covered in *Fulltext Sources Online*, Winter 1989

BRS Information Technologies (United States)	Mead Data Centeral (LEXIS and NEXIS) (United States)
Data-Star (United Kingdom)	NewsNet (United States)
Datatimes (United States)	PROFILE (United Kingdom)
DIALOG (United States)	STN International (United States, Japan, West Germany)
Dow Jones News/Retrieval (United States)	VU/Text (United States)
Financial Post Information Service (Canada)	WESTLAW (West Publishing Company) (United States)
G-CAM Serveur (now SINORG) (France)	
Infoglobe (Canada)	
Infomart Online (Canada)	

Ruth M. Orenstein, ed., *Fulltext Sources Online: For Periodicals, Newspapers, Newsletters & Newswires*. Needham Heights, Mass.: BiblioData, 1989.

scanned complete texts of articles from over 200 of their journals. All graphics including photographs are included, and articles printed from the Adonis disc have the typefaces, format, and all aesthetic appeal of the originals. In 1989 a CD-ROM version of Compton's Encyclopedia was introduced. It includes text, graphics, and sound in the first widely available multimedia full text publication.

Table 1–4 lists the titles of all the CD-ROM full text databases that were identified for the 1988 edition of the *Optical Publishing Directory*. Only those products that could be purchased as of mid–1988 are included; products in prototype or under development were specifically excluded. Since CD-ROM was still relatively new in 1988 the number of new titles is expected to increase rapidly. By 1989 there were over 500 titles, with over 700 expected by mid–1990. More innovations in full text databases are under development and will be appearing soon in the marketplace.

Table 1–3
CD-ROM Databases by Type

TYPE	NUMBER	%
Reference	55	28%
Bibliographic	54	28
Bibliographic with abstracts	25	13
Full Text	35	18
Statistical, numeric	18	9
Images, supplementary data	7	4
Music and sound effects	2	1
TOTAL	196	*

Compiled from Richard A. Bowers, ed. *Optical Publishing Directory*, 1988, 3rd ed. (Medford, N.J.: Learned Information, Inc., 1988).

* Total is greater than 100% because of rounding.

ORGANIZATION OF THIS BOOK

The major online systems that offer full text and their full text databases are described in more detail in Chapter 2. Chapter 3 provides an overview of the search and display features on the major online systems that are particularly suited to full text searching. Chapters 4, 5, 6, and 7 turn to research results. Chapter 4 introduces and provides an overview of the types of full text research that have been done. The next three chapters describe in detail the methodology and findings of some full text research projects that the authors have undertaken.

We mentioned earlier that the results of the research described in this book were in a large part practical. Chapters 8 and 9 bring together the practical aspects of the research described in the preceding chapters and offer useful advice for searchers, database producers, and online system developers. The information is of immediate use for searching today's full text databases, but also offers ideas for improvements in the near future.

Finally Chapter 10 focuses on the future of full text research. Many areas where further research is needed were identified in the earlier research studies. These areas are summarized and ideas for future research are given in Chapter 10. Additional ideas for research can be found in many of the articles included in the extensive bibliography at the end of the book. The bibliography includes articles specifically about full text databases, but also

Table 1–4
Full Text Databases on CD-ROM, 1988

Bible Library
Bookshelf
Compact Library: AIDS
CCINFOdisc
Construction Criteria Base
Daily Oklahoma
Decision Series: Northwest
Diocles Juridisc
Electronic Encyclopedia
Enflex Info
Federal Procurement Disc
First National Item Bank and Test Development System
Harrap's Multilingual Dictionary
International Dictionary of Medicine and Biology
International Encyclopedia of Education
Italian Tax Law Database
Kirk-Othmer Encyclopedia of Chemical Technology
LaserROM
Luther Bible
McGraw-Hill CD-ROM Science & Technology Reference Set
Merriam Webster Ninth New Collegiate Dictionary
MSDS
Oncodisc
OPTEXT Issue No. 101, 102 and 103
PDQ (Physicians' Data Query) CD-ROM
Personnet
Pravda on Disc
Science Helper k-8
Small Business Consultant
State Education Encyclopedia
Texas Attorney General Documents
TLG Databank of Ancient Greek Texts
Wall Street Journal

As categorized by Richard A. Bowers, ed. *Optical Publishing Directory,1988*, 3rd ed. (Medford, N.J.: Learned Information Inc., 1988).

citations to research studies that used methodology particularly appropriate to full text research.

NOTES

1. *Directory of Online Databases* 10, No. 1 (January 1989) (New York: Cuadra/ Elsevier, 1989).

2. Ibid., p. viii.

3. Ibid., p. vii.

4. Seldon W. Terrant, "Computers in Publishing," *Annual Review of Information Science and Technology* 15 (1980): 191–219.

5. F. Wilfred Lancaster, "Electronic Publishing: Its Impact on the Distribution of Information," *National Forum* (Summer 1983): 3.

6. Ibid., pp. 3–5. See also F. Wilfred Lancaster, *Libraries and Librarians in an Age of Electronics* (Arlington, Va.: Information Resources Press, 1982).

7. Magazine ASAP is produced by Information Access Company, which holds the copyright to the electronic version. *Sunset* magazine is copyrighted by Lane Publishing, Menlo Park, California.

8. Carol Tenopir, "Users and Uses of Full Text Databases," *Proceedings of the International Online Meeting, London, December 1988* (Oxford: Learned Information, Ltd., 1988), pp. 263–270.

9. As tabulated by Fran Spigai and Peter Sommer, *Guide to Electronic Publishing* (White Plains, N.Y.: Knowledge Industry Publications, Inc., 1982), p. 7.

10. Based on a random sample of 435 titles from the January 1989 edition of the *Directory of Online Databases* (New York: Cuadra/Elsevier).

11. Ruth M. Orenstein, ed., *Fulltext Sources Online: For Periodicals, Newspapers, Newsletters & Newswires* (Needham Heights, Mass.: BiblioData, Winter 1989).

12. Richard A. Bowers, ed., *Optical Publishing Directory, 1988*, 3rd ed. (Medford, N.J.: Learned Information, Inc., 1988).

Figure 2–1
Growth in Databases and Online Systems

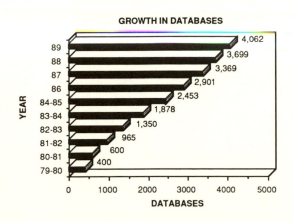

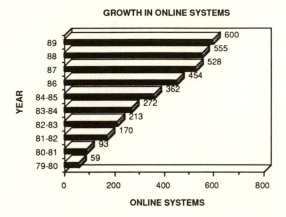

Figures from Cuadra/Elsevier <u>Directory of Online Databases</u>, January 1989.

Source: *Directory of Online Databases,* January 1989. Copyright 1989 by Elsevier Science
Publishing Co., Inc. Reprinted by permission of the publisher.

ONLINE SYSTEMS

DIALOG Information Service Inc.

DIALOG is used by more libraries than any other online system and is
an established part of many intermediary search services in all types of
libraries. It is likely to continue to be because of its variety of database

2

Online Systems and Full Text
Databases

The growth in the number of databases mentioned in Chapter 1 has been paralleled by the growth in the number of online systems that make these databases searchable. The Cuadra/Elsevier *Directory of Online Databases* shows an almost tenfold increase in online systems during the 1980s, as illustrated in Figure 2–1.[1] Many of these online systems offer full text databases. Some of the systems specialize in full text, while others include full text along with bibliographic or other databases. Some are used worldwide, others primarily in their host country. Some are used heavily by the library/information center market; others are not so well known to librarians.

As discussed in Chapter 1 and shown in Table 1–2, *Fulltext Sources Online* lists fifteen online systems that have substantial full text offerings and that are widely used by the library and information center market.[2] Of these fifteen, five are among the most heavily used online systems in the information center/library market in the United States: BRS Information Technologies, DIALOG, Mead Data Central's LEXIS and NEXIS, STN International, and WESTLAW. The use data shown in Figure 2–2 comes from *Information Market Indicators* and is derived from a sample of libraries and information centers in the United States.[3] Most of this chapter discusses these five systems with descriptions of some of the most popular full text database offerings on each. The other ten systems covered in *Fulltext Sources Online* are discussed briefly. Although many of the systems are available through gateway systems in addition to direct access and many of these systems provide gateway services to other online systems, gateway access is not included in this discussion. Chapter 3 covers search features available on the systems; this chapter concentrates on description of the systems and selected databases.

Figure 2–2
Uses and Revenues for Online Systems in the Library and Information Center Marketplace

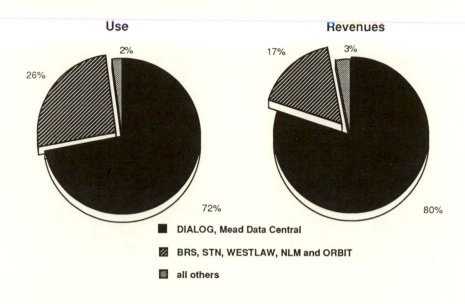

Use

Revenues

2%
26%
72%

17% 3%
80%

■ DIALOG, Mead Data Central

▨ BRS, STN, WESTLAW, NLM and ORBIT

▨ all others

Figures supplied by Martha E. Williams, Information Market Indicators.

offerings, availability around the world, and widespread use in instructional programs for future intermediary searchers. In two recent studies of online instruction in graduate schools of library and information science, all schools that responded indicated that they taught their students to use DIALOG.[4]

DIALOG first became commercially available in 1972, after development in the late 1960s by Lockheed Missiles and Space Company under contract with the National Aeronautics and Space Administration.[5] The first databases on DIALOG were bibliographic (e.g., ERIC, Chemical Abstracts, BIOSIS, NTIS, Computerized Engineering Index, Agricola, and so on), and the first users were intermediaries. DIALOG continued to market primarily to libraries, especially academic and special libraries, until the early 1980s when the proliferation of microcomputers expanded the potential user base for online systems. In 1988 Lockheed sold DIALOG to Knight-Ridder, which also owns the VU/TEXT full text online system.

By the beginning of the 1990s DIALOG has grown to over 300 databases, including full text, directory, and numeric in addition to bibliographic. The 1989 DIALOG database catalog shows 290 separate databases with bib-

Table 2–1
DIALOG Databases by Type, January 1988

TYPE	NUMBER	%
Full Text	54	18.6%
Bibliographic	164	57.0
Directory*	68	23.4
Numeric only**	4	1.0
TOTAL	290	100.0%

*If a database was listed by DIALOG as a bibliographic and a full text database or as a bibliographic and a directory database, it was counted as full text or as directory, not as a bibliographic database.
**If a database was listed by DIALOG as a numeric database and also under any of the other three categories, it was counted under the other type, not as a numeric database.

liographic still the most common, but 18.6 percent (54 databases) are full text in whole or in part (see Table 2–1). Roger Summit, president of DIALOG, said at a 1988 press conference at the Online '88 meeting in New York that the company is planning to continue to expand the number of databases on DIALOG and has targeted full text particularly for growth.

The 54 full text databases in DIALOG's 1989 catalog include a variety of subjects and types of text. There are no legal statutes in DIALOG, but all other major categories of full text are represented. Categories with example databases are: (1) government publications (e.g., *Commerce Business Daily, Cendata, IRS Taxinfo*), (2) news releases (e.g., Businesswire, Washington Presstext), (3) research reports (e.g., Arthur D. Little Online, Investext), (4) newspapers (e.g., *Chicago Tribune, Washington Post* Online, *Financial Times* Fulltext), (5) newswire services (e.g., AP News, UPI News, Reuters, PR Newswire, Japan Economic Newswire Plus), (6) newsletters (e.g., PTS Newsletter Database, Online Chronicle), (7) reference books (e.g., *Academic American Encyclopedia, Everyman's Encyclopedia, Bible*, Drug Information Fulltext, *Facts-on-File*, Kirk-Othmer Online), (8) scholarly or technical journals (e.g., Business Dateline, Computer ASAP,

Harvard Business Review, McGraw-Hill Publications Online), (9) magazines (e.g., *Consumer Reports*, Trade & Industry ASAP, Magazine ASAP), and (10) DIALOG documentation (e.g., Chronolog Newsletter, DIALOG Bluesheets).

Subjects vary from business, to medical, to interdisciplinary. Many of DIALOG's full text databases are business-related, with many newswires and newspaper databases as well. Some databases cover a single source publication (e.g., *Harvard Business Review*); others mix many different sources (e.g., Trade and Industry ASAP). Together over 600 full text publications are available online on DIALOG. These are published by a wide variety of print source publishers or database publishers; DIALOG itself does not create any databases.

Mead Data Central LEXIS and NEXIS

In the late 1960s Data Corporation in Dayton, Ohio, began working with the Ohio State Bar Association to develop a legal information retrieval system for Ohio law.[6] The new system, called OBAR, contained texts of Ohio law but was relatively primitive in search capabilities by today's standards. In 1969 Data Corporation became a part of The Mead Corporation, a large paper and forest products company, and Mead Data Central was born. (The parent company still produces paper at the same time that it is one of the top providers of electronic information!)

Mead improved and expanded the OBAR system, and the LEXIS service first became commercially available in 1973. It included at first only Ohio and New York codes and cases, the United States Code, and selected federal cases. Now, more than fifteen years later, LEXIS generates more revenues than almost any other online textual system in the world. It includes the full texts of laws for all federal courts and all fifty states plus many specialized state and federal legal libraries such as tax laws, patent laws, insurance laws, congressional voting records, and Securities and Exchange Commission (SEC) filings. Laws from France, the United Kingdom, Australia, New Zealand, Ireland, and other countries are online in LEXIS as well. A total of over 11 million statutes, judges' opinions, and agency decisions are available through LEXIS.

Although most of the full text on LEXIS falls into the category of legal statutes, the database also includes some other government publications such as the *Federal Register* and many legal journals. In its specialized medical libraries (MEDIS) LEXIS includes other types of information, such as: (1) full texts of many medical journals (e.g., *Cancer, JAMA, Annals of Internal Medicine*), (2) textbooks and other medical reference books (e.g., *Current Emergency Diagnosis and Treatment, Handbook on Injectable Drugs, Drug Information Fulltext, Accreditation Manual for Hos-*

pitals), and (3) newsletters (e.g., all *F-D-C Reports Newsletters, American Health Consultants Newsletters*).

The NEXIS service was started in 1979 to complement LEXIS. NEXIS offers full text of news information in a broad sense, including magazines, journals, newspapers, and newswires. LEXIS subscribers also have access to NEXIS, but NEXIS can be accessed alone for a lower monthly fee in those organizations that do not also want the legal resources.

NEXIS provides access to thousands of sources, each of which can be searched separately on the system. In addition, users can group sources together as they wish or select a pregrouped file that puts together materials related by date, type of material, or form. NEXIS files include: (1) news-papers (e.g., *Crain's Chicago Business, Christian Science Monitor, New York Times, Women's Wear Daily*), (2) magazines (e.g., *People, American Libraries, Money, Saturday Evening Post, Sports Illustrated*), (3) journals (e.g., *ABA Banking Journal, Chemical Engineering, Journal of Small Business Management*), (4) newsletters (e.g., *Platt's Oilgram News and Price Report, Daily Report to Executives, Social Security Bulletin*), (5) newswires (e.g., Reuters, UPI, AP), and (6) a few reference books (e.g., *Almanac of American Politics, Who's Who in Television & Cable*). LEXIS and NEXIS together provide access to over 40 million documents. Table 2–2 shows the major categories of databases available on LEXIS and NEXIS.

WESTLAW

WESTLAW is the computer-assisted legal research service of West Publishing Company, the well-known Minnesota-based publisher of printed legal materials. For over 100 years West Publishing has been an important name in legal research; its WESTLAW division is the new kid on their block, since it has been available "only" since 1975.[7]

When WESTLAW first became available, it was not a full text system but consisted entirely of the West Headnotes (summaries and citations to cases). To stay competitive with LEXIS, WESTLAW began to build full text databases in December 1976. The system was completely redesigned in the late 1970s and early 1980s, including enhancements to databases, reprogramming of software, and improvements to hardware. Now WEST-LAW is directly competitive with LEXIS and includes the full text of federal case law, federal statutes and regulations, administrative law, and special topics such as taxation, insurance, immigration, and others. Case law, administrative law, and other laws are available for all fifty states, as are statutes, public utilities reports, and attorney generals' opinions.

WESTLAW is not limited to laws, statutes, and regulations. Also included are (1) newsletters (e.g., *Tax Notes Today, Westlaw Today*, many Bureau of National Affairs (BNA) newsletters), (2) a small but mixed

Table 2–2
Categories of LEXIS/NEXIS Databases

THE LEXIS SERVICE

    General Legal Libraries
    Specialized Legal Libraries
    Specialized Medical Libraries (MEDIS libraries)
    United Kingdom and Commonwealth Legal Libraries
    French Legal Libraries (in French)
    Complementary Research Tools (e.g., Shepard's Citations Service)

THE NEXIS SERVICE

    NEXIS Library (magazines, newspapers, etc.)
    The Information Bank Library
    Advertising and Public Relations Library
    U.S. Patent and Trademark Office Library
    Computers and Communications Library
    Government and Political News Library

SPECIAL SERVICES

    The LEXIS Financial Information Service, Company Library
    The LEXIS Country Information Service, Country Analysis Reports
        Library and International News Library
    The Associated Press Political Service
    The National Automated Accounting Research System

---

variety collection of reference books (e.g., *Directory of Online Databases*, *McGraw-Hill Encyclopedia of Science and Technology*, *Black's Law Dictionary*), and (3) over 200 law reviews and bar journals (some include only selected coverage, while others include all articles published in the journal). Table 2–3 shows the major categories of information found on Westlaw.

The unique contribution of WESTLAW to the highly competitive area of full text legal systems is its mixed role as both a vendor and a creator of information. The databases on Westlaw are a combination of full texts with intellectual analysis of the text.[8] West's manuscript department and editorial staff add value to the full text of the decisions on WESTLAW just as they do to their printed products. Online this system is called "Full-Text Plus." Material added to texts includes synopses, headnotes, correc-

Table 2–3
Categories of WESTLAW Databases

General Materials: State and Federal

Specialized Materials (e.g., <u>Billcast</u>, <u>Directory of Online</u>
<u>Databases</u>, <u>Index to Legal Periodicals</u>)

Antitrust

Communication

Energy and Utilities

Environmental Law

Financial Services

Government Contracts

International Law

Labor

Securities

Taxation

Bureau of National Affairs: Highlights, Individual, and Tax

Calendar and Legislation Databases

---

tions to original opinions (with the agreement of the judges writing the opinions), parallel citations and textual updates, and digest topic and Key Number information.

Synopses are narrative summaries of each case written by a West lawyer-editor. Headnotes are brief summaries of each point of law in an opinion and the numerical citations to statutes that have been interpreted in a case. The Key Number System is a classification system that arranges points of law by main topics and subtopics under seven main categories and thirty-two subheadings.

BRS Information Technologies

Like DIALOG, BRS is a supermarket system that includes databases on all subjects and of different types. It grew out of the State University of New York's (SUNY) Biomedical Communication Network (BCN) in the 1970s to provide inexpensive access to Medline and a few other widely used bibliographic databases.[9] BCN used a modified version of the IBM STAIRS software package. In 1977, when BCN funds were threatened, the founders of BCN started BRS as a commercial database service. BRS

Table 2–4
BRS Databases by Type

TYPE	NUMBER	%
Full Text	34	24.6%
Bibliographic/other	94	68.1
Directory	10	7.3
TOTAL	138	100.0%

originally stood for Bibliographic Retrieval Services, reflecting its early reliance on bibliographic databases. The original and biggest market for BRS was libraries, especially high-volume users such as large academic libraries. BRS was the first of the supermarket systems to offer a subscription plan that provides substantial connect hour discounts for high-volume use.

BRS was also the first of the supermarket systems to make a commitment to full text databases and to the end user market. Beginning in the early 1980s, BRS began adding many full text databases, initially in the field of medicine. They saw this as a natural addition to services that would be used in the home or office by the end user who might not have ready access to a library collection.

In 1980 BRS was purchased from its original owners and became part of Thyssen-Bornemisza's Information Technology Group. In 1989 Macmillan Inc. acquired BRS. Macmillan is owned by Robert Maxwell, who also owns Pergamon InfoLine and Orbit search services. Since April 1, 1989, BRS has been one branch of Maxwell Online (the other online branch is Pergamon-Orbit Search Service).

By the early 1990s there are nearly 150 databases available on BRS. The 1989 catalog shows that 34 of the 138 databases listed (approximately 24.6 percent) are full text. As can be seen in Table 2–4, the rest are either directory or bibliographic. BRS is targeting full text as a special area of growth and holds seminars and provides course materials devoted to full text searching on BRS.

The thirty-four full text databases listed in the 1989 BRS catalog include sources in business, science/technology, and multidisciplinary topics, but there is special strength in medical topics. Eighteen of the BRS full text offerings are targeted to the medical community. Many of the nonmedical databases are also available on DIALOG and NEXIS. BRS includes different types of materials, with the strongest coverage in magazines, jour-

Table 2–5
STN International Databases by Type

TYPE	NUMBER	%
Full Text	10	14.3%
Bibliographic	49	70.0
Directory, Properties or Structures	11	15.7
	—	——
TOTAL	70	100.0%

nals, and reference tools. Legal materials and government publications are not included.

Sample BRS full text offerings include: (1) reference books (e.g., *Academic American Encyclopedia*, *Comprehensive Core Medical Library* [CCML] *Medical Books*, *Kirk-Othmer Encyclopedia of Chemical Technology*), (2) journals (e.g., CCML journals, *New England Journal of Medicine*, *Harvard Business Review*, AIDS articles from CCML), and (3) magazines (e.g., Magazine ASAP III, Trade & Industry ASAP III).

STN International

STN is an international information network that provides worldwide access to scientific and technical information. Formed in the mid–1980s, it is operated by three nonprofit organizations: in North America by Chemical Abstracts Service (CAS), a division of the American Chemical Society; in Europe by FIZ Karlsruhe; and in Japan by the Japan Information Center of Science and Technology (JICST). In the United States it enhanced the offerings of the relatively new CAS Online, an online system formed especially to provide access to the databases created by *Chemical Abstracts*.

The CAS Online files (bibliographic and registry) are still the premier offerings on STN International, but the system also has some full text, other bibliographic, and directory files. The approximately seventy databases all relate to science or technology, with an emphasis on chemistry, chemicals, and chemical engineering. Some of the databases are in German.

Table 2–5 shows that STN International has a mixture of bibliographic, properties or structures, directory, and full text databases. A majority (approximately 83 percent) fall into the former three categories, and approximately 17 percent are full text.

The full text offerings are strongest in scholarly journals, but a few other types are available. Full text on STN includes: (1) unpublished materials (e.g., Conferences database that includes press releases, calls for papers, and so on for scientific conferences; several databases that describe, in German, ongoing research projects), (2) reference books (e.g., Beilstein, several books of physical properties including *National Bureau of Standards Tables of Chemical Thermodynamic Properties* and the *Design Institute for Physical Property Data Compilation*), (3) scholarly journals (e.g., Chemical Journals of the American Chemical Society, Chemical Journals of the Association of Official Analytical Chemists, Chemical Journals of the Royal Society of Chemistry, and Chemistry Journals of John Wiley & Sons, Inc.)

Other Systems

The other ten systems covered in *Fulltext Sources Online* are from the United States (4), Canada (3), the United Kingdom (2), and France (1). They are discussed briefly below grouped by country of origin. Many of these systems are not used frequently or so widely as the five systems above, others (notably Dow Jones News/Retrieval) are highly successful and widely used systems that target a slightly different audience than the library and information center marketplace surveyed in the Williams study quoted above.

Dow Jones News/Retrieval (DJN/R) is marketed primarily to the end user, both at home and within the corporate environment. It is widely used in business and corporate libraries as well. Within the corporate market-place it is one of the major and longest used online systems. Its creators claim to serve 82 percent of the 500 largest industrial corporations in the United States and 85 of the leading banks.

The system began in 1974 when Dow Jones & Company of Princeton, N.J., a well-known business publisher, began providing online access to its business information in *The Wall Street Journal*, *Barron's*, and its Dow Jones News Service. Later it added stock quotes and financial databases to DJN/R. There are now approximately fifty databases, some created by Dow Jones and some merely marketed by them.

Most of the databases on DJN/R are business-related. A few general interest databases such as Cineman Movie Reviews, the *Academic American Encyclopedia*, and Peterson's College Selection Service cater to the home end user. A majority of the databases are full text, with some directory and numeric. Full text includes newspapers (notably *Wall Street Journal* and the *Washington Post*), newswires (Japanese and U.S.), business newsletters, and selected articles from over 150 national and regional business magazines and journals.

DataTimes is available via Dow Jones News/Retrieval or from the DataTimes company in Oklahoma City. It specializes in full text for the corporate end user and contains regional, national, and international sources. Included are the full text of articles from over thirty regional newspapers, several national newspapers (e.g., *USA Today* and the *Washington Post*), wire services, approximately fifteen business or computer magazines, journals, or newsletters; and several newspapers from Australia. Also available from DataTimes are gateways to Infomart Online, Profile Information, and Dow Jones News/Retrieval.

The NEWSNET system of Pennsylvania specializes in newswires and newsletters for the business and industry marketplace. It includes the full text of over 300 newsletters that span a wide range of topics and industries. Almost every profession and type of business will find its industry newsletters in NEWSNET's collection, including such diverse sources as: *Military Space*, *Daily Petro Futures*, *Student Aid News*, American Banker Fulltext, *Television Digest*, Catholic News Service, *Satellite News*, *Tax Notes Today*, and *Middle East Business Intelligence*. Over 70 percent of these sources are not available elsewhere online.

Newswires on NEWSNET include American sources such as PR Newswire, AP and UPI plus Jiji from Japan, Xinhua from China, and Reuters from Europe. Newsnet also includes stock and commodity quotes, TRW Business profiles, and the *Official Airlines Guide*.

VU/TEXT is a Knight-Ridder Company headquartered in Philadelphia. It is exclusively full text, specializing in regional newspapers. Over forty regional newspapers are available, including well-known titles such as the *Los Angeles Times, Boston Globe*, and *Chicago Tribune* as well as lesser-known small-city papers like the *Ft. Lauderdale News*, *Fresno Bee*, *Akron Beacon Journal*, and *Allentown Morning Call*.

In addition to newspapers, VU/TEXT provides access to Business Dateline with 150 regional business publications, some wire services such as AP and PR Newswire, and the Wall Street Transcript. Since VU/TEXT and DIALOG are both owned by Knight-Ridder, cooperative arrangements are being made between the two systems.

Infomart Online of Canada specializes in regional Canadian newspapers, Canadian newswires, and other Canadian business full text sources. Newspapers covered include *The Gazette* of Montreal, the *Ottawa Citizen*, *Toronto Star*, *Vancouver Sun*, and the *Windsor Star*. Newswires include the Business Information Wire and Canadian Press Wire. Other sources access press releases and other unpublished information from Canadian corporations (Canada Newswire), financial forecasts (*Financial Times of Canada*), and the U.S.-Canada Free Trade Agreement. *Maclean's*, Canada's weekly news magazine, is also accessible on Infomart.

FP Online is the online product group of the Financial Post Information Service of Toronto, Canada. Most of the sources directly available on FP Online are produced by the *Financial Post*, not just sold by it. Although the sources on FP Online are few in number, like many of the online systems, they actively market gateway access to additional services.

FP Online is marketed primarily to the Canadian corporate customer and includes three main directories: of Canadian industrial companies; of mining, petroleum, and energy companies; and of directors of Canada's top companies. Also available are the Financial Post Electronic Edition and *Maclean's* magazine.

Info Globe is the online service of the Toronto–based *Globe and Mail.* It includes about a dozen databases, which are a mix of bibliographic, numeric, directory, and full text. Like Dow Jones News/Retrieval in the United States it provides full text information produced by the online provider, and it includes stock market quotes.

The premiere full text source on Info Globe is the newspaper the company publishes. The Globe and Mail Online corresponds to the *Globe and Mail* newspaper and is updated daily. It has been online since 1977. Another notable full text database on Info Globe is the Key Government Documents Database, which includes French and English language versions of all Canadian federal government news releases, legislation, motions, speeches, and appointments to key government posts.

PROFILE information of England specializes in wire services, newspapers, newsletters, and magazines produced in the United Kingdom. It includes some international full text sources as well. Newswires include the AP European output, TASS, and the Asahi News Service. Newspapers are all British including the *Telegraph* (daily and Sunday), the *Guardian*, and the *Times* and *Sunday Times*. Several newsletter series from the Financial Times are included as are several trade weeklies aimed at the business market. Magazines include *Media Week*, *Business Week* (U.S.), and *Campaign*.

PROFILE has several interesting full text databases that provide news summaries. The BBC Summary of World Broadcasts, Keesing's Record of World Events, McCarthy Online: Press Cuttings Service, and Mintel Daily Digest all attempt to summarize the world's news events and business news for the busy executive. The target audience for such services is end users in the corporate environment.

Data-Star, a service of Radio-Suisse, is located in Bern, Switzerland, but the service is available worldwide, with marketing offices in the United States (Wayne, Pennsylvania), London, Paris, Frankfurt, Tokyo, and Gothenburg. It is a popular service in Europe and is growing in popularity worldwide. Data-Star includes over 200 databases on many different topics, with specializations in business, biomedical, chemical, and technical subjects. Many of these offerings are the same sources available on the major U.S. systems, including such popular bibliographic databases as BIOSIS, Chemical Abstracts, Excerpta Medica, Compendex, Predicasts, and others.

As of 1989 there were seventeen full text databases available on Data-Star. These include reference books (*Kirk-Othmer Encyclopedia* and *Ac-*

ademic American Encyclopedia), newsletters (*F-D-C Reports* and *Predicasts Newsletters*), journals and magazines (*Harvard Business Review* online and *American Banker*), government reports (Diogenes includes Food and Drug Administration documents), and research reports or previously unpublished information (*ICC Stockbroker Research, Investext*, and Diogenes).

SINORG (formerly G-CAM Serveur) of Paris is primarily a French-language online service that specializes in providing access to the literature produced in France or in French on all topics. It includes mostly bibliographic databases, but has some full text offerings also, notably the Agora database family. Agora is made up of five files that together provide the full text of all daily or weekly newswire stories produced by the Agence France Presse. Stories in English and French cover such areas as economic news, international and French news events, sports news, and background on events and personalities in the news.

SELECTED DATABASES

It would be folly to begin to describe all full text databases available on the fifteen systems described above, or even one or two databases from each in any meaningful detail. Instead, in this section, we describe as examples several full text databases that are referred to in later chapters of this book. Described here are those databases that have been studied in detail in the various research projects related in Chapters 4 to 8. This descriptive information will help you understand the research projects better and give a feel for the structure and arrangement of full text databases. The databases represent a mixture of subjects and types and are available on several different online systems.

Harvard Business Review/Online

Harvard Business Review/Online (HBR/O) is available on BRS, Data-Star, DIALOG, and NEXIS (among others). It was one of the first full text journal databases available on the first three primarily bibliographic systems listed above and was the database used in the studies reported in Chapters 5 and 6. The printed equivalent is published by the Graduate School of Business Administration at Harvard University, but the online version is distributed by John Wiley & Sons, Electronic Publishing Division.

The HBR/O database contains the full texts of all articles published in the *Harvard Business Review* from 1976 to the present. *Harvard Business Review* is issued six times a year with approximately ten to fifteen full-length articles of 4,000–8,000 words each per issue. The online version excludes all letters to the editor and begin including book reviews with the

November/December 1982 issue. Some early classic articles are also included in the online file. The BRS and DIALOG versions also have bibliographic citations without full text for articles from 1971–1975.

Each of the full text records corresponds exactly to the word portions of the printed journal. All text, captions to graphics, and references are included, but the graphics themselves are not online. Figure 2–3 reproduces a sample record of HBR/O as it appears in BRS. The information in the records is a combination of descriptive information needed to identify the article and value-added information to aid retrieval. Fields can be described in five groups: (1) bibliographic description, (2) abstract, (3) extracted information, (4) descriptors, and (5) full text.

Bibliographic description information includes title, author (including subjects of interviews), author's affiliation, source (containing month, year, and beginning page of the article in the print copy), series title, accession number, ISSN, and translation information. It is used to identify the printed equivalent, for citation purposes, or to order a print copy.

The abstract field contains an informative abstract of approximately 100–250 words. The abstracts are written by one of four manuscript editors who are instructed not to add any evaluation or interpretation. The abstracts are fully searchable in all the online systems.

Extracted information is a series of controlled fields to assist consistent retrieval of information even if it is inconsistently used by authors in texts. All company names, organization names, products and services, geographic areas, or industry categories mentioned in the text of an article are extracted from the text, checked against controlled vocabulary lists to be put into a standard form by the HBR/O staff, and placed in special fields for searching. In addition, graphic material is described in a controlled way. HBR maintains controlled lists for all these fields as part of a total of eight controlled vocabularies. In addition to the controlled fields, the HBR/O user manual includes personal names and cited references as extracted information fields, although they undergo no translation to controlled form. Each is given its own field tag and is fully searchable.

In addition to the six controlled vocabularies for extracted information, there are two subject descriptor vocabularies. Corporate Functions and Subject and Management Terms are both used to index major subjects in each article. The vocabularies were created in 1980 by a consulting firm hired by HBR when automation began. The firm started with the limited broad terms that had been used in the past at HBR and added more specific standard business terms and terms encountered in the indexing of a backlog of several hundred articles. One person now does all of the indexing and maintenance of the vocabulary.

For articles appearing since 1976 the full text is available in the online file exactly as it appears in the printed journal (but without any graphics). Grammatical paragraphs and sentences are maintained as they are in print.

Figure 2–3
Sample HBR/O Record from BRS

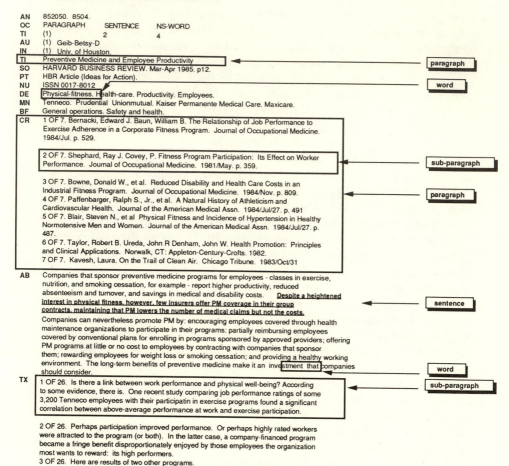

AN	852050. 8504.		
OC	PARAGRAPH	SENTENCE	NS-WORD
TI	(1)	2	4
AU	(1) Geib-Betsy-D		
IN	(1) Univ. of Houston.		
TI	Preventive Medicine and Employee Productivity		
SO	HARVARD BUSINESS REVIEW. Mar-Apr 1985. p12.		
PT	HBR Article (Ideas for Action).		
NU	ISSN 0017-8012		
DE	Physical-fitness. Health-care. Productivity. Employees.		
MN	Tenneco. Prudential Unionmutual. Kaiser Permanente Medical Care. Maxicare.		
BF	General operations. Safety and health.		
CR	1 OF 7. Bernacki, Edward J. Baun, William B. The Relationship of Job Performance to Exercise Adherence in a Corporate Fitness Program. Journal of Occupational Medicine. 1984/Jul. p. 529.		
	2 OF 7. Shephard, Ray J. Covey, P. Fitness Program Participation: Its Effect on Worker Performance. Journal of Occupational Medicine. 1981/May. p. 359.		
	3 OF 7. Bowne, Donald W., et al. Reduced Disability and Health Care Costs in an Industrial Fitness Program. Journal of Occupational Medicine. 1984/Nov. p. 809.		
	4 OF 7. Paffenbarger, Ralph S., Jr., et al. A Natural History of Athleticism and Cardiovascular Health. Journal of the American Medical Assn. 1984/Jul/27. p. 491		
	5 OF 7. Blair, Steven N., et al Physical Fitness and Incidence of Hypertension in Healthy Normotensive Men and Women. Journal of the American Medical Assn. 1984/Jul/27. p. 487.		
	6 OF 7. Taylor, Robert B. Ureda, John R Denham, John W. Health Promotion: Principles and Clinical Applications. Norwalk, CT: Appleton-Century-Crofts. 1982.		
	7 OF 7. Kavesh, Laura. On the Trail of Clean Air. Chicago Tribune. 1983/Oct/31		
AB	Companies that sponsor preventive medicine programs for employees - classes in exercise, nutrition, and smoking cessation, for example - report higher productivity, reduced absenteeism and turnover, and savings in medical and disability costs. **Despite a heightened interest in physical fitness, however, few insurers offer PM coverage in their group contracts, maintaining that PM lowers the number of medical claims but not the costs.** Companies can nevertheless promote PM by: encouraging employees covered through health maintenance organizations to participate in their programs: partially reimbursing employees covered by conventional plans for enrolling in programs sponsored by approved providers; offering PM programs at little or no cost to employees by contracting with companies that sponsor them; rewarding employees for weight loss or smoking cessation; and providing a healthy working environment. The long-term benefits of preventive medicine make it an investment that companies should consider.		
TX	1 OF 26. Is there a link between work performance and physical well-being? According to some evidence, there is. One recent study comparing job performance ratings of some 3,200 Tenneco employees with their participatin in exercise programs found a significant correlation between above-average performance at work and exercise participation.		
	2 OF 26. Perhaps participation improved performance. Or perhaps highly rated workers were attracted to the program (or both). In the latter case, a company-financed program became a fringe benefit disproportionately enjoyed by those employees the organization most wants to reward: its high performers.		
	3 OF 26. Here are results of two other programs.		

Labels (right margin): paragraph · word · sub-paragraph · paragraph · sentence · word · sub-paragraph

Figure 2–3 continued

---

4 OF 26. A Canadian insurance company that furnished a work site with exercise facilities reported an absenteeism rate 22% below normal for the six-month measurement period after the start of the experiment.

5 OF 26. Prudential Insurance Company launched a similar exercise program in Houston and found that disability absence days declined 20%. The company estimated that it saved $1.93 in medical and disability costs for every $1 invested.

6 OF 26. Much evidence shows that physical fitness makes people healthier--and so, by inference, more reliable and productive employees. Of two studies released last year, for example, one identified high blood pressure as the best predictor of coronary attack, with inadequate exercise the strongest predictor on a community basis; while the other found that the less physical fit are 1 1/2 times as likely as the physically fit to suffer from high blood pressure.

7 OF 26. Programs for smoking cessation, better nutrition, and exercise can dramatically reduce deaths from cancer and heart disease, especially among the middle-aged. Researchers report that obese smokers triple the risk of heart attack in comparison with slim nonsmokers, and the combined probabilities of cancer and heart disease reduce smokers' life expectancy more than seven years.

8 OF 26. And what do such programs do for organizations? They reduce both turnover from early death or disability and absenteeism. Smokers, for example, miss work 33% to 45% more often than nonsmokers, according to government statistics derived from academic studies.

9 OF 26. SECTION HEADING: Insurers' position. Although ubiquitous joggers on the sidewalks and rows of health food items in the supermarkets testify to a heightened interest in physical fitness, most corporations do little to promote or underwrite it. Apathy on the part of some managers and employees is no doubt one reason.

10 OF 26. In view of the mounting cost of insurance claims, however, it is curious that few insurers offer coverage of preventive medicine (PM) programs. Group insurance generally pays for treatment after a diagnosis turns up a health problem. To shed light on insurers' reasons for not offering more PM coverage in their group contracts, I surveyed all U.S. health insurance carriers. I received responses from 263 companies, just over half of those contacted.

11 OF 26. Some PM producers are covered by insurance but only under certain conditions in most cases. For example, programs of monitored exercise are legitimate claims for 40% of all carriers. But almost all policies contain two provisos: first, some illness must have already been diagnosed, making the exercise particularly desirable; second, an M.D. must prescribe it.

12 OF 26. Considerably fewer companies provide any coverage for other PM undertakings. Only 11 of the carriers write for programs to help employees stop smoking. Most of these require diagnosis of an illness that smoking could aggravate, and require that an M.D. or other licensed professional (probably a psychologist) provide the program. For other preventive medicine--monitored exercise, nutrition education, stress management, weight control, and health risk appraisals--11% to 40% of all carriers offer coverage and conditions are similar: an M.D. prescribes it and a licensed professional supplies it. Except for the health risk appraisal, which few policies cover, a previous diagnosis of illness is required for payment by most carriers.

13 OF 26. Is coverage so limited because insurers doubt that PM works? That doesn't seem to be the case. I asked the insurance executives to project the effect on claims of employee participation in PM in the short term (two to five years) and the long term (six to ten years) if participation were not insurance financed. They believe that such participation would lower the number of claims in both time frames.

Figure 2–3 continued

14 OF 26. The distinction, though, between PM use and coverage of that use is key. Given the same time durations, the executives think that covering PM would raise their claims in constant dollars an average of 6% in the short term, and that even in the longer term claims would be 1.4% higher. In other words, these executives think PM reduces illness but not enough to cover its cost--at least as long as ten years. So they see no dollar payoff if they must depend merely on claims reductions to justify coverage beyond present levels.

15 OF 26. Would insurers then offer PM coverage as a higher premium option for companies that want it? Most say they would, if large employers asked. They are more likely to take that position if they view health maintenance organizations or self-insurance by large employers as their competition.

16 OF 26. With a few exceptions, however, such as Unionmutual in Portland, Maine, most carriers are not looking for PM business. They believe there is great resistance among employers to additional rises in premiums. Furthermore, they say, their function is risk spreading, not "dollar swapping," where the employer's dollar goes to pay for a purely elective program.

17 OF 26. SECTION HEADING: Employers' choices. Companies that cannot get PM coverage from the insurance carriers or that do not self-insure can nevertheless encourage employee participation in preventive medicine programs in many ways. The benefits to the organization, as I suggested before, may be considerable. Here are some steps.

18 OF 26. Encourage employees covered through health maintenance organizations to participate in their PM programs. Since HMOs are financially responsible for treating illness, they have a big stake in cost-effective PM. Kaiser Permanente and Maxicare, two of the largest HMOs in the country, offer (besides health risk appraisals) classes in stress reduction, weight control, smoking cessation, nutrition, and parenting.

19 of 26. For employees who have chosen conventional insurance coverage instead of an HMO, consider a 50-50 reimbursement plan if they buy PM from a list of "approved" providers. Some carriers are understandably nervous about drawing up such lists, considering the practice to be an invitation to lawsuits. In a city, however, it may be possible to require that a provider serve a local HMO or community college. If necessary, the company can fall back on the "licensed provider" criterion.

20 OF 26. Offer PM programs yourself, at limited or no cost to employees, by hiring or contracting with companies that provide them--as a reported 200 U.S. corporations do for weight-control programs. Naturally you run the risk of giving the PM equivalent of a party where nobody comes; employees may not attend. Even those who do attend and get the message may not follow the advice or maintain the regimen. Publicity and wholehearted support from executives are the least you should do to further the effort.

21 OF 26. Pay employees for results, not for programs. Weight loss is measurable, as is reduction in blood pressure. Employee smoking during working hours can be monitored, and abstinence rewarded, based on the reasonable expectation that 40 hours per week without a cigarette indicates smoking reduction. Companies that refund part of employees' health insurance premiums if they make no claims during a year are attempting this same approach, but less efficiently since the employees may fail to see their doctors for illness and thus compound the problem.

22 OF 26. Structure the work environment to "teach" preventive medicine by example. In Houston, for instance, Tenneco not only offers health risk appraisals, an exercise center, and programs on stress management, nutrition, and weight control, but also extends concern for employee "wellness" to its cafeterias. The caloric content of all dishes is marked; a suggested low-calorie menu is offered both at breakfast and lunch; no butter is used in cooking; beef sausage is offered as an alternative to pork at breakfast; and low-sugar desserts are on the menu daily.

Figure 2–3 continued

23 OF 26. SECTION HEADING: Logic of the dollar. For some executives, interest in PM for employees is unlikely. This is certainly true in industries where today's worker will not be tomorrow's worker. In the building trades, for example, the unions allocate workers to employers and the unions are the medium for group insurance policies.
24 OF 26. For companies with conventional work forces, however, it is reasonable at least to consider incentives for employee use of PM. The issue for any organization is effectiveness per dollar, whether that dollar goes to higher premiums for insurance coverage of PM, to direct employee reimbursement, or to employer-provided programs.
25 OF 26. It is likely that pressure from workers and society and quite possibly the logic of long-term cost savings will at least bring the preventive medicine insurance issue up for consideration in many companies. The time to gather data on what your insurance carrier will provide at what cost, or to investigate the alternatives available as I have outlined them, may be at hand.
26 OF 26.

Depending on the online system that is mounting the file, the HBR/O fields are searchable in groups or separately. In BRS, for example, the descriptor field includes terms from both the Subject descriptors thesaurus and the Industry Categories list. The BRS identifier field incorporates personal names and terms from three extracted information controlled vocabularies: geographic areas, company names, and organization names. A "super field" allows all these fields to be searched together. Corporate functions, Products and Services, and Graphical Data are each put into a separate field.

On DIALOG, on the other hand, the descriptor field includes subject descriptors, geographic descriptors, company names, organization names, industry categories, and products and services. Graphical data are in a separate field as are Corporate Functions. The full text on both BRS and DIALOG is treated as one field. On BRS subfields corresponding to grammatical paragraphs are labeled TX 1 of x, TX 2 of x, and so on. On NEXIS, HBR/O is structured quite differently. The following segments (fields) are available: publication, date, page, length, headline, byline, abstract, body, editor-note, correction date, correction, bibliography, and graphic.

The studies reported in detail in Chapters 5 and 6 used the BRS version of HBR/O. They compared results from searching using the various controlled vocabularies with searching on abstracts, complete texts, and text paragraphs.

Chemical Journals Online

The American Chemical Society (ACS) was a pioneer in testing the feasibility of online full text retrieval of scientific journals. In a series of tests with BRS in the early 1980s (described in Chapter 4) they determined the feasibility and desirability of making their scholarly journals available online. In June 1983 the complete texts of eighteen ACS journals became commercially available on BRS as the ACS Primary Journal Database, which was later changed to ACS Journals Online, and still later to CJACS (Chemical Journals of the American Chemical Society) part of a larger effort known as Chemical Journals Online. Chemical Journals Online (CJO) is now available only on STN International.

CJO is an umbrella name for a group of full text scientific journal files, each of which corresponds to the journals of a particular publisher. In addition to the Chemical Journals of the American Chemical Society, CJO includes the Chemical Journals of the Royal Society of Chemistry (CJRSC), the primary polymer journals of John Wiley & Sons (CJWILEY), the Journal of the Association of Official Analytical Chemists (CJAOAC), and the International English edition of Angewandte Chemie from VCH Verlagsgesellschaft (CJVCH). Others are planned under the CJO umbrella.

CJACS includes articles from nineteen ACS journals, eighteen of them from 1982 to the present and the nineteenth (Langmuir) from 1985. It is the largest of the CJO files; as of 1989 it included over 41,000 articles (over 70,000 records) with approximately 350 added biweekly. The journals are aimed at the scientist in chemistry, chemical engineering, biochemistry, or biomedical science. They include such titles as *Analytical Chemistry, Biochemistry, Energy & Fuels, Inorganic Chemistry, Journal of Chemical Information and Computer Science*, and *Journal of the American Chemical Society*.

The online file includes the full text of all articles, communications, and notes published in the print versions of the journals, excluding graphics and some chemical or mathematical equations. Figure 2–4 shows a sample record from the CJACS file as loaded on STN International. Fields include the descriptive information fields of accession number, document number, source (location in printed journal), title, author(s), and corporate source. Although there are no descriptors as such, a registry number field provides controlled access to chemical names. There is a searchable abstract in addition to the full text. The text field maintains the grammatical paragraphs as subfields labeled TX (1) of x, and so on. Footnotes are searchable in a separate Reference field, as are titles of all tables.

The other CJO files are much smaller than CJACS, but the fields and structure are very similar. CJRSC contains all articles, communications, notes, and so on from the ten journals of the Royal Society of Chemistry. This file is newer and contains articles only from 1987 to the present for a total of over 2,500 documents as of 1989. Updates are biweekly with approximately fifty documents added per update.

CJWILEY covers five polymer journals of John Wiley & Sons (*Biopolymers, Journal of Applied Polymer Science*, and *Journal of Polymer Science* Parts A, B, and C.) Coverage is from 1987 to the present with approximately 1,500 records in 1989. Updates are biweekly with approximately fifty documents added per update.

CJAOAC is the full text of a single journal, the *Journal of the Association of Official Analytical Chemists*. It includes all approximately 500 articles from 1987 to the present, with biweekly updates. CJVCH is also a single-title file, corresponding to the research papers published in the International English Edition of *Angewandte Chemie*. It began in 1988, includes approximately 150 records, and is updated monthly.

All CJO files are aimed at the research scientist in fairly identifiable fields. The users are expected to be familiar with the printed equivalents and with the subject area and language used in the literature in which they are searching.

Magazine ASAP

Information Access Company's Magazine ASAP (MASAP) database includes the full texts of articles, editorials, columns, reviews, product

Figure 2–4
Sample CJACS Record from STN International

```
A N    84:98  CJACS
DN     OM840541Q
SO     Orgnometallics, (1984), 3(12), 1916-1917. CODEN: ORGND7. ISSN:
       0276-7333
T I    Facile C-Mercuration of Bis(diphenylphosphino)methane
A U    (1) Lusser, Maria; (2) Peringer, Paul (*)
CS     (1,2) Institut fur Anorganische und Analytische Chemie der
       Universitat Innsbruck, Innrain 52a A-6020 Innsbruck, Austria
A B    The reaction of CH2(PPh2)2 with Hg(OAc) and [Hg(Me2SO)6](03SCF3)2 leads to {(AcOHg)
       nCH2-n[PPh2(HgOAc)]2} (03SCF3)2 (n = 1, 2), which were characterized with 199 Hg and
       31 P NMR spectroscopy.
T X    TX(1) of 5.  Most metal complexes of deprotonated bis (diphenylphosphino)methane (dppm) are
       coordinated via the phosphorus atoms of the ligand either in a chelating (i) or in a bridging mode (ii). `1
       .Footnote.  .General Graphic.  This is true for transition metals including Au, Ni, Pd, and Pt 2-6
       .Footnote. as well as for lithiated dppm that adopts structure i according to 31 P and 6 Li NMR
       measurements. 7 .Footnote. Coordination through the methylene carbon is known only in a few cases.
       8-12 .Footnote.  The complexes were generated from the deprotonated ligand and appropriate metal
       compounds or by deprotonation of the coordinated ligand.  We report here further examples of C-
       substitution in various mercury complexes of dppm.

       TX(2) of 5.  The reaction of dppm with Hg(OAc)2 and [Hg(Me2SO)6] (O3SCF3)2 13  .Footnote.
       according to eq :  .Equation. in methanol at ambient temperature affords the C-metalated product
       1 almost quantitatively within a few minutes. 14   .Footnote.   The compound was isolated and
       crystallized as an Me2SO solvate. 15 .Footnote. The structure is evidenced by 199 Hg and 31 P NMR
       spectroscopy. 16   .Footnote. The 199 Hg{1H} NMR spectrum (199Hg, I = 1/2, abundance 16.8%) of 1
       shows two different mercury sites: one doublet attributable to the mercury bound to phosphorus and a
       1:2:1 triplet for the carbon-bound mercury being coupled to two equivalent phosphorus atoms via two
       bonds. This is confirmed by the 31 P NMR spectrum. The NMR data are summarized in Table I. .Table.

       TX(3) of 5.  The reaction of one further equivalent of Hg(OAc)2 according to eq 2 .Equation. leads
       under the same conditions almost quantitatively to the dimercurated product 2, which was
       characterized similarly to 1 (Table I).  14,17   .Footnote.  Particulary conclusive is the nearly doubled
       intensity of the 199 Hg satellite pattern due to 2 J(199Hg, 31 P) in the 31 P NMR spectrum according
       to a statistical abundance of 19.37% for the isotopomer 2a .General Graphic;. compared with that of
       1a (11.56%).  The mercury-199 resonance of the C-bound mercury is at high frequency relative to
       that of 1 in keeping with the results for the series CH4-n(HgX)n. 18  .Footnote.
                                                     .
                                                     .
RN     RN(1) of 5.    93254-20-7      CN(1)    1
       RN(2) of 5.    93254-22-9      CN(2)    2
       RN(3) of 5.    2071-20-7       CN(3)    Ph2PCH2PPh2
       RN(4) of 5.    1600-27-7       CN(4)    Hg(CAc)2
       RN(5) of 5.    76703-09-8      CN(5)    [Hg(Me2O)6] (03SCF3)2
RE     RE(1) of 21.   1 Puddephatt, R. J. Chem. Soc. Rev. 1983, 99.
       RE(2) of 21.   2 Schmidbaur, H.; Mandl, J. R. Angew. Chem. 1977, 89, 679. Schmidbaur, H.;
       Mandl, J. R. ; Bassett, J. M. ; Blaschke, G.; ZimmerGasser, B. Chem. Ber. 1981, 114, 433.
                                                     .
```

---

evaluations, and recipes from over a hundred general interest magazines. Coverage dates vary by title, but most begin with articles from 1983. Some titles (i.e., *Ladies Home Journal* and *Rolling Stone*) are no longer being added to the file, but old articles remain. As of 1989 there were over 200,000 records in the MASAP file, with approximately 3,500 records added each month.

Most magazines on MASAP are nonscholarly, popular titles such as you might purchase at a newsstand. They can be further subdivided into the following categories: news (i.e., *Time* and *Newsweek*), business (i.e., *Forbes* and *Money*), hobby (i.e., *Popular Photography* and *Popular Mechanics*), political/commentary (i.e., *New Republic* and *Nation*), women's (i.e., *Ladies' Home Journal* and *Redbook*), entertainment (i.e., *Sports Illustrated, Teen,* and *Rolling Stone*), and science (i.e., *Science* and *Psychology Today*).

The writing style and length of the articles varies tremendously among the magazines, but most are aimed at the general or nonspecialist reader. Most of the originals do not include footnotes, but if they do, the references are searchable online. The printed versions do include many photographs and other illustrations, but these are not available online. Captions from photographs, graphs, or charts are searchable, however.

MASAP is available on DIALOG, BRS, and NEXIS. The coverage is slightly different on each system, with the DIALOG version containing the most magazine titles.[10] The other versions are labeled Magazine ASAP III on BRS, and Magazine ASAP II on NEXIS to differentiate.

Figure 2–5 is a sample record from the DIALOG version of MASAP. As can be seen, records include basic descriptive information including: accession number, title, author(s) if present, source, and length. Picture captions are present and searchable. In addition, MASAP has several value-added features, added by the IAC indexing staff as needed. Unclear titles are annotated with words in parentheses (i.e., recipe or book review). Precoordinated controlled vocabulary descriptors are assigned to each article. Other controlled fields include: CODEN for standardized access to journal names, document type, named persons, Standard Industrial Classification (SIC) codes, geographic codes, and geographic locations. There are no abstracts in MASAP records. The text is treated as one long field. On BRS the grammatical paragraphs are numbered and treated as subfields. Figure 2–6 shows how Mead mounts the MASAP database on NEXIS.

A companion file to MASAP is the Magazine Index database. Magazine Index is a bibliographic-only database that includes indexing and citation information for articles from over 450 magazines from 1959 to the present. All the approximately one hundred magazines that are in full text in MASAP are also indexed in Magazine Index. The two files are linked, so that when a user retrieves a record in Magazine Index that has the full text in the ASAP file, he may print the full text without leaving the index file. The full text is only searchable from the MASAP file, however.

Trade & Industry ASAP

Trade & Industry ASAP (T&IASAP), also from Information Access Company, has the same sort of companion arrangement with the bibliographic Trade & Industry Index database. The full text file includes articles,

Figure 2–5
Sample MASAP Record from DIALOG

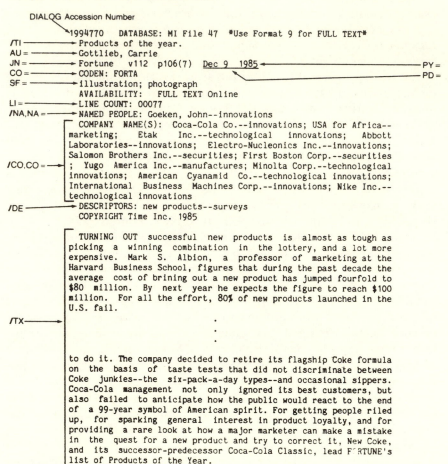

trade news, reviews, new product announcements, editorials, and columns from over 120 magazines in the broad subject areas of business and industry. Periodicals vary in style and scope, including such disparate titles as *Automotive Industry, Datamation, Dallas-Fort Worth Business, Fortune, Monthly Labor Review, Playthings*, and *PC Week*. In addition, it includes press releases from PR Newswire and Kyodo News International. Coverage of the full text is from 1983 to the present for most titles.

The bibliographic-only Trade & Industry database indexes over 300 pe-

Figure 2–6
Sample MASAP Record from Mead (NEXIS)

SCIAMR / Scientific American Copyright (c) 1986 Information Access Company
Copyright (c) Scientific American, Inc. 1986

TITL: Taking the waters. (testing the physiological benefits of warm mineral baths)

REFR: Scientific American Vol 254 pp 66B(2)

DATE: April, 1986

TERM: DESCRIPTORS mineral waters, physiological aspects; baths, warm, physiological aspects

LENG: Original Source: 26 lines

TEXT: Taking the Waters

Bath, Baden Baden, Saratoga Springs and many other old spas testify to the great age of the notion that immersion in warm mineral water is good for what ails you. Yet little work has been done over the centuries to find out what the precise physiological effects of the treatment are. Eight workers at the British Royal Infirmary in Bristol have now looked into the matter. They report their results in the British Medical Journal....

ADDITIONAL TEXT OMITTED

....with tap water maintained at 35 degrees C. produces essentially identical results.

NOTE: ORIGIN MAGIND

IDEN: CODEN SLAMA

ACCE: 01771285

LOAD: June 13, 1986

Source: *Access to Access: An Online User's Guide to IAC Databases,* 3d ed. Copyright 1986, Information Access Company, Foster City, California 94404. Used with permission.

riodicals from 1981 to the present, including all of those in full text on T&IASAP.

Like the other full text databases, graphics are not included, but captions are searchable. T&IASAP records look very much like MASAP records, as can be seen in Figure 2–7. This sample record from the DIALOG version shows descriptive fields such as accession number, title, author, source,

Figure 2–7
Sample T&IASAP Record from DIALOG

1506800 DATABASE: TI File 148 *Use Format 9 for FULL TEXT* Dollar
descending; a weaker dollar is expected to boost the outlook for a domestic travel
boom. (Travel Weekly's Economic Survey of the Travel Industry)
    Beason, Catherine
    Travel Weekly v45 p16(6)
    Jan 31 1986
    illustration
    AVAILABILITY: FULL TEXT Online
    LINE COUNT: 00161
    SIC CODE: 4722
    NAMED PEOPLE: Mills, Anne—forecasts; Shilling, A. Gary—forecasts; Holland,
Daniel—forecasts; Martin, Neil—forecasts; Paul, Pamela—forecasts; McNeal,
Anne—forecasts; Rust, Richard P.—forecasts; Kenle, Arthur—forecasts;
Wynegar, Don—forecasts
    DESCRIPTORS: dollar, American—rates; tourist trade—forecasts; foreign ex-
change—forecasts; executives—forecasts
    COPYRIGHT Murdoch Pub. Co. 1986
    Dollar descending
    A weaker dollar is expected to boost the outlook for domestic travel boom.
    Last winter's super dollar all but guaranteed another boom year for foreign travel.
But there are no guarantees this year. At its strongest, the last two weeks of
February, the
dollar bought nearly three and a half deutsche marks and over 260 yen, while the
one-dollar pound was very nearly a reality. Travelers returning with tales of $30
cashmere sweaters and $25 Italian leather gloves made Europe a prime
destination.
    Nearly 4 million Americans traveled to Europe in the first six months....

Source: *Access to Access: An Online User's Guide to IAC Databases*, 3d ed. Copyright 1986,
    Information Access Company, Foster City, California 94404. Used with permission.

and so on in addition to the value-added fields of SIC code, named people,
and descriptors. The title is annotated by the IAC indexers.

T&IASAP is available on BRS, DIALOG, and NEXIS, with slightly
different coverage on each. Like MASAP, the DIALOG version is the
most complete. NEXIS does not repeat any sources available elsewhere
in the NEXIS system. The BRS version is known as T&IASAP I and the
NEXIS version as T&IASAP II. The DIALOG version is merely
T&IASAP. Figures 2–7 and 2–8 are sample records from the DIALOG
and BRS versions of T&IASAP respectively.

SUMMARY

Although there are hundreds of online systems commercially available
throughout the world, fifteen of them are identified by being major providers of full text databases and are covered in the directory *Fulltext Sources*

Figure 2–8
Sample T&IASAP Record from BRS

AN   1392100 8604.
DB   BIZZ.
TI   Dollar descending; a weaker dollar is expected to boost the outlook for
     domestic travel boom. (Travel Weekly's Economic Survey of the Travel
     Industry).
AU   Beason-Catherine.
SO   Travel Weekly, volume 4, Jan 31, 1986, pg16(6)
PD   860131.
IL   illustration.
SC   SIC CODE: 4722
DE   dollar-American; rates. tourist-trade; forecasts. foreign-exchange:
     forecasts. executives: forecasts.
AV   FULL TEXT AVAILABLE ONLINE.
LN   ARTICLE LENGTH (APPROX. LINE COUNT): 00161.
CP   COPYRIGHT Murdoch Pub. Co. 1986.
TX   (1 Of 51) Dollar descending.
     (2 Of 51) A weaker dollar is expected to boost the outlook for a domestic
     travel boom.
     (3 Of 51) Last winter's super dollar all but guaranteed another boom year for
     foreign travel. But there are no guarantees this year.
     (4 Of 51) At it's strongest, the last two weeks of February, the dollar bought
     nearly three and a half deutsche marks and over 260 yen, while the one-
     dollar pound was very nearly a reality.
     (5 Of 51) Travelers returning with tales of $30 cashmere sweaters and $25
     Italian leather gloves made Europe a prime destination.

Source: *Access to Access: An Online User's Guide to IAC Databases*, 3d ed. Copyright 1986,
Information Access Company, Foster City, California 94404. Used with permission.

Online. Of these fifteen, five are among the most heavily used online
systems in the library/information center market. Two of these (LEXIS
and WESTLAW) specialize in legal information, one (STN International)
is scientific/technical, and the others are "supermarket" systems with a
variety of types of information and subjects (DIALOG, BRS, and Mead's
NEXIS). Some of the full text databases on these five systems overlap;
others are unique. The systems are in competition and share many of the
same features. System search features are described in Chapter 3.

NOTES

1. *Directory of Online Databases* 10, no. 1 (January 1989) (New York: Cuadra/
Elsevier, 1989).

2. Ruth M. Orenstein, ed., *Fulltext Sources Online: For Periodicals, Newspapers, Newsletters & Newswires* (Needham Heights, Mass.: BiblioData, 1989).

3. Martha E. Williams, *Information Market Indicators* (Monticello, Ill.: Information Market Indicators, periodically).

4. Carol Tenopir, "Education for Database Intermediaries: How Library Schools Have Changed (and How They Haven't," *Online* 13 (November 1989): 55–63; and Martha E. Williams, "Preparing for Online Searching Through Education and Training," *Proceedings of the National Online Meeting, New York, May 1988* (Medford, N.J.: Learned Information, Inc., 1988).

5. For more historical information see M. Lynne Neufeld and Martha Cornog, "Database History: From Dinosaurs to Compact Discs," *Journal of the American Society for Information Science* 37 (July 1986): 183–190; and Roger C. Palmer, "Chapter 1: Introduction," in: *Online Reference and Information Retrieval*, 2d ed. (Littleton, Colo.: Libraries Unlimited, 1987).

6. For more historical information see: William G. Harrington, "A Brief History of Computer-Assisted Legal Research," *Law Library Journal* 77, No. 3 (1984–1985): 543–556.

7. Ibid.

8. The debate still rages over the relative merits of just full text as found on LEXIS and enhanced full text as found on WESTLAW. For an interesting view of the debate see Daniel P. Dabney, "The Curse of Thamus: An Analysis of Full-Text Legal Document Retrieval," *Law Library Journal* 78 (Winter 1986): 5–40, and the responses to that article including Jo McDermott, "Another Analysis of Full-Text Legal Document Retrieval," *Law Library Journal* 78 (Spring 1986): 337–343; Craig E. Runde and William H. Lindberg, "The Curse of Thamus: A Response," *Law Library Journal* 78 (Spring 1986): 345–347; Scott F. Burson, "A Reconstruction of Thamus: Comments on the Evaluation of Legal Information Retrieval Systems," *Law Library Journal* 79 (Winter 1987): 133–143; and Jon Bing, "Performance of Legal Text Retrieval Systems: The Curse of Boole," *Law Library Journal* 79 (Spring 1987): 187–202.

9. For more information see Neufeld and Cornog, "Database History," and Palmer, "Introduction."

10.   Ruth Pagell, "Searching IAC's Full-Text Files: It's Awfully Confusing," *Database* 10 (October 1987): 39–47.

3

System Features for
Full Text Searching

Even though many of the online systems described in Chapter 2 were originally developed for bibliographic database searching, almost all now have special search and display features especially designed for full text. The need for such features has been recognized as users search and gain experience with full text. Their successes and failures suggest new or different search features. System designers also watch their competitors, so that a good idea offered by one system often appears later in a slightly altered form on another. Rarely does the development of a full text search system progress logically or systematically. Online systems add, alter, or delete features almost continually as they gather reactions from users or try out new ideas or new features offered by competitors.

Many of the special search and display features offered by today's full text systems were tested for effectiveness in the research studies described in Chapters 4, 5, 6, and 7. Other studies tested experimental features that are not yet available on major commercial online systems. Together the results of these studies led to many of the recommendations for online systems and database producers in Chapter 9. This chapter describes the major search and display features currently available on one or more of the five major full text online systems covered in Chapter 2. Many are familiar to searchers, as they are standard features that have been available on online systems for almost thirty years. Anyone who has ever done an online search knows about such things as truncation, Boolean logic, and so on that are described in this chapter. What is different here is that we point out which features are especially useful or recommended for full text searching and give examples of how the major full text systems implement the various features.

Figure 3–1
Two HBR/O Records in the Linear File on BRS

Sample BRS/HBRO Citations

```
AN  834160, 8307.
CC  PARAGRAPH    SENTENCE    NS-WORD
    AN (1)        4           2
    PT (1)        2           3
AU  (1) ROSEN-BENSON; (2) RYNES-SARA; (3) MAHONEY-THOMAS-A.
IN  (1) UNIV. OF NORTH CAROLINA; (2) CORNELL UNIV. NEW YORK
    STATE SCHOOL OF INDUSTRIAL RELATIONS; (3) VANDERBILT
    UNIV.OWEN GRADUATE SCHOOL OF MANAGEMENT.
TI  COMPENSATION, JOBS, AND GENDER.
SO  HARVARD BUSINESS REVIEW. JUL-AUG 1983. P 170.
PT  HBR ARTICLE (PROBING OPINIONS).
NJ  ISSN 0017-8012.
DE  WAGES-AND-SALARIES. EQUAL-EMPLOYMENT-OPPORTUNITY.
    SEX-DISCRIMINATION. COMPENSATION-ADMINISTRATION.
    WOMEN-IN-BUSINESS.
MN  HARRIS (LOUIS) & ASSOCIATES. HARVARD BUSINESS REVIEW.
    EQUAL EMPLOYMENT OPPORTUNITY COMMISSION. NA-
    TIONAL ACADEMY OF SCIENCES. NORTON, ELEANOR
    HOLMES.
BF  COMPENSATION. PERSONNEL RELATIONS.
EX  PROFILE OF HBR SURVEY PARTICIPANTS.
    IMPORTANCE FACTORS SHOULD HAVE IN SETTING SALARIES
    (PERSONNEL).
    FACTORS THAT CONTRIBUTE TO THE SALARY GAP BETWEEN
    MEN AND WOMEN (PERSONNEL).
    PROSPECTS AND PRESSURES FOR CHANGE IN COMPENSA
    TION POLICIES (PERSONNEL).
    EFFECTIVENESS OF PROPOSED REMEDIES (PERSONNEL),
    LIKELY CONSEQUENCES OF ATTEMPTS TO REDUCE THE SAL-
    ARY GAP (PERSONNEL).
    A LEGAL HISTORY OF COMPARABLE WORTH (BOX).
CR  1 OF 6. MILKOVICH, GEORGE T. CITED BY LIVERNASH. E. ROB-
    ERT. THE EMERGING DEBATE/IN COMPARABLE WORTH: ISSSUES
    AND ALTERNATIVES. WASHINGTON, DC:  EQUAL EMPLOYMENT
    ADVISORY COUNCIL 1980.
    .
    .
    6 OF 6. TREIMAN, D.J. JOB EVALUATION: AN ANALYTIC RE-
    REVIEW. WASHINGTON, DC: NATIONAL ACADEMY OF SCIENCES.
    1979.
AB  A SURVEY OF 5,000 HBR SUBSCRIBERS, OF WHOM 910 RE-
    PLIED, SHOWS THAT: (1) MALE AND FEMALE READERS DISA-
```

```
AN  834030, 8307.
CC  PARAGRAPH    SENTENCE    NS-WORD
    AN (1)        4           2
AU  (1) BHIDE-AMAR.
IN  (1) MCKINSEY & CO.
TI  BEYOND KEYNES: DEMAND-SIDE ECONOMICS.
SO  HARVARD BUSINESS REVIEW. JUL-AUG 1983. P 100.
PT  HBR ARTICLE
NJ  ISSN 0017-8012.
DE  INDUSTRIAL-POLICY. BUSINESS-GOVERNMENT-RELATIONS.
    ECONOMIC-POLICY. COMPETITION. REGULATION. ELECTRI-
    CAL-AND-ELECTRONIC-INDUSTRIES. COMPUTER-INDUSTRY.
MJ  MINISTRY OF INTERNATIONAL TRADE AND INDUSTRY (JA-
    PAN).
MN  MIT. CALIFORNIA INSTITUTE OF TECHNOLOGY. NASA. DEPT
    OF TRANSPORTTION. INTERNATIONAL POSTAL UNION. EU-
    ROPEAN COMMUNITY. FCC. TOYOTA MOTOR. SEARS ROE-
    BUCK. ZENITH RADIO. RCA. IBM. PEUGEOT-CITROEN
    (FRANCE), RENAULT-PEUGEOT (FRANCE). WANG. INTEL. DIGI-
    TAL EQUIPMENT. PRIME COMPUTER. TANDEM COMPUTERS.
    HEWLETT-PACKARD. POLAROID. HONDA MOTOR (JAPAN).
    SONY(JAPAN). SHARP(JAPAN). WESTINGHOUSE ELECTRIC.
    MITSUBISH MOTOR. FORTUNE. DRAPER. HITACHI (JAPAN).
    MATSHSHITA ELECTRIC INDUSTRIAL (JAPAN). SYNTHETIC
    FUELS. GENERAL MOTORS. DELCO. CHRYSLER. LOCKEED.
    MCDONNELL DOUGLAS. BOEING. NISSAN MOTOR (JAPAN).
    FEDERAL RESERVE BANK. SMITH. ADAM. THUROW. LESTER.
    REICH. ROBERT. ROHATYN. FELIX. HART. GARY. BIC. MARCEL
    WILSON. HAROLD.
BF  GOVERNMENT AND BUSINESS
EX  A LOOP STANDARD (BOX).
CR  1 OF 4. JEQUIER, NICOLAS CITED BY VERNON. RAYMOND. ED.
    COMPUTERS/IN BIG BUSINESS AND THE STATE. CAMBRIDGE,
    MA: HARVARD UNIVERSITY PRESS. 1974.
    .
    .
    4 OF 4. BHADKAMKAR NEAL PORTER. MICHAEL E. THE U.S.
    TELEVISION SET MARKET. 1970-1979 (ICCH 9-380-181). BOS-
    TON, MA:HBS CASE SERVICES.
AB  PLEAS FOR A U.S. INDUSTRIAL POLICY OFTEN FOCUS ON
    SUPPLY-SIDE MEASURES. SUCH AS CAPITAL GRANTS. INTER-
```

GREE ABOUT THE CAUSES OF THE GAP IN MEN'S AND WOMEN'S EARNINGS AS WELL AS ABOUT THE PROBABLE CONSEQUENCES OF REQUIRING A COMPARABLE WORTH APPROACH TO PAY; (2) WOMEN TEND MORE THAN MEN TO ATTRIBUTE SALARY DIFFERENCES TO ORGANIZATIONAL SELECTION AND COMPENSATION PRACTICES, WHILE MEN ARE MORE LIKELY TO BLAME WOMEN FOR CHOOSING LOW-PAYING JOBS; (3) READERS OF BOTH SEXES AGREE THAT WOMEN'S GROUPS ARE MORE LIKELY THAN PERSONNEL SPECIALISTS, UNIONS, OR THE FEDERAL GOVERNMENT TO ADVOCATE COMPARABLE WORTH, ALTHOUGH RESPONDENTS SEE WOMAN'S GROUPS AS LACKING THE NECESSARY CLOUT TO EFECT MAJOR CHANGES; AND (4) READERS DISAGREE ABOUT THE DESIRABILITY AND FEASIBILITY OF ADOPTING A COMPARABLE WORTH APPROACH TO PAY...

TX 1 OF 74. DO MALE GUARDS DESERVE HIGHER SALARIES THAN PRISON MATRONS? A RECENT NATIONAL ACADEMY OF SCIENCE STUDY REPORTS THAT DESPITE 20 YEARS OF ANTIDISCRIMINATION LEGISLATION, THE EARNINGS OF WORKING WOMEN IN THE UNITED STATES AVERAGE LESS THAN 60% OF MEN'S EARNINGS. MOREOVER, IN 1978 THE AVERAGE MALE HIGH SCHOOL DROPOUT EARNED MORE THAN A FEMALE COLLEGE GRADUATE. ALTHOUGH PEOPLE DISAGREE ABOUT HOW MUCH OF THE EARNINGS DISPARITY BETWEEN MEN AND WOMEN THEY SHOULD ATTRIBUTE TO DISCRIMINATION IN PAY-SETTING PRACTICES, ECONOMIC AND SOCIOLOGICAL STUDIES INDICATE THAT EVEN AFTER ADJUSTING FOR DIFFERENCES IN EDUCATION AND WORK EXPERIENCE APPROXIMATELY HALF THE GAP REMAINS.

. . .

74 OF 74. FURTHER COMPARISONS CAN APPROXIMATE THE EFFECTS ON PAYROLL EXPENDITURES ON THE BASIS OF THESE PROJECTED BENEFITS AND COSTS. CORPORATE DECISION MAKERS CAN BETTER JUDGE THE KIND AND EXTENT OF COMPENSATION POLICY REVISIONS THAT ARE PRACTICAL IN THEIR ORGANIZATIONS. OPEN-MINDED EFFORTS ON THE PART OF MANAGERS TO EXAMINE THE ISSUES AND EXPLORE THE ALTERNATIVES REPRESENT AN IMPORTANT FIRST STEP TOWARD CREATING FAIR AND EQUITABLE REWARD SYSTEMS FOR ALL EMPLOYEES.

EST RATE SUBSIDIES, ACCELERATED DEPRECIATION ALLOWANCES, AND FUNDING FOR R&D, WHICH FAIL TO DELIVER ON THE STRUCTURAL CHANGES THEY PROMOSE AND LEAVE A TRAIL OF WASTE, INEQUITY, AND ANIMOSITY THE MINISTRY OF INTERNATIONAL TRADE AND INDUSTRY HAD LITTLE INFLUENCE ON THE SUCCESS OF JAPAN'S AUTOMOBILE AND ELECTONICS INDUSTRIES. FRANCE'S SERIES OF FIVE-YEAR PLANS TO SUPPLY CAPITAL TO PROMISING INDUSTRIES HAS FAILED TO MAKE THAT COUNTRY INTERNATIONALLY COMPETITIVE.

POLICES THAT AFFECT THE QUALITY AND MAGNITUDE OF DEMAND CAN CHANGE INDUSTRY STRUCTURE. THEY ADOPT THE PERSPECTIVE OF THE CONSUMER. RELY ON INDIVIDUAL INITIATIVE, AND REFLECT MARKET FORCES. DEMAND-SIDE POLICES IN JAPAN HAVE HELPED THE ELECTRONICS AND OTHER INDUSTRIES GROW. THE U.S. GOVERNMENTS SUCCESSFUL INDUCEMENT OF CONSUMERS TO REDUCE ENERGY DEMAND IN THE 1970S WHEN OIL SUPPLIES WERE JEOPARDIZED DEMONSTRATES THE POWER OF DEMAND-SIDE POLICIES.

TX 1 OF 77. MODERN WISDOM HAS IT THAT INDUSTRIAL POLICY DOES NOT EXTEND BEYOND DOMESTIC SHORES, NEXT QUARTER'S EARNINGS, OR YESTERDAY'S TECHNOLOGY. AND EVEN WHEN THE EYE IS FARSIGHTED. THE HAND OFTEN LACKS THE MUSCLE TO STEER THE RIGHT COURSE. MANAGERS MAY KNOW THE IMPORTANCE OF NEW TECHNOLOGY. MODERN PLANT, OR GLOBAL MARKET SHARE ONLY TOO WELL BUT LACK THE RESOURCES TO DO ANYTHING ABOUT IT. DEE-ROOTED STRUCTURAL DEFECTS OF THE MARKETPLACE REQUIRE GOVERNMENT TO GO BEYOND ITS TRADITIONAL ECONOMIC ROLE AND. REACHING DOWN TO THE LEVEL OF SPECIFIC INDUSTRIES. TO PLAY AN ENERGETIC PART IN GUIDING THEIR EVOLUTION.

. . .

77 OF 77. INDUSTRY AND GOVERNMENT ARE NOT IN A ZERO-SUM GAME WITH EACH OTHER. OR WITH CONSUMERS. IT IS NOT IN THE SELF-INTEREST OF POLITICIANS OR BUSINESS PEOPLE TO CONFRONT OR COERCE VOTERS OR CUSTOMERS. THE ULTIMATE SOURCE OF BUSINESS PROFITS AND GOVERNMENT SUCCESS IS THE SATISFACTION OF THE NEEDS OF THE PEOPLE. THE OBJECT OF INDUSTRIAL POLICY MUST BE TO FACILITATE THAT SATISFACTION.

SEARCH FEATURES

All the online systems described in Chapter 2 follow the same de facto standards for basic search features that grew out of developments of the 1960s and early 1970s. Some were refined or enhanced especially for full text retrieval, but all represent a gradual development process based on a certain set principles. All major commercially available online systems of today rely on inverted index file structures and the search features promulgated by this structure. Inverted indexes are described briefly here; for more details check any beginning online searching textbook.[1]

All articles in a full text database are structured according to the rules and specifications agreed to by the database producer and the online system on which the file will be loaded. Fields are specified and tagged, separation is made between fields, and delimiters are placed between different values in a single field (i.e., multiple descriptors). Searchable fields are marked. The resulting records are loaded in the online system and maintained in accession number order in a so-called linear file. Figure 3–1 could be two records in the linear file of the HBR/O database on BRS.

When a user wishes to retrieve records on a given topic, it is impractical for the computer to search sequentially through every character in every searchable field in each record in the linear file given the huge size of commercial databases and the hardware limitations of today's database systems. Instead of relying on sequential scanning of the linear file, all major commercial online systems create a separate inverted index file (or dictionary file) that stores just the searchable data elements from each record with pointers back to the appropriate record in the linear file. Figure 3–2 shows part of an inverted file on BRS created from linear file records such as those illustrated in Figure 3–1.

Some systems (for example, DIALOG) create more than one inverted index file. As can be seen in Figure 3–2, in DIALOG all words or phrases from subject-related fields are put into one alphabetically ordered inverted index called the Basic Index. Values from nonsubject fields (e.g., author, journal name, and so on) are put into separate alphabetically ordered indexes. The searcher must explicitly tell the system to search in these separate inverted indexes. Other systems (such as BRS, Mead, and WESTLAW) create only a single inverted index with values from all fields interfiled.

An inverted file is an index to the searchable words or phrases in each record in a database. Each term is extracted automatically from each record and placed in alphabetical order with a numerical pointer to another file that contains information about each term. The information retained about each term typically includes the accession number of each record that contains the term, the fields where the term is found in each record, and the placement of each term in each field. Searching on inverted file systems is speedy because the system does a binary search of the alphabetically

Figure 3–2
Creation of a Dictionary (Inverted) File

Sample Title:

Telecommunications Technology in the 1980's: Computers and Advances in Communications Systems.

SAMPLE DICTIONARY FILE

Term	Document Number	Paragraph Label	Sentence Number	Word Number
ADVANCES	1	TI	1	5
COMMUNICATIONS	1	TI	1	6
COMPUTERS	1	TI	1	4
SYSTEMS	1	TI	1	7
TECHNOLOGY	1	TI	1	2
TELECOMMUNICATIONS	1	TI	1	1
1980S	1	TI	1	3

System Assignment of Word Numbers:

- Numbers are assigned sequentially to each "word" within each "sentence"
- "Stopwords" are not assigned word numbers

Example:

TELECOMMUNICATIONS (1) TECHNOLOGY (2) ~~IN~~ ~~THE~~ 1980'S (3) COMPUTERS (4)

~~AND~~ ADVANCES (5) ~~IN~~ COMMUNICATIONS (6) SYSTEMS (7)

Source: "How a Database Is Constructed," *Dialog System Seminar Manual*, 1989. Copyright © DIALOG* Information Services, Inc. All rights reserved. Reproduced with permission (*Service mark Reg. Pat. & TM Off.)

Figure 3–2 continued

How a Database is Constructed

> 2. DIALOG creates the database's BASIC INDEX, the alphabetical list of subject words (excluding STOP WORDS). Each record is divided into FIELDS (parts), each field is labelled, and the position of each word within a field is noted.

Term	Location	Term	Location
a	30249 AB2	in	30156 AB34
	30249 AB12	industries	30156 AB31
	30156 TI10	is	30249 AB9
actions	30249 AB22	kentucky	30156 AB19
	30249 TI5	kinds	30249 AB18
age	30156 AB17	labor	30156 AB36
as	30249 AB11		30156 TI1
attitudes	30249 DE2	metropolitan	30156 AB5
behavior	30249 DE4		30156 TI5
	30249 TI8	model	30249 AB3
characteristics	30156 AB26	nonfarm	30156 AB7
comparative	30156 TI11	nonmetropolitan	30156 AB8
compare	30156 AB21		30156 TI6
complaint	30249 AB21	occupations	30156 AB29
	30249 TI4	participation	30156 TI3
consumer	30249 AB20	personal	30156 AB22
	30249 DE1	postpurchase	30249 AB5
	30249 DE3		30249 TI1
	30249 TI2	presents	30249 AB1
consumer attitudes	30249 DE1DE2	processes	30249 AB7
consumer behavior	30249 DE3DE4	repurchase	30249 TI7
data	30156 AB2	rural	30156 DE7
different	30249 AB17	rural environments	30156 DE7DE8
employment	30156 DE1	socioeconomic	30156 AB23
employment status	30156 DE1DE2	status	30156 DE2
environments	30156 DE6	study	30156 TI12
	30156 DE8	theoretical	30249 AB13
evaluation	30249 AB6	urban	30156 DE5
evaluations	30249 TI3	urban environments	30156 DE5DE6
examined	30156 AB1	used	30249 AB10
explaining	30249 AB16	which	30249 AB8
family	30156 AB25	women	30156 AB12
farm	30156 AB11		30156 AB33
	30156 TI8		30156 TI9
females	30156 DE4	yrs	30156 AB15
force	30156 AB37	1231	30156 AB10
	30156 TI2	18	30156 AB13
framework	30249 AB14	3631	30156 AB6
human	30156 DE3	65	30156 AB14
human females	30156 DE3DE4	937	30156 AB4

STOP WORDS		
an	for	the
and	from	to
by	of	with

Figure 3–2 continued

> 3. DIALOG creates the database's ADDITIONAL INDEXES of remaining searchable fields. These indexes are searched with PREFIXES.

```
AU=Bokemeier, Janet L.              30156
AU=Francken, Dick A.                30249
AU=Keith, Verna                     30156
AU=Sachs, Carolyn                   30156
DC=11470                            30249
DC=11480                            30249
DC=17196                            30156
DC=23450                            30156
DC=45040                            30156
DC=54940                            30156
DT=Journal Article                  30249
                                    30156
JN=Journal of Economic Psychology   30249
JN=Rural Sociology                  30156
LA=English                          30249
                                    30156
PY=1984                             30249
                                    30156
UD=8505                             30156
UD=8506                             30249
UD=9999                             30249
```

Source: "How a Database Is Constructed," *Dialog System Seminar Manual*, 1989. Copyright © DIALOG* Information Services, Inc. All rights reserved. Reproduced with permission (*Service mark Reg. Pat. & TM Off.)

arranged inverted file rather than scanning the complete linear file. Using the index, most major retrieval systems first report the number of records that contain a search term (called *hits* or *postings*), and the accession numbers of the records that satisfy a given search request are put into a group called a set. (Set building is discussed in more detail later.) Not until the searcher enters a display command for a given set does the system use the accession numbers to access the linear file records.

Inverted index entries are typically created for every nontrivial word in a full text record, allowing very fast response time even for very long articles or books. Trivial words are defined by the online system and range in number from the nine stopwords defined by DIALOG (an, and, by, for, from, the, to, with, or) to the over seventy on BRS (see Table 3–1). The full text is almost always word indexed (or word parsed), meaning that every string of characters recognized as a separate word is available for searching. Usually a word is defined as a string of characters or numbers surrounded by a blank or by punctuation marks. Different systems employ different definitions of words for word parsing, which may affect retrieval capabilities. Table 3–1 shows the BRS text editing decisions for word parsing. Note that BRS differentiates between the apostrophe and other punctuation marks. Other systems treat all punctuation marks as blanks. Tests reported in Chapter 7 show how this variation affects full text retrieval.

Table 3–1
BRS Rules for Text Editing

BRS performs text-editing functions when creating a dictionary file for a database.

Punctuation

Naturally occurring punctuation and special characters are generally omitted for searching purposes, but they do appear when the documents are printed.

Example:

To retrieve	Enter
input-output	input adj output
i/o	i adj o
alzheimer's	alzheimers

Hyphens

Hyphens are inserted or retained in certain paragraphs, such as, controlled vocabulary and authors. (Note: varies with database. Check database guide or AidPage)

Example:

To retrieve	Enter
C. R. Kyle	Kyle-c-r (author's name)
elementary education	elementary-education (controlled vocabulary)

Stopwords

Certain common words are omitted for searching but they do appear when the documents are printed. Searching for stopwords will usually result in a "SEARCH TERM NOT FOUND" message. (Note: In some databases stopwords are searchable in certain paragraphs. Check database guide.)

Example:

	To retrieve	Enter
quality of life	quality adj life	(free-text)
	quality with life	(free-text)
	quality-of-life	(controlled vocabulary)

Table 3–1 continued

A	FOR	MUST	THROUGH
ABOUT	FOUND	•••	TO
AMONG	FROM	N O	TOWARD
ALL	FURTHER	N OT	•••
AN	•••	•••	UPON
AND	HAS	OF	USED
ARE	HAVE	ON	USING
AS	HOWEVER	OR	•••
AT	•••	••	•••
•••	IF	SAME	WERE
BE	IN	SEVERAL	WHAT
BEEN	I NTO	SOME	WHICH
BETWEEN	IS	SUCH	WHILE
BOTH	IT	•••	WHO
BY	ITS	THAN	WILL
•••	•••	THAT	WITH
DO	MADE	THE	WITHIN
DURING	MAKE	THEIR	WOULD
•••	MANY	THESE	•••
EACH	MAY	THEY	
EITHER	MORE	THIS	
•••	MOST	THOSE	

Fields other than the full text that are word parsed typically include titles, abstracts, notes, and headlines.

Some full text databases also include controlled fields, where a human indexer or inputter has indicated that the words in a phrase go together as a bound phrase. Phrase-parsed entries are separated by some special delimiter (such as a semicolon), so that the computer will know where one phrase ends and the next begins. Phrases in the inverted index include all spaces and punctuation. Fields that are often phrase-parsed include authors, journal names, and geographic location. To search a phrase-parsed field, the searcher must enter the entire phrase exactly as it is in the database, punctuation and all. Note in Figure 3–2 that all entries with more than one word come from phrase-parsing.

If a full text database includes descriptor terms or subject headings, these fields are usually both word and phrase parsed. Magazine ASAP, Harvard Business Review/Online, and Trade & Industry ASAP all have controlled vocabulary descriptors. Bound phrases are kept together in the inverted index, but they are also separated into single words. This allows searchers to use the intellectual decision involved in creating a controlled vocabulary descriptor, but allows individual words to be searched if a user does not know the correct form of a descriptor.

The inverted index file structure and parsing decisions for each field greatly impact the search features that are necessary and/or available in online systems. The features discussed here are truncation, vocabulary control, viewing the inverted index, proximity operations, Boolean operations, set building, field specification comparison operations, and record or file linking.

Truncation

Most online systems allow the searcher to use word stemming (called truncation) to search for all terms or phrases that begin with the same character stem. This is usually indicated to the system by the searcher placing a special truncation symbol at the end of a word stem. Thus, placing a truncation symbol after the stem COMPUT will find entries in the inverted index under COMPUTING, COMPUTE, COMPUTER, COMPUTERS, COMPUTATION, COMPUTATIONS, COMPUTATIONAL, and so on. Different systems use different symbols to indicate truncation, such as ?, #, :, $, !, and others. Most allow the option of unlimited stemming or specification of a certain number of following characters (e.g., COMPUTE$2 on BRS) to provide more precision.

Such righthand truncation is easily handled with inverted index systems. The system locates a group of alphabetically related terms with the same initial stem and places them in a single set. Most systems allow some variation on righthand truncation so that the user can specify how many characters can come after the initial stem. By specifying a single letter after the stem COMPUTER, the system would retrieve only the singular and plural and eliminate some potential false drops. This is also fairly easy with inverted indexes. All the online systems mentioned in Chapter 2 provide righthand truncation.

Truncation is especially important with full text systems because of the variations in the language used by different authors and the many possible word endings in the free-text English language. Some online systems have thus added more refinements to truncation features. A fairly common refinement is the ability to use internal truncation or wild card characters within a word stem. Internal truncation specifies that any number of characters can occur in the middle of a word, so long as the word begins and ends with the characters specified by the searcher. Thus LAB#R will retrieve LABOR and LABOUR (but also LABRADOR, LABORER, and others). Of the five major full text systems discussed in Chapter 2, only Mead offers unlimited internal truncation.

Wild card searching is a more common variation on internal truncation. A special character is inserted in the middle of a word for a one-to-one replacement. LAB#R will thus retrieve only LABOR. This is obviously more restrictive, but is useful in special plural cases such as WOMAN and WOMEN or TEETH and TOOTH. All five systems offer wild card searching.

A few systems offer lefthand truncation, although that is not as easily done with inverted indexes. Lefthand truncation is especially important in certain subjects such as chemistry, where a searcher may wish to retrieve all words that contain a common stem, such as OXIDE or VINYLS. STN offers lefthand truncation on some databases.

Since truncation is so essential in the free-text searching that usually makes up a full text search, the systems that offer substantial numbers of full text databases have gone one step further. Automatic stemming, or automatic truncation, allows users to retrieve such common variations as both singular and plural forms of a word automatically without entering a special truncation symbol. Mead, WESTLAW, and BRS all provide automatic searching of singulars and plurals (in BRS the function has to be turned on by the searcher; in WESTLAW it is automatic but can be disabled; in Mead it is automatic.)

Word Equivalency Control

An extension of the concept of automatic truncation is the automatic searching of other common word-form variations. Again the impetus for this feature comes from full text searching where words and word forms are uncontrolled and vary from record to record. In a few cases, the online system helps impose some order on this inconsistency by having word equivalency tables that are checked as words are searched. On Mead and WESTLAW for example, there are equivalency tables for standard abbreviations (Oct = October, Sat = Saturday), for numbers (two = 2, first = 1st), and other common abbreviations (regulation = reg). Mead has equivalencies for government agencies (OSHA = Occupational Safety and Health Administration), for variations in British and American spelling (labor = labour, tire = tyre), and for variations in Chinese romanization schemes (Beijing = Peking). No matter which variation the searcher enters, the system will find all occurrences of either form. This may lead to some false drops, of course, because a searcher cannot turn the feature off, but it puts the burden of variations in language on the computer system rather than on the user. In BRS the searcher can turn on automatic British-American equivalency.

Viewing the Inverted Index

Many systems allow the searcher to view specified portions of the inverted index online. By looking at the inverted index, the searcher can see what words or phrases are in the records and are available for searching, see the many term variations that occur, and find the exact form to search. This can help eliminate false drops caused by truncation by showing the impact of truncating a given stem. For phrase-parsed fields such as authors, viewing the inverted index is especially helpful because phrases may be long or complex and they must be entered exactly as they are found in the records, including all spaces and punctuation.

If the database includes a descriptor field, the descriptors may come from a controlled vocabulary thesaurus. The standards for thesaurus construction specify the inclusion of broader terms, narrower terms, related terms, and *see* and *see also* references to help the indexer assign the correct term and to help the user select appropriate terms. In a few databases on DIALOG the thesaurus is mounted online, so that the searcher can view it directly. In some bibliographic systems it can be automatically invoked, but this is not a common feature in full text systems. Many full text databases do not even have descriptors or a thesaurus. When the capability is available, as it is on DIALOG, and a controlled vocabulary descriptor field is present, as it is on Magazine ASAP, the ultimate decision as to whether to put the thesaurus online rests jointly with the database producer and online system. An online thesaurus is not yet implemented for most full text databases.

Proximity Searching

More important than controlled vocabulary descriptors for full text databases is the capability for the searcher to join words in the text to make phrases. Such "post-coordination" allows word parsed fields like the full text to be searched with more precision. Proximity operations, or the capability of specifying multiword phrases at the time of searching, are considered essential for full text databases. Some variation of proximity operations is available on all of the major online systems that offer full text.

Proximity operations are possible because of the positional information that is recorded by the online system at the time the word-parsed inverted index is created. The positional information indicates the field and where in the field each term occurs so a user can specify, for example, the word MANAGEMENT right next to the word INFORMATION next to the word SYSTEMS.

The rules that govern the word parsing on each system impact how the proximity operations work. On DIALOG, for example, stopwords are counted in the positional count; on BRS they are not. MANAGEMENT right next to OBJECTIVES will not retrieve Management by Objectives on DIALOG, but it will on BRS. (On DIALOG you would have to specify MANAGEMENT with one intervening word before OBJECTIVES.) Tests of these variations are described in Chapter 7.

Since proximity operations are so important with full text, the full text systems typically have many possibilities that allow searchers to incorporate the grammatical structure of the documents. In addition to the term adjacency noted above (which is available on all systems) DIALOG, Mead,

WESTLAW, and STN allow the searcher to specify a given number of intervening words. These will retrieve any and all variations up through the specified limit. For example, ONLINE (2w) CATALOGS on DIALOG or STN will retrieve Online Public Access Catalogs, Online Library Catalogs, and Online Catalogs (and also "online searching for catalogs").

On BRS the adjacency operator requires that the words be in the documents in the order given by the searcher. On all of the others there is one operator that requires specified order (+ on WESTLAW, (W) on DIALOG and STN, pre/ on Mead) and another that will search for words in either order. Thus, ENVIRONMENTAL w/2 IMPACTS on Mead or ENVIRONMENTAL /2 IMPACTS on WESTLAW will retrieve Environmental Impacts and Impacts of an Environmental nature, but ENVIRONMENTAL pre/2 Impacts on Mead or ENVIRONMENTAL +2 IMPACTS on WESTLAW will only retrieve the former (and variations on the former). On STN, bidirectional proximity is specified by the (A) or (nA) operator, on DIALOG it is (N) or (nN), while on both the (W) word operator demands words are in the order specified.

Some systems offer proximity operators that recognize grammatical form. STN offers the widest range of grammatical operators. It supports within the same sentence or a specified number of sentences and within the same paragraph or within a specified number of paragraphs. On BRS the WITH operator means within the same sentence (sentences are designated by a full stop . and two spaces). The BRS SAME operator demands that words appear in the same paragraph. In the full text the paragraphs correspond to grammar, in other fields a paragraph equals a field (e.g., the abstract paragraph, the title paragraph, and so on). WESTLAW and Mead allow same paragraph or same sentence. DIALOG only has a paragraph operator (S). Many of these were tested in studies described in the following four chapters.

Boolean Logic

Boolean logic searching is another form of post-coordination, but it works at the document level rather than at the word, section, or field level. The main Boolean operators AND, OR, and NOT are available on all major online systems and have been the standard for database searching since the 1960s. Boolean operators are a backbone of full text searching, just as they have been for bibliographic searching, with some exceptions as noted below.

As illustrated in Figure 3–3 AND designates that all terms specified must be present in the same record, but does not say where in the record the terms must be. In bibliographic databases AND is the normal way to link concepts in a search. For full text searching, most online systems and database producers recommend replacing the AND operator with a more

Figure 3–3
Venn Diagram of the Boolean AND Operator

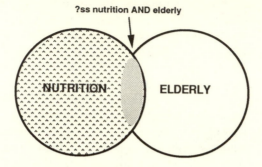

Venn Diagram of the Boolean OR Operator

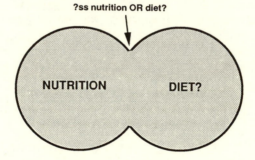

Venn Diagram of the Boolean NOT Operator

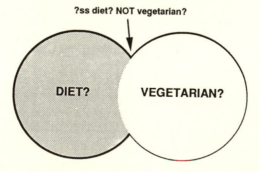

precise proximity operator. (This advice is tested in several studies reported in later chapters.) The assumption is that STRESS w/10 EXECUTIVES will yield more precise results than STRESS AND EXECUTIVES, where the words could be anywhere in the text with no relationship to each other.

The AND operator is necessary in full text searching when a searcher specifies different fields for searching (e.g., publication year AND words in the text.) This is described in more detail below in the section on Field Specification.

The OR operator (Figure 3–3) is as important in full text searching as it is in bibliographic searching. OR is used to specify synonyms or other equivalent terms for the same concept so that a document will be retrieved if one or more of the words is used in it. In full text searching it compensates for variations in words used by different authors to describe the same subject. STRESS or TENSION or HYPERTENSION will retrieve documents that use any of those terms.

The third Boolean operator that is available on all of the major online systems is the NOT operator (Figure 3–3). NOT is used to exclude concepts or terms and can be used in full text searching to eliminate some false drops (i.e., SQUIRREL not SQUIRREL MONKEYS).

An alternative to Boolean logic searching is offered by Dowquest, a new interface to Dow Jones News/Retrieval aimed at end users. Dowquest uses innovative methods such as relevance feedback and natural language input made possible by parallel computer architecture (all discussed briefly in Chapter 4). It is not yet known if Dowquest outperforms standard search techniques.

Set Building

As mentioned earlier, when a user enters a word or phrase to be searched, the system goes to the inverted index file. If the term is found in the inverted index, the corresponding record numbers are placed in a numbered group called a set. On the major online systems, once sets are created, they can be referred back to by set number and combined with new sets or terms. Boolean operators and/or proximity operators can be used to join set numbers.

Set building allows interaction in searching, as users can easily modify results by referring back to previous sets. The systems vary as to how many sets are created in a search. Only DIALOG gives the option of creating a separate set for each term or part of a term entered in a single search statement. The other systems create a single set for each statement. Using the SELECT STEPS command on DIALOG the statement SS (EXPERT(W)SYSTEMS OR ARTIFICIAL(W)INTELLIGENCE) AND MANAGEMENT(W)INFORMATION(W)SYSTEMS would create eleven sets. On the other systems it would create only one.

The advantages of multiple set building are greater flexibility to make modifications and correct errors; the disadvantages are a potential of too many sets for meaningless words or parts of phrases.

Field Specification

All major online systems segment each document into fields. As mentioned earlier, the field specifications are agreed on by the database producer in conjunction with the online vendor. Some online systems try for consistency in field specification among databases, while others have many differences among databases. All systems, however, allow a user to specify a particular field or fields for searching.

The full text as a field can be specified, but more likely with field specification a searcher will select a narrower, more precise field because of the nature of the search question. For example, a searcher may be looking for a particular judge in WESTLAW's JU field, or an article by a certain author (.AU. in BRS), or for something written in a given year (PY= in STN). WHITE$.au. in BRS will search only on the author field and will eliminate records with words such as whitewash, whitewalls, and the like elsewhere in the text.

Field specification can be used with Boolean operators to pose complex queries. The values with the proper field specification are searched, and a Boolean AND is used to link additional concepts searched in other fields or in the complete record. EXECUTIVE? (S) STRESS and PY=1989 in DIALOG will retrieve only those articles on the topic written in 1989.

Comparison Operations

Some systems allow arithmetic or comparison operators to be used in a search statement. Specifying dates greater than (or less than) a certain date is less cumbersome than entering a range of dates, which is the usual alternative. Comparison operations usually occur on specific fields such as date or numeric fields such as gross income. STN, for example, allows equal, ranging, less than, greater than, less than or equal to, and greater than or equal to for date or numeric fields. In full text searching these comparisons are usually one concept that may be linked to a subject word search on the text.

DISPLAY FEATURES

The display of retrieved documents is almost as important in full text systems as are the search and retrieval capabilities. Because of the length of full text documents, there have had to be many refinements in record display beyond the features offered for bibliographic databases. Display features described here are format specification, key-word-in-context display, browsing, word frequency ranking, and record linking.

Format Specification

Most online systems have certain set formats, often expressed in format numbers, that display selected parts of each retrieved record. In BRS and DIALOG for example, Format #6 will display only the titles of the retrieved items. Format #5 is the full record, or in some databases, the full record except the full text field. Mead's CITE format displays only titles and authors or legal citations.

In addition, most systems allow the user to define formats using field tags. Specifying just AU and TI in a display command in BRS, STN, or DIALOG will display only authors and titles. These features allow some customization of output based on individual preferences or needs. Because they operate at the full field level, however, and because the full text is treated as one field in all these systems, specifying TX in a display command will display the *entire* text of the document. This is not conducive to browsing or to scanning for relevance. Some special format options are available just for full text databases.

Key-Word-in-Context Display

In most online systems that have large numbers of full text databases one can view just those portions of the documents that contain the terms or concepts searched. In Mead and DIALOG this feature is called Key-Word-in-Context (KWIC); in BRS it is called HITS. We generically refer to this feature as KWIC display.

A KWIC display is meant to facilitate relevance judgment, since only those portions of a document that include a search term are displayed. The amount of text displayed around the search terms varies from system to system; on DIALOG thirty words of text surround the words, but the number can be set anywhere between two and fifty. On BRS the entire paragraph is displayed. Search terms are highlighted on most systems or the highlighting feature can be turned off or on by the user.

How the KWIC is invoked varies among systems. In WESTLAW and Mead there is a special KWIC function key that makes display easy. In BRS and DIALOG KWIC display is just another format option that must be entered in the correct position in a display command. For example, on DIALOG the TYPE command is followed by a set number/format option/ documents. The command might look like this: TYPE sl/kwic/1–3. On BRS the form is very similar, the . .print command is followed by a set number, format option and documents (. .print 1 hits 1–3).

Both DIALOG and BRS allow the KWIC display to be combined with other fields in the records as specified by the user. Thus, a user who wished to view the title and KWIC portions of three documents on DIALOG would enter: TYPE sl/ti, kwic/1–3. On BRS it would be . .print 1 ti, hits 1–2. This allows more customization in output depending on what fields in a given database might be useful for a given user.

Browsing

The display commands described above are issued for a set number and go for all documents specified in the command. If a user wishes to browse dynamically through documents, many systems allow a shortcut command to be entered that will display the next record in the previously specified format. If a user wishes to view more of a particular document in the midst of a display sequence, the systems vary in flexibility.

On Mead and WESTLAW, for example, function keys or commands allow a user to view more or less of a document at the time it is being viewed in the previously specified format. The "next page" key will override the KWIC display for one document, but it allows the user to return to KWIC viewing of subsequent documents by simply pushing the "next document" key. A user can scroll forwards and backwards in the documents. In addition, WESTLAW offers half-page scrolling backwards or forwards and statutory documents preceding the one currently in view.

On DIALOG, STN, and BRS, however, a user who wishes to view more of a document in the midst of a display sequence must exit that display sequence, enter another display command for the desired document, and then enter a third display command to return to the original viewing format. Users cannot ask to see the next paragraph of a given document or any additional portions of the document without issuing a new command. To view portions of the full text other than complete text or KWIC (HITS) portions, the user must specify a text subfield number in a display command.

Display Order

The default document order for display of a retrieved set is LIFO (last in first out) in almost all systems. This means the most current information (or documents that were most recently added to the database) will be displayed first. If a user wishes to change the order of display, some systems allow sorting of a retrieved set by specified fields in some databases. For example, the records retrieved in a search on Magazine ASAP on the DIALOG system can be sorted before display by author, journal, title, or publication year. A primary and secondary sort can be specified.

WESTLAW (and VU/TEXT) are unusual in their support of display of records by word frequency ranking as an output option. As discussed in

Chapters 4 and 6, the number of times search words occur in a document is assumed to provide some clue to the relevance of the document to the search request. It is assumed that documents where the search words occur more times will be more relevant, or the likelihood of relevance will be greater. To display documents in ranked order, the online system must be able to count the number of times search words occur in a document and then reorder search results according to this number. Most systems do not do either, although number of occurrences would be possible to count from the information in the inverted index of almost all systems. The standard in Boolean systems has been to place a document in a set if search words occur one or more times and not to differentiate between number of times.

BRS does not reorder display of records but it does use word-frequency information. It has a feature called an *occurrence table* that can be invoked in a ". .print" command by specifying OC as the format. The occurrence table shows in chart form in what fields and how often search terms occur in each document. It is then up to the user to decide potential relevance based on this word occurrence information and issue a customized print command to view the documents with the greatest likelihood of relevance.

Record Linking

A few databases on some systems are beginning to link records from more than one database for display purposes. Notable are the Information Access Company family of files where there is a close relationship between a bibliographic and full text file. For example, Magazine Index is a bibliographic database that contains citations and indexing for articles from over 450 magazines from 1959 to the present. The smaller full text Magazine ASAP includes complete texts of articles from over 100 of those 450. If a user is searching the bibliographic Magazine Index and there is a full text article in Magazine ASAP of a retrieved record, the full text can be displayed (not searched) from the bibliographic file.

BRS has a LINK command that allows the searcher of a bibliographic database to request a print-out of the full article if it is present in a BRS full text file. Such LINK features facilitate full text document delivery, but do not relate to searching on full texts.

SUMMARY

The major online systems for full text follow the same general principles of inverted file structures, set building, and field segmentation. This structure facilitates certain search features such as righthand truncation, Boolean logic, proximity operations, field specification, and so on. Display tends to be somewhat static, using set format options and display commands or function keys.

NOTE

1. See for example, Carol Tenopir, "Database Design and Management," in *Principles and Applications of Information Science for Library Professionals*, ed. John Olsgaard (Chicago: American Library Association, 1989); Roger Palmer, *Online Reference and Information Retrieval*, 2d ed. (Littleton, Colo.: Libraries Unlimited, 1987).

4

Research on Full Text
Database Retrieval

Since the number of full text databases has grown rapidly in the past several years, they have not, except for legal and some news full text databases, been studied extensively. Research on full text databases has focused on three main areas: (1) user opinions on their feasibility and capability, (2) evaluation of their retrieval effectiveness or efficiency, and (3) modification of databases and search systems to improve the effectiveness or efficiency of retrieval.

User studies tell about the market for a database and provide some indications of how full text is used online. As more full text databases become available online, many experienced searchers have expressed opinions about retrieval performance, suggested searching strategies for best results, and recommended new searching features to improve performance. Database and system specialists also have presented design considerations that need to be taken into account to provide user-friendly systems and improved performance. However, most of the recommendations are based on experience and observation rather than results of systematic research.

A few studies have been conducted on retrieval performance of full text databases. Research that evaluates full text search methods allows improved search techniques and systems to be developed. Several projects have studied methods for modifying search systems to improve the effectiveness of full text retrieval using automatic indexing, weighting and ranking algorithms, and changing record structures. Most are laboratory rather than field experiments. Research on full text database retrieval is in the initial stages of investigation and is still a professional art based on a rather loosely stated set of experiences.

A few comprehensive literature reviews have appeared, among them reviews of research on

- retrieval characteristics of lengthy full text journal article databases, by Tenopir[1]
- full text legal information systems, by Beard,[2] Bull,[3] Larson and Williams,[4] and Bing[5]
- electronic publication for creating and developing full text databases, by Terrant,[6] Lerner et al.,[7] and Hjerppe.[8] The last two are beyond the scope of this book.

This chapter begins with a summary of the research that predicted the feasibility of offering full text databases. After that, treated in sequence are: user studies and opinions, experimental research on the retrieval performance of full text databases, and research on the methods for modifying search systems to improve the retrieval performance of full text.

RESEARCH PREDICTING THE FEASIBILITY OF FULL TEXT DATABASES

The possibility and acceptability of full text information retrieval systems was predicted by research on natural language retrieval systems using titles or abstracts of documents and on automatic indexing from full texts of documents. These studies hypothesized that natural language systems that allow searching on titles or abstracts or automatic indexing systems on full texts are not inferior to human-assigned index language systems.

Research on text-based natural language retrieval systems has focused on the relative effectiveness of document surrogate searches. An early study by Salton shows no significant differences in search performance between the use of natural language words from titles or abstracts and the use of controlled indexing terms.[9] Later studies by Keen and McGill confirm these findings.[10] Olive and associates found that the use of controlled index terms increased recall more than the titles, but the precision was equivalent.[11] King and associates found only a slight difference in recall when free text terms versus controlled vocabulary terms were used.[12]

Other studies, however, have found significant differences in performance levels. The second Cranfield Project and studies by Parker and Aitchison and associates concluded that natural language often has retrieval advantages over controlled vocabularies.[13] Natural language performs best when some level of elementary control is imposed, such as consistent word endings for plurals and singulars. Cleverdon also pointed out the economic advantages of simple natural language, now a major concern for full text database producers.

Cleverdon found that natural language searches on titles or abstracts had significantly higher recall ratios than controlled vocabulary searches but had little difference in precision ratios.[14] Markey found that free text search strategies result in higher recall while controlled vocabulary formulations result in higher precision.[15] Studies by Charton, Rowlett, Carrow, Henzler, Calkins, and Byrne, however, agree that neither titles nor abstracts nor controlled vocabulary descriptors alone provide complete retrieval.[16] A combination of controlled vocabulary and free text yielded the best results in Markey's and Calkins's studies.

Williams, Smith, and McGill found that there is low overlap of documents retrieved from free text searching based on titles or abstracts and controlled vocabulary searching.[17] Weinberg examined the controlled vocabulary indexing terms assigned to documents to determine the percentage of the controlled vocabulary terms found in the abstract or full text of the articles, and found an overall increase of 23 percent when going from abstracts to full texts.[18]

Even though these studies are based on titles or abstracts of documents, the results of the studies could predict performance of full texts because the full text of a document is a more complete and representative surrogate of a document than the title or abstract. Retrieval systems based on full texts eliminate not only indexing bias but also abstracting bias.

Studies on automatic indexing using full texts of documents have also predicted the value of text words selected from full text as subject content words. Studies in this field could be categorized into three types: (1) those that focused on what percent of index terms manually assigned to a given document is found in the cluster of text words extracted from the full text of the document by automatic indexing[19] (2) those that compared full text words extracted by automatic indexing with manual index terms or other clusters of text words extracted from titles or abstracts by automatic indexing[20] and (3) those that compared different automatic indexing theories using full texts of documents.[21]

The results of the studies show that full text words extracted by automatic indexing are unlikely to degrade performance.[22] They are characterized variously as "not significantly different from manual index words," "better than abstract words," "superior to title words," "holds some promise," "has significant value."[23] The results show that full text words could be accepted as more descriptive content words for a document than title words or abstract words. Weighting algorithms used in automatic indexing could be applied to improve retrieval effectiveness of full text databases for ranking algorithms.

USER STUDIES

Before publishers went to the expense and trouble of making a publication available online for full text search and retrieval, some conducted descriptive user studies to determine the potential market for such searching. The most extensive user tests were conducted by the Books and Journals Division of the American Chemical Society (ACS) and BRS from 1979 to 1982.[24]

The first test was conducted to determine the feasibility of creating an ACS primary journal online database. An original test file of approximately 1,000 full text articles and their abstracts from the *Journal of Medical Chemistry* was made available online by BRS in 1980. Twelve self-selected persons, most of whom were experienced in searching online bibliographic databases, were asked to use the system for three months and to report its usefulness. Overall impressions of the searchers were that the full text database was very useful. Their reactions to this initial file justified the expansion of the test database to include the full text of sixteen ACS journals. The second test was conducted on this expanded online file with about 300 volunteers. In 1982 a continued test involved another 250 participants and 25,000 articles from eighteen ACS journals.

Reactions to the test files were generally positive. Most participants felt they would use the databases and that a chemist with no online searching experience could search the full text file after an hour or two of training or self-instruction. They indicated that full text searching was more powerful than other methods. Searchers could find specific factual information from the text of articles when no term indicating the presence of this information could be found in the titles or abstracts of the articles. However, a cost of $100 per hour was too high, and users were disappointed with the absence of graphics in the online journal. The positive reactions to these test files led ACS to make its journals available online through BRS as of June 1, 1983. The studies also revealed that the online journal was not being used as a replacement for the printed journal. Users did not read or browse entire articles online; instead they mainly used the system as a bibliographic service, to find an article and decide whether it was relevant. Then they went to the shelves to find it.

Even without graphics, the subjects testing the ACS full text test database identified several advantages of having the full text of the journals online:

1. Direct access to specific data (e.g., physical constants, biological testing data, full experimental details, etc.) as they appear in the primary literature.

2. Rapid access to these data, generally within seconds.

3. The ability to locate valuable information that is peripheral to the main focus of the paper. Because secondary services index only major concepts, this information is often missed and users are not even aware of the loss.

4. Timely information, available online at about the same time the printed journals are available. Coverage by secondary sources is delayed by several weeks or months.

5. Ease of use for inexperienced searchers (especially end users such as chemists), probably because searching is accomplished through authors' natural language rather than a limited indexing system that presupposes knowledge of the indexing process.

A similar study was conducted by Elsevier Science Publishers on their ESPL full text journal database.[25] To test technological and marketing aspects of producing a commercially viable primary journal online, the test took place at twenty-five sites (eighteen in the United States) from May 1983 through September 1983. Scientists and librarians at the sites were trained to search the database on the BRS search system and search time was provided at no cost. Users' reactions and suggestions were gathered via questionnaires and interviews. The scientists most frequently complained about the absence of the current journal issues or the lack of specific journal titles. All users requested additional titles. As in the ACS studies, they saw full text as an enhancement of the searching process rather than as an alternative to the paper copy. Full texts were used to locate interesting articles, to find particular experimental methods used in a study, or to search the footnotes or references. The major problem was considered to be the absence of graphics and illustrations, a problem more serious to cell biologists than to molecular biologists. The most powerful aspect of full text searching was considered to be the ability of a user to judge relevance immediately.

Before MEDIS, the full text medical information retrieval system, was added to Mead Data Central's system, Mead tested a MEDIS prototype.[26] During the three months from May to July 1984 more than 500 health care professionals conducted 9,377 searches using computer terminals located in seven hospital and medical centers. With one or two hours of training, the majority of respondents to a questionnaire given during the test period said they would continue to use the service during the pilot test, and only about 1 percent reported the search process difficult to use or not user-friendly. As expected, when users became more experienced, the mean time for a search decreased from 16.8 minutes (for the first two searches) to 6.9 minutes for the users who had requested more than twenty-four searches.

The pilot test demonstrated the feasibility of a computerized online retrieval system for full text medical literature. It also revealed that users felt limited by what they perceived to be an inadequate medical literature database and the inability to retrieve graphs and images. Although graphs and images are still not available, MEDIS has grown from thirteen publications in the pilot system to more than one hundred publication files of textbooks and journals by 1989. Users' comments about the insufficient contents of the database are probably no longer as valid.

While the studies on ACS, ESPL, and MEDIS full text databases focused on subject-expert users of scholarly journal articles, some other studies looked at popular literature and its users. Two recent articles by Pagell are a first look at the uses of the Magazine ASAP database.[27] Pagell found that not everything in the printed journal is included in the database version. Not only are graphics left out, but entire sections of the magazines are omitted from the online file. For some magazines only feature articles and columns are included, dates of coverage vary, and journal titles included in Magazine ASAP vary according to what online system loads the file. She concluded that Magazine ASAP is "useful for individuals looking for the full text of selected articles" but the electronic versions "cannot serve as substitutes for the journals themselves."

Using the same database, Tenopir investigated the potential users and uses of full text popular magazine databases in an academic environment.[28] After a two-hour initial training session, eleven end-user volunteers searched any topic for any purpose for up to a total of five hours through DIALOG. While the potential popularity of browsing has been underestimated in other studies on full text scholarly journal articles, this study found that a popular use of the database was to browse through articles or portions of articles for background information on a topic. The majority of use was found to be to locate a set of documents on a particular subject. The participants preferred to download entire articles rather than find the original magazine in the library. Browsing and downloading entire articles online were by far the most common uses in this study. Most of the participants indicated that they would not download or browse as much if they were paying, but they would pay up to $50 for a work-related search if it would meet an urgent, important, and unique need. This finding suggests that if the pricing issue could be solved, full text browsing could become an important use. (Chapter 7 discusses this study in detail.)

RESEARCH ON RETRIEVAL PERFORMANCE OF FULL TEXT DATABASES

User studies have been conducted to assess the feasibility and capability of full text service and user acceptability of the service. They indicate the feasibility and capability of full text retrieval and general satisfaction with online versions of journals, textbooks, and patents. The second category of experimental studies has focused on evaluating retrieval performance of full text databases using evaluation measurements such as recall and precision.

Experiments on Legal Literature

As mentioned in Chapter 2, the field of law has been the leader in online full text retrieval. In law most of the research tests on full text performance have compared database searching with the manual conventional techniques of index lookup.

The first test was conducted to evaluate the LITE system in the United States.[29] The test lasted six months in 1964 and was conducted on a database of approximately 17 million words using 215 questions. The findings were that

1. in 7.5 percent of the total searches the computer retrieved fewer relevant citations than were discovered by a manual search.
2. in 44.1 percent of the total searches the same number of relevant citations were retrieved by both methods.
3. in 48.4 percent the LITE system retrieved more relevant citations than were discovered manually.

Summing up the results shows that the computer full text retrieval system worked on a 92.5 percent effectiveness rate, while manual retrieval worked at a 51.6 percent effectiveness rate. The relative recall ratio of computer retrieval was 93.5 percent while manual retrieval was 62 percent.

The Joint American Bar Foundation and International Business Machine Project was conducted in 1966–1967 to test the computerized full text retrieval as compared with manual retrieval.[30] The database consisted of 5,800 appellate court decisions and the question set consisted of forty questions taken from the files of practicing lawyers. It was found that the retrieval system and the manual search performed about equally well in terms of recall and that the manual search was about twice as effective in terms of precision. The study also found often intense disagreement about relevance judgments among the four evaluators (lawyers).

In England, the first research on full text was conducted by a lawyer, Colin Tapper; it has become known as the Oxford Experiment.[31] Two databases were prepared for the purpose of the experiment. The first was the All England Law Reports, a general series of reports of decisions in the High Court, and the second was the Commissioner's Decisions, a series of administrative decisions in the field of insurance claims for industrial injuries. The two databases consisted of about 2 million and 1 million words respectively.

The results in terms of recall and precision were that computer full text retrieval had on the average 70 percent recall and 29 percent precision while manual index look-up search had on the average 49 percent recall and 92 percent precision. The computer search retrieved 496 documents,

144 of which were relevant, while the manual search retrieved 109 documents, 100 of which were relevant. The full text system produced inferior precision values.

The Responsa project was an attempt to make the huge Responsa literature available for research through a full text retrieval system.[32] The Responsa span seventeen centuries and are written mainly in Hebrew and Aramaic. The system was tested on an initial database consisting of the 518 Responsa (558,864 words) by Rivash. In all, sixteen questions were run and the results were gratifying: 100 percent recall was achieved for all questions, and the average precision was 34 percent. These performance figures are not directly comparable to the other performance figures because of the abnormal procedure used. Before the query was constructed, the searcher spent a full day researching the database in order to acquaint himself with the relevant vocabulary.

Some other research on full text retrieval is available, but the results were measured using effectiveness measurements other than recall and precision. In 1961, Fels tested the first full text retrieval system developed by the Health Law Center of the University of Pittsburgh.[33] In this test two systems were compared: retrieval by computer versus retrieval by manual search. Mooers's ratio was computed.[34] The full text retrieval got 0.700 crucial-documents ratio, 0.575 relevant-documents ratio, and 0.300 irrelevant-document ratio, while the manual search got 0.750 crucial-documents ratio, 0.818 relevant-documents ratio, and 0.000 irrelevant-documents ratio.

A recent study by Blair and Maron examined the well-known automatic text-retrieval system STAIRS as applied to a collection of 40,000 legal full text documents (equivalent to some 350,000 pages of text) to answer forty different user queries.[35] In STAIRS, words extracted from document texts have been broadened using truncation, then each word may be supplemented by lists of synonyms supplied by the user. When synonyms are specified, a search based on a particular term automatically extends to all the synonyms. The STAIRS system also includes a ranking feature that orders retrieved sets of less than 200 documents in decreasing order based on total document weights, which are calculated by adding the weights of the query terms contained in each retrieved document. In addition, it provides ranking functions that permit the user to order retrieved sets of 200 documents or less in either ascending or descending numerical (e.g., by date) or alphabetic (e.g., by author) order. In the STAIRS retrieval test conducted by Blair and Maron, an average precision value of about 75.50 percent and an average recall value of 20.26 percent were obtained with weighting. The unweighted average value turned out to be 79 percent for precision and 20 percent for recall.

This study includes a lengthy discussion on the unexpected recall and precision results. It was assumed that full text searching would yield high recall and low precision. As mentioned by Blair and Maron, one reason for their high precision and low recall was the lawyers' fear that they could get output overload from such a large database. Consequently the users-narrowed search formulations by adding intersecting terms. The process of continuing to add intersecting terms to a query until the size of the output reaches a manageable number, was reported to be necessary because of the large size of the database. Search queries employing four or five intersecting terms were not uncommon among the queries used in Blair and Maron's test. (Salton objected to the idea that a large collection results in too large an output.[36])

Another reason for high precision and low recall mentioned by Blair and Maron was the difficulty of predicting the words and phrases in the field of law that are used by all relevant documents in order to retrieve a document by subject. One request resulted in the identification of three key terms or phrases that were used to retrieve relevant information; later another twenty-six words and phrases that retrieved additional relevant documents were found. If all the missed words were used to retrieve all the relevant documents by full text searching in this study (i.e., 100 percent recall), what would its precision value be? Ro answered that "the Responsa project suggested the possible answer, i.e., 34 percent precision."[37]

One interesting finding is that misspellings kept relevant documents from being retrieved. The misspellings "flatening," "guage," "gage," "memoes," and "correspondance" instead of the search words like "flattening," "gauge," "memos," and "correspondence" meant that relevant documents containing the errors could not be retrieved. It was suggested that searchers foresee the whole range of possible misspellings, letter transpositions, and typographical errors that are likely to be committed.

On later discussion, Blair presented an additional finding that the scale of relevance judgments affects the retrieval effectiveness.[38] With relevance judgments on the scale of one to four where the relevant documents were judged to be either "marginal," "satisfactory," or "vital," the effectiveness turned out to be 79 percent for precision and 20 percent for recall. However, when only documents judged "vital" were counted as relevant documents, the recall went up significantly (from 20.0 percent to 48.2 percent) and the precision down (from 79.0 percent to 18.2 percent).

One difference between Blair and Maron's study and other studies in the field of law is that Blair and Maron evaluated only retrieval performance of a full text database, while others evaluated retrieval performance of a full text database compared with manual look-up. Another difference between it and most other full text retrieval performance studies described in the remainder of this book is that Blair and Maron used an absolute recall value by which the total number of relevant documents in the database was assessed based on the number of relevant documents in a sampled subset of the database. Other studies used a relative recall value by which the total number of relevant documents was defined as the number of relevant documents in the union of sets retrieved by several searches on the same topic. It is possible that absolute recall values may sometimes be lower than relative recall values.

Experiments on Other Literature

Unlike research in the field of legal documents, most studies with journal articles evaluated the retrieval performance of full text documents compared with that of controlled vocabulary descriptors. Full texts of documents in this research field varied from a document collection of one-page review articles to a collection of long journal articles.

Early studies were conducted with full texts of short papers. Swanson tested three retrieval systems based on a subject heading index, full text, and thesaurus in addition to the words obtained by the document text; this study used one hundred nuclear physics articles selected from the *Physical Review* and fifty questions.[39] He found that the effectiveness of full text searching could be improved through the requestor's use of certain "retrieval aids" such as a thesaurus. He discussed techniques for systematically improving these aids as a result of collecting experimental data. However, he reported the superiority of retrieval performance of a system based on automatic text analysis over a conventional system based on a manually assigned subject heading index.

The SMART system has been used to test automatic indexing procedures using various intellectual aids in the form of synonym dictionaries, hierarchical arrangements of subject identifiers, statistical association methods, syntactic analysis, request-document matching, and others.[40] A series of tests for automatic indexing was conducted with three document collections. One collection out of three, a set of eighty-two short papers presented at the 1963 Annual Meeting of the American Documentation Institute, was used to test full texts of documents with thirty-five search requests. The comparison between document abstracts (an average of fifty-nine words in length) and full texts (an average of 1,380 words in length) was done in two fields of processing, a word stem dictionary and synonym dictionary (thesaurus). The results show that full text processing is superior to abstract processing in both word stem and synonym dictionaries. But Salton and Lesk pointed out that the increase in effectiveness is not great enough to reach the unequivocal conclusion that full text processing is always superior to abstract processing.

The studies in 1969–1970 by Hersey and colleagues[41] of the Smithsonian Institution Science Information Exchange (SSIE) reported a negative effectiveness of online full text retrieval compared with that of subject indexing codes, from a database of 4,600 documents in four subject areas. By searching thirty-nine questions, they found that average recall values were 30–40 percent higher, and relevance values were 15–20 percent higher for subject index code use as compared with text word use. But, since the database consisted of one-page summaries of research projects, it has many of the characteristics of a lengthy abstract database rather than full text.

Since these early studies were conducted with full texts of short papers, the results should be only cautiously extrapolated to lengthy full text documents. Swanson used review articles averaging 1,000 words, the SMART system used ADI short papers averaging 1,380 words, and the SSIE study used one-page summaries of research projects. Several studies have been conducted with full texts of lengthy articles.

In 1975–1976, Rinewalt ran a series of experiments designed to evaluate various features of a full text information retrieval system in a controlled environment.[42] The test evaluated a minicomputer-based experimental retrieval program known as EUREKA with two databases: (1) a collection of thirty-seven technical articles on information retrieval containing approximately 1 million characters, and (2) a set of state statutes containing approximately 20 million characters. Three groups of students had access to the full text of EUREKA, a restricted version of EUREKA, and the original printed documents respectively, to look for documents that answered questions in a quiz. The online full text searching group did not perform significantly better on the quizzes than other groups.

Cleveland, Cleveland, and Wise compared searching on various combinations of less than full text document surrogates with full text searching.[43] Thirty-eight articles on epidemiology were randomly selected and their references were used to create a database of over 700 documents. The query documents were used to extract search terms for indirect searching of the database for related articles, a technique developed by Goffman.[44] The extracted terms were searched in the full text field and the less than full text fields of abstracts, references and titles, and combinations of abstracts/references, titles/abstracts, titles/references, and title/abstracts/reference. The best results in both recall and precision came from the combination title/abstract/reference searches. The full text ranked third.

Besides these laboratory experimental studies, a few field experimental studies have concentrated on the retrieval performance of commercially available online full text systems. Stein and others evaluated hands-on use by end users of the Patent and Trademark Office Full Text Database.[45] The tests consisted of three studies: (1) concept representation in patent full text, (2) end user online searching of the entire full text of patents, and (3) end user online searching of commercially available patent text databases. To study the concept representation, six expert patent classifiers were asked to conduct twelve searches each on a LEXIS database of 50,000 patents. After the searches were completed, each query was examined to determine where in each patent the search terms occurred and what term variants occurred. The combinations of summary and description provided the best search results, that is, 87 percent of the retrieved documents from full text searching were retrieved if a search was limited to them. To test end user online searching of the entire full text, 102 examiners (end users) were trained for three hours, and twelve users received an additional two hours of advanced training. Twelve users from each group were selected randomly to participate in manual versus full text search. It was found that any useful reference from full text searching was considered a quality and productivity enhanced, cross-fertilization reference, since such a reference would not have been found in a manual search. For the third test, three systems through ORBIT, DIALOG, and INFOLINE were tested. Two groups of users were trained on three vendors' systems for fifteen weeks and three months respectively. There was no significant difference in performance from different durations. Overall performance for the three systems was ranked as follows: Derwent (ORBIT) > IFI/Plenum (DIALOG) > Pergamon (INFOLINE).

The Tenopir study (described in detail in Chapter 5) evaluated full text searching compared with searching on different fields in the Harvard Business Review Online database on the BRS search system using thirty-six queries from the history file of two libraries.[46] She studied not only the effectiveness but also the overlap and unique documents retrieved from each search. Her conclusion was that full text searching had higher recall and retrieved a greater total number of documents, but it had a lower precision than abstract or controlled vocabulary searching. Nearly 75 percent of the total number of unique documents retrieved were retrieved by searching the full text alone. But since Tenopir used the SAME paragraph operator rather than searching the entire full text search with the Boolean operator AND, her conclusions pertain to paragraph searching in full text rather than searching the full text as a whole.

In 1984, Abbott and Smith compared two American Chemical Society databases: full text ACS Journals Online (CFTX) and the bibliographic CA Search (CHEM).[47] Both databases are available through BRS. CFTX at that time contained the full text of approximately 30,000 citations from eighteen ACS journals dating from 1980. CHEM is an online version of *Chemical Abstracts* containing indexed citations to the world's chemical literature. Twenty-five chemists submitted one search query each and evaluated the retrieved articles for relevance. Searches were first run in CHEM and then modified until the desired citation set was retrieved. The searches were saved and executed in the CFTX file and modified as needed. CHEM resulted in an average precision value of 53 percent and took an average connect time of 0.325 hour per search while CFTX had 36 percent and took 0.217 hour. It was found that the search strategies suitable for use in the bibliographic file usually were not suitable for re-execution in the full text file. To increase the contextual affinity among search terms, the SAME, WITH, and ADJ operators were more successful. However, care must be exercised not to become too restrictive. Over 50 percent of the relevant citations found using SAME were lost when the search was further qualified by WITH.

In the post-search questionnaires, users pointed out the coverage limitation of CFTX. Seven users thought that CFTX was sufficient to survey the literature on their search topic, while eighteen answered negatively. The most frequent reason given for insufficiency was that CFTX covers too few journals. One biochemist indicated only one CFTX journal, *Biochemistry*, concerned his area, while CHEM covered *Cell, Journal of Molecular Biology*, and other biochemical journals. A need for dissertations, patents, and foreign language materials not available from CFTX was indicated. Users felt that the years of coverage were too few.

In spite of its coverage limitation, CFTX retrieved many additional relevant citations that were not retrieved in CHEM. There was no overlap between the relevant CFTX results and the relevant CHEM results in eight of the searches. Where overlap was found, seven searches had less than 40 percent overlap, and five searches had 50 to 80 percent of the CFTX citations previously retrieved in the CHEM results. In eight searches all the relevant documents retrieved from CFTX were new additional documents not retrieved from CHEM. In seven searches more than 60 percent of the relevant documents retrieved from CFTX were new (not retrieved from CHEM), and in five searches 50 to 80 percent of the relevant CFTX citations were new (not retrieved from CHEM). Five users did not respond to this question.

In order to examine a common perception that full text databases give a significant amount of irrelevant information, Love and Garson conducted another research study using the ACS Journal Online on BRS, a full text database containing nineteen ACS journals.[48] The results of forty searches show that the ACS Journal Online file gave retrieved information on a highly precise level. Twenty-three percent of the searches had 100 percent precision; 35 percent of the searches had 90–100 percent precision; and 88 percent of searches had 50–100 percent precision.

Several suggestions for searching full text chemical databases are given. The first is to discuss the search requests with the client and to read through several relevant documents in order to identify unique terms that describe the interrelationships sought by the search query. Searches using broad terms having many synonyms were reported to give poor information retrieval. Using chemical names as search terms was reported to yield imprecise results because chemical names usually have a number of synonyms. Using molecular formulas as search terms was also reported to yield imprecise results because of imperfections in the parsing routine as implemented at BRS. The second recommendation is to use the proximity operators ADJ, WITH, and SAME to retrieve reference information on a very precise level instead of the Boolean AND operator.

Wagers investigated the factors affecting decisions to use full text as a searchable field of Magazine ASAP on BRS.[49] To determine the contribution of text to searching, Wagers mapped various terms and phrases upon controlled vocabulary in order to represent fairly exact correspondences, and broader, narrower, and related text appearances. The study then investigated how structure of the subject area, search terminology, the specificity and depth of the controlled vocabulary, and document characteristics affect the decision to search in various fields. The study recommended that when searchers believe documents may cover a topic in general and may have general titles, index terms, and possibly abstracts, but contain significant discussions of specific matters directly related to the search topic, they should strongly opt in favor of text searches. When they believe the indexing language is too limited to capture a variety of expressions for a searchable concept, they should look to text to meet this need. Finally, when searchers believe the documents will be highly specific on various topics with specific titles and index terms, and their search is about general concepts hierarchically of a higher order, they should consider text as a searchable field. When a searcher wants to retrieve complete documents or large portions of documents or to find specific facts, lists, answers to questions, or succinct explanations and expects only a portion of each document will contain the required information, full text searches could be preferred.

The Tenopir study (described in detail in Chapter 7) investigated the effectiveness of various search strategies for full text databases.[50] Four methods of combining concepts in full text searching of Magazine ASAP on DIALOG were compared (1) Boolean AND, (2) within the same grammatical paragraph ((S) operator), (3) within ten words in either order ((10N) operator), and (4) within five words in either order ((5N) operator). Recall was much higher when concepts were linked with AND, but the large number of false drops (low precision averaging 49.3 percent) made the cost-effectiveness of this method low. Same paragraph searching on the average offered the best balance between recall and precision and provided a more cost-effective way to retrieve a set of relevant documents. In several questions, however, important partially relevant documents were not retrieved with the (S) operator because all concepts of a topic were not mentioned in the same paragraph. On the average 47.9 percent of the relevant documents retrieved from AND searching were not retrieved from same paragraph (S) searching. Paragraph (S) searching had higher precision and much higher recall than (10N) and (5N). Often the (10N) and (5N) techniques eliminated relevant documents while retaining some of the false drops. The operator (5N) had a lower precision score than (10N) in some questions and on the average had lower precision and much lower recall than paragraph searching.

A mixture of different types of magazines and articles seemed to pose problems with search strategy. News summary stories and book or movie reviews resulted in false drops for all the techniques. Footnotes also resulted in some false drops. The journals themselves might be a predictor of relevance to a certain degree. For example, in a question on AIDS, relevant documents came from science magazines, but not from hobby magazines. This study suggests that optimum search strategy needs to vary with the purpose of the search (fact or document retrieval), writing style of documents makes a difference in retrieval, and searchers should be able to make use of this by the ability to exploit grammar, style, and word frequency in search strategies.

A study by Shu compared retrieval effectiveness of proximity operators on the different vendor systems, DIALOG and BRS.[51] The (10N) and (S) operators on DIALOG were compared with the WITH and SAME operators on BRS using Trade and Industry ASAP database. The (10N) on DIALOG retrieved on the average three more records than the WITH on BRS, but they were often false drops. Since the WITH operator requires all the concepts on a topic to be within the same sentence while the (10N) operator ignores the . (period) sentence delimiter and counts only word proximity, the BRS WITH operator had better precision overall than DIALOG's (10N). This suggests that the author's grammatical structure of sentences is useful to help improve precision. There was less variation between DIALOG's (S) operator and the BRS SAME operator, since they both use the grammatical structure of paragraph. Documents were uniquely retrieved on DIALOG because the DIALOG version was more up-to-date than the BRS version. In both versions the type of article was often a predictor that an item would be a false drop. Precision could be improved by using the Boolean NOT to exclude certain types of articles in predefined or user-defined categories. This study also found the BRS HITS format together with the occurrence table to be better for relevance judgment, but more display enhancements are needed by both systems.

Studies on information-seeking and search behavior of online searchers, especially of end users, is essential to design and implement effective and efficient "user-friendly" retrieval systems. Marchionini examined information-seeking strategies by novice users searching a full text electronic encyclopedia on CD-ROM.[52] The research was conducted from a cognitive process perspective. Two groups of elementary school children conducted two assigned searches after two forty-five-minute demonstration sessions on use of the electronic encyclopedia. Older searchers (sixth graders) were more successful and took less time in finding required information than younger searchers (third and fourth graders). Analysis of search patterns showed that novices used a heuristic, highly interactive search strategy. Most searchers used sentence and phrase queries and accepted system defaults. Marchionini suggests that "perhaps a viable strategy in a full text, no-connect-charge environment is a scan and select technique where the searcher uses one general term or phrase to locate a title list and then uses scanning methods and frequency count feedback to judge quickly which articles to examine; followed by scanning of the article by using the high-lighted terms in the text to focus on relevant information and locate other terms to use in subsequent queries."[53]

RESEARCH ON METHODS FOR MODIFYING SEARCH SYSTEMS TO IMPROVE RETRIEVAL

Even though user studies indicate the feasibility and general satisfaction with online full text database retrieval, experimental studies suggest that full text searching must be done with caution. As more full text databases become available online, many experienced searchers and database and system designers see potential problems as well as strengths in searching full text databases.

Milstead describes full text news databases and news indexing tools, emphasizing that the two are separate and usually accessed through different systems. Her experience with searching both types of systems led her to conclude that with full text databases "all the problems of lack of vocabulary control and bulk which might be anticipated are encountered, with the obvious advantages of speed and completeness as tradeoffs."[54]

Implementation of a broad controlled vocabulary to full text databases was advocated in many articles. As described by Duckitt, controlled indexing with the advantage of synonym control can supplement the advantages of full text searching for end users as well as for intermediaries because end users are in general not used to thinking of synonyms or terms related to the words that first come into their minds.[55] Controlled indexing systems based on a hierarchical thesaurus might correspond very well with the basic human mental processes used in conceptualizing and formulating problems. While full text searching looks only for the presence of words and their positional relationship to each other, controlled indexing systems have a limited amount of syntax by indicating links, roles, and other relations between terms.

Duckitt argues for the use of controlled indexing systems to enhance free text searching of full texts. For MARTINDEX, a full text drug information databank designed solely for an online system without hard copy abstracting or indexing services, she proposed the production of a hybrid between a thesaurus and a database user guide.

Perez also believes that the limitations of relying totally on free text searching of natural language text are becoming apparent.[56] Major problems exist, including the cost and effort of augmenting text and the design of a consistent and efficient text enhancement methodology. Text enhancement is expensive and still requires a major effort by the database producer. Perez recommends a "pragmatic compromise" of combining the ability to do full text/free text retrieval with the addition of words from small or abbreviated controlled vocabularies, in order to reap the benefits of both approaches. Several newspaper full text databases offer this compromise that allows retrieval of broad or general concepts with controlled indexing in addition to the specific concepts that can be retrieved by words from the text.

Sprowl also advocates this broad or "coarse" indexing approach in legal text databases. By providing even coarse indexing, searchers will not have to browse irrelevant cases. Broad indexing allows a portion of the database to be isolated, and "one may then search through only a portion of the collection using words and phrases, and many totally irrelevant cases from the remainder of the collection that by chance contain the same words and phrases are screened out by the indexing."[57]

Tousignaut introduced another broad subject indexing approach, "concept (or facet) indexing," used on the full text drug databases Drug Information Full Text and Consumer Drug Information.[58] In a compilation of drug descriptions there are recurring concepts in each such as Dosage, Dosage Form, Drug Interactions, Uses, Adverse Reactions, Allergies, Stability Data, and others. A list of terms representing these recurring ideas became the concept terms in the concept indexing scheme. A four-digit hierarchical number was assigned to the concept terms. It enables the user to search the file for a concept and find the precise location in a drug description for that concept.

Besides the implementation of a broad controlled vocabulary, some considerations that need to be taken into account when designing full text databases and systems providing user-friendly systems and enhancing retrieval systems have been presented by database and system specialists. Jackson reviews existing search system features and research that seeks to improve results from searching full text databases.[59] She mentions simplified and dedicated terminals with function keys, menu-driven systems or common command languages, the addition of controlled language to the text at the time of document creation, and automated language enhancements as system enhancements to facilitate and improve full text retrieval. Automated language enhancements implemented to date include truncation that allows automatic searching for different forms of words, string searching to retrieve variant spellings, the ability to view a list of synonyms or even to search automatically for synonyms, word proximity searching, document ranking and clustering based on word occurrences, and artificial intelligence techniques for automated translation or indexing or natural language query formation.

Zuga also offers design considerations for the database vendor.[60] She recommends providing abstract or controlled vocabulary searching to be used as "filters" to search for major concepts and needs. She also suggests more proximity operators than are usually available on most systems—not only document, field, subfield, and word operators—but operators to search a section or chapter of text, a subsection, a paragraph, a sentence, and within a user-defined segment of N words. She also recognizes the importance of the appearance of the online text display, especially readability and scanning capability. Readability and aesthetic considerations can make a difference in user acceptance and are as important as search features. Useful display features that Zuga suggests include blank lines between paragraphs, special treatment of headings and section headings, highlighted search terms, the ability to define how much text is viewed on either side of the search terms, and clearly labeled fields. The user should be able to scan search words in context and stop scanning at any point to read more of a particular document.

The enhanced quality of text display was also recognized by Jennings.[61] Dramatically increasing the amount of information actually available for viewing, reading larger blocks of text into the terminal RAM, different print styles, sizes and weights, and other techniques such as preserving page references in stored data were recommended.

Evaluative studies on the effectiveness of full text retrieval argue for sophisticated search techniques to improve the effectiveness of full text retrieval. Some experienced searchers also provide their experience in developing the best search strategy on a full text system to improve the retrieval effectiveness. Klinkroth discussed the use of full text databases in health sciences and recommended use of proximity operators to increase precision, to print occurrence tables that show location and frequency of search terms in a record and give a clue to relevance before printing hits, to use the text field when searching for a narrow and specific concept, to avoid the text field and rely on title with abstract and descriptor fields if necessary when searching for a broad concept, to use synonyms liberally in full text files lacking descriptors and consider their use in other files as well (especially if descriptors are very general or assigned sparingly), to check carefully the vendor's and producer's documentation before embarking on a full text search, and to look for information in tables that are available in some full text databases.[62] Preference of proximity operators to the Boolean AND operator for high level of precision was supported by Tenopir, Huth, Love and Garson, and others.[63] Huth concluded that searching texts of articles is the best way to zero in on new concepts, jargon, and fads. Tenopir also suggested use of term occurrence data. The major contribution of the full text was reported to be made when an article is of broader scope than the search question or when one facet of a question is mentioned only as one possible factor in a broader issue.

Improving full text searching requires additional carefully designed research into database and system design considerations for effective retrieval and display. Research on methods for enhancing text or modifying search systems to improve retrieval from full text databases focuses on (1) automatic extraction of index terms from text, (2) use of weighting to match queries to document contents, (3) combination of menu-driven and query-driven systems, and (4) changing computer architecture and document record structures to improve retrieval of specific content.

Use of Ranking Algorithms

A ranking algorithm defines an ordering on a set of documents retrieved by a search query in terms of the similarity between each document and the query. A ranking algorithm consists of three major components: (1) weighting of terms in the document, (2) weighting of terms in the query, and (3) a similarity measure between query and document. There are many possible ranking algorithms, using different combinations of these three components.

Document-term weighting algorithms based on word frequency were originally proposed and tested for automatic indexing. Some were proposed for extracting keywords from abstracts, and some were proposed and tested for full text of documents. The algorithms can be categorized into four types: (1) absolute frequency, (2) relative frequency, (3) inverse document frequency, and (4) probabilistic theory.

Noreault, McGill and Koll introduced and tested twenty-one document-term weighting algorithms with a binary query-term weighting and twenty-four similarity measures.[64] Robertson, Rijsbergen and Porter tested probabilistic document-term weighting algorithms with a binary query-term weighting and a probabilistic similarity measure.[65] While both of these studies tested ranking algorithms using a document collection of abstracts and titles, Sager and Lockemann tested the relative effectiveness of ranking algorithms using a document collection of full texts.[66] They tested the relative effectiveness of nineteen document-term weighting algorithms with one query-term weighting (binary one) and one similarity measure of vector ($R_n = x_m \, y_m$, where x_m = query weight vector, and y_m = document weight vector). With the binary query term weighting used in the study, the similarity between a document and a query, R_n = the sum of the weights of each search term used for the query in the document, since zero is assigned to terms not occurring in the query and one is assigned to terms occurring in the query.

In the experiment thirty-four test queries in a database of 1,003 decisions (in German) of the Federal Constitutional Court were searched on IBM STAIRS software. Of nineteen document-term weighting algorithms, some performed better than no weighting. However, some other algorithms based on absolute frequency performed worse than no weighting. The results of this study indicated that ranking algorithms are of considerable help:

—to inexperienced users who formulate their queries in a very general way and hence end up with a large number of documents retrieved;

—to experienced users who are interested in a few highly relevant documents but care little for a complete survey;

—to users who look for a complete bibliography but wish to start out with a first impression.[67]

The Norwegian Research Center for Computers and Law has conducted a number of the NORIS (Norwegian Studies in Legal Informatics) projects on full text retrieval since 1970.[68] Research was tested on different strategies for identical search requests, different surrogates for identical strategies, ranking algorithms, and so on. A NORIS project compared binary document-term weighting with absolute-frequency weighting under the same conditions of binary query weighting and vector similarity measure. A ranking algorithm highlighted as a new search strategy was to rank documents based on conceptor frequency, that is, the number of different word types of a concept appearing in a retrieval document. The performance of conceptor ranking strategies was compared to the results of a straight word-frequency ranking, that is, ranking based on the total number of frequency tokens of all word types for a concept occurring in the document, and an incidental ranking based on the dates of the documents.

The results in the recall-precision graphs showed that ranking by the number of word types of a concept performed better than word-frequency ranking, and word-frequency ranking performed better than chronological ranking. In other words, the conceptor method was best. This result verified the finding of Sager and Lockemann that showed superiority of the binary document-term weighting algorithm to the absolute frequency weighting under the conditions of binary query weighting and the vector similarity.

While these two experiments were conducted with the full text of legal documents in German and in Norwegian, respectively, another research study tested ranking algorithms with English journal articles. To investigate methods intended to improve the precision of full text retrieval, Ro tested relative performance of twenty-nine ranking algorithms based on twenty-nine document-term weightings and a binary query-term weighting.[69] A ranking approach used in fuzzy-set retrieval was applied for similarity measures under the Boolean environment. This study found that the use of ranking algorithms achieved significantly higher levels of precision than full text searching without the use of such algorithms. The relative performance of individual algorithms was found to depend on level of recall and search strategy. (Chapter 6 presents this research in detail.)

Bernstein and Williamson proposed a very successful ranking algorithm for a full text retrieval system they called ANNOD (A Navigator of Natural Language Organized Data).[70] ANNOD is a retrieval system that combines use of probabilistic, linguistic, and empirical means to weight and rank individual paragraphs of full text for their similarity to natural language queries proposed by users. ANNOD deletes stopwords, stems word roots, expands queries with a thesaurus, and applies a complex empirical ranking algorithm. The system was tested using a prototype Hepatitis Knowledge Base (HKB) and fifty-one questions. The similarity of individual HKB paragraphs to the query entered by the user was based initially on manipulation of empirically derived weightings of five factors: query word root weighting, paragraph word root weighting, entire HKB word root weighting, additional weighting for expansion by a thesaurus, and a correction for paragraph length. The weighting score (called Raw Score) was then recalculated by adding a bonus for percent match with original query roots.

This study shows that information needed to answer 85–95 percent of the queries was located and displayed in the first few selected paragraphs. It was successful in locating information in both the classified (listed in the table of contents) and unclassified portions of text. This system bridges the gap between complete scanning of full text and the indexing of discrete content and illustrates the potential of word root matching algorithms for full text access. Many researchers draw attention to the value of weighting documents on the basis of the frequency with which they contain specific query terms, but Rowbottom and Willett suggest that such methods will give varied results depending upon the subject matter of the documents.[71]

Combination of Boolean and Menu Systems

The current retrieval software on the major commercial online search services falls generally into two classes: hierarchical menu-driven and Boolean query driven (also referred to as command driven), each appealing to different classes of users. While typical full text retrieval systems provide query access based on the Boolean combination of keywords and/or manually prepared subject codes, menu access could be an attractive alternative. The query driven systems, such as DIALOG and BRS, offer flexible searching. These systems have important advantages in power and efficiency compared to menu driven systems. Boolean retrieval permits users to browse the database by posing general queries. It also allows users to formulate specific queries by logically adding a number of terms together to form a very precise query. However, Boolean retrieval has been criticized for its rigidity, lack of ranking of results, and need for vocabulary control. It is too rigid in that if a query logically ANDs three terms together as in, A AND B AND C, and if one of the terms is not present in a database passage, the result is "false." Although the result was "almost true," as two of three terms are present, Boolean logic does not recognize this condition. (Both DIALOG and BRS have a menu interface option. However, both require users to input search terms with Boolean logic after a series of preparing menus, so are not included in our discussion of pure hierarchical menu systems.)

Menu retrieval is widely used where the database has a hierarchical structure and the user population is expected to be familiar with the subject area but not with computer processing.[72] This may occur in applications such as inventory control and videotex systems in which the databases may be hierarchically structured and the users are familiar with the subject area but not with computer processing or with the contents and organization of the database. Menu driven systems permit only highly structured retrieval, through a hierarchical tree structure of menus and prompts. These systems have the important advantage of being very simple to use, which appeals to end users who may not have training or motivation to master more sophisticated systems. However, menu driven retrieval has been also criticized as being tedious, time-consuming, and frustrating. It can be particularly frustrating when incorrect choices lead the user down the wrong branch of the hierarchy. Because of the pros and cons of menu or query driven systems, some database producers, such as Business Research Corporation, provide both for full text databases.[73]

Geller and Lesk compared keyword and menu access to two textual databases: an online library catalog and stories from a newswire service.[74] They found that users preferred keyword access to the library catalog but menu access to the news stories. The difference was based on the degree of user fore-knowledge of the database and its organization. Menus are preferred when the user does not know what is available.

Bochmann, Gecsei, and Lin combined Telidon videotex menus with a keyword system to alleviate some of the frustrations of a pure menu system.[75] Watters and associates introduced the possibility of such integration in a full text retrieval system.[76] They described a prototype system which has integrated Boolean combinations of keywords, menu, and direct access methods for the retrieval of passages from full text databases. The integration is based on the hierarchical structure inherent in such databases as legal statutes and regulations and engineering standards. The full text of the database has been segmented into separate records on the basis of their function within the text. The user may switch freely among access methods to develop the most appropriate search strategy.

A user may access a passage of text directly if its identification code is known. This code may be determined from various sources: previous accessed "see" references in retrieved passages, menus, or from the original document. According to Watters and colleagues, menus might be the initial choice of access method by those familiar with the subject area but not familiar with the contents and/or organization of the database itself. Boolean retrieval might be the initial choice of access by those familiar with the contents of the database. This approach may be especially valuable with textbooks and other documents in which the subject matter is hierarchically ordered.

Changing Computer Architecture and Record Structure

Although the usual method of organizing a full text database is to construct an inverted index of all words it contains, the inverted index file has problems of unsatisfactory response time in the case of large databases with conventional computer architecture. Stanfill and Kahle presented a new implementation of free text searching that takes advantage of the possibilities offered by a massively parallel computer, the Connection Machine (CM), with up to 65,536 processing elements.[77] In this implementation, the representation of the documents in memory permits a very fast search for the presence of a word in a document. With the CM, each processing element stores between one and three documents; queries are then broadcast to the entire machine and the results collected. Because of the massive parallelism, the resulting system is fast enough to permit exhaustive methods not previously feasible for large databases. Two applications of this technology were a benchmark test of the Connection Machine as a query evaluator, and a prototype of an interactive document-retrieval system using a technique called relevance feedback to produce an interface that is fast and easy to use and produces high-quality searching. A benchmark of the Boolean query algorithm was performed on a 16,384 processor prototype of the CM with a test database of 31,993 documents, totaling 18 Mbytes. The combined use of simple queries and the relevance feedback techniques was tested on a database of 16,000 articles (totaling approximately 32 Mbytes) from the Reuters Wire Service.

The results of the test shows that it combines high precision and recall with ease of use and fast response and represents an advance over existing free-text database search technology given sequential machines and inverted databases. For a database of 18 Mbytes on a 16,384 element machine, the measured time to execute a query varies from 0.004 seconds for a Boolean query with 25 terms to 0.295 seconds for a Boolean query with 20,000 terms (computer time only). Salton and Buckley reported that a comparison of parallel text-search methods to alternative available search strategies that use serial processing machines (that is, nonparallel vector matching processes) suggests that parallel methods do not provide large-scale gains in either retrieval effectiveness or efficiency.[78]

Dowquest, an end user system from Dow Jones News/Retrieval, is the first commercially available system to use parallel methods and relevance feedback. It is too early to know if Dowquest performs more successfully than Dow Jones's more conventional News/Retrieval interface.

SUMMARY

Two obvious questions in full text research are how full text retrieval performs and how to improve the retrieval performance of full text databases. Most previous studies compared the retrieval performance of full text databases with the performance of other search methods to make the general question—how full text retrieval performs—specifically: how full text retrieval systems perform compared with other retrieval in terms of effectiveness and efficiency. Recently there has been increased interest in improvement of full text retrieval. Research on full text databases in this area has been incorporated with ranking or weighting algorithms based on word occurrences, combined menu driven and query driven systems, and improvement of computer architecture and record structure for databases.

Since full text databases, with the exception of legal literature, have only recently become widely available online, research is in some cases not sufficient to draw any definitive conclusion on full text retrieval. Research that evaluates full text search methods will allow improved search techniques and systems to be developed.

NOTES

1. Carol Tenopir, "Full-Text Databases," *Annual Review of Information Science and Technology* 19 (1984): 215–246.

2. Joseph J. Beard, "Information Systems Application in Law," *Annual Review of Information Science and Technology* 6 (1971): 369–396.

3. Gillian Bull, "A Brief Survey of Developments in Computerized Legal Information Retrieval," *Program* 15, No. 3 (1981): 109–119.

4. Signe E. Larson and Martha E. Williams, "Computer Assisted Legal Research," *Annual Review of Information Science and Technology* 15 (1980): 251–286.

5. Jon Bing, "Text Retrieval in Norway," *Program* 15, No. 3 (July 1981): 150–162.

6. Seldon W. Terrant, "The Computer and Publishing," *Annual Review of Information Science and Technology* 10 (1975): 273–301; and Idem., "Computers in Publishing," *Annual Review of Information Science and Technology* 15 (1980): 191–219.

7. Rita G. Lerner et al., "Primary Publication Systems and Scientific Text Processing," *Annual Review of Information Science and Technology* 18 (1983): 127–149.

8. Roland Hjerppe, "Electronic Publishing: Writing Machines and Machine Writing," *Annual Review of Information Science and Technology* 21 (1986): 123–166.

9. Gerard Salton, "The Evaluation of Computer-Based Retrieval Systems," in *Automatic Information Organization and Retrieval*, ed. Gerard Salton (New York: McGraw-Hill, 1968), pp. 280–349.

10. Michael E. Keen, "The Aberystwyth Index Language Test," *Journal of Documentation* 29, No. 1 (March 1973): 1–35; and Michael McGill, *An Evaluation*

of Factors Affecting Document Ranking by Information Retrieval Systems (Syracuse, N.Y.: Syracuse University Press, 1979).

11. G. Olive, J. E. Terry, and S. Datta, "Studies to Compare Retrieval Using Titles with That Using Index Terms," *Journal of Documentation* 29, No. 2 (June 1973): 108–191.

12. Donald W. King et al., *Comparative Evaluation of the Retrieval Effectiveness of Descriptor and Free-Text Search Systems Using CIRCOL* (Rockville, Md.: Westat Research, Inc., 1972).

13. C. W. Cleverdon, J. Mills, and E. M. Keen, *Factors Determining the Performance of Indexing Systems*, 2 vols. (Cranfield, England: College of Aeronautics, 1966); J. E. Parker, "Preliminary Assessment of the Comparative Efficiencies of an SDI System Using Controlled or Natural Language for Retrieval," *Program* 5 (1979): 26–34; and T. M. Aitchison et al., *Comparative Evaluation of Index Language. Part II: Results* (London: The Institution of Electrical Engineers, 1970).

14. C. W. Cleverdon, *A Comparative Evaluation of Searching by Controlled Language and Natural Language in an Experimental NASA Data Base* (Washington, D.C.: National Technical Information Service, 1977).

15. Karen Markey, Pauline Atherton, and Claudia Newton, "An Analysis of Controlled Vocabulary and Free Text Search Statements in Online Searches," *Online Review* 4, No. 3 (1982): 225–236.

16. Barbara Charton, "Searching the Literature for Concepts," *Journal of Chemical Information and Computer Science* 17 (1977): 45–46; Russell J. Rowlett, Jr., "Keywords vs. Index Terms," *Journal of Chemical Information and Computer Science* 17 (1977): 192–193; Deborah Carrow and Joan Nugent, "Comparison of Free-Text and Index Search Abilities in an Operating Information System," in *Information Management in the 1980s: Proceedings of the American Society for Information Science 40th Annual Meeting: Sep.26–Oct.1, 1977* (White Plains, N.Y.: Knowledge Industry Publications, 1981): pp. 131–138; Rolf G. Henzler, "Free of Controlled Vocabularies: Some Statistical User-Oriented Evaluations of Biomedical Information Systems," *International Classification* 5, No. 1 (1978): 21–26; Mary L. Calkins, "Free Text or Controlled Vocabulary? A Case History Step-By-Step Analysis . . . Plus Other Aspects of Search Strategy," *Database* 3 (1980): 53–67; and Jerry R. Byrne, "Relative Effectiveness of Titles, Abstracts, and Subject Headings for Machine Retrieval from the COMPENDEX Services," *Journal of the American Society for Information Science* 26, No. 4 (1975): 223–229.

17. Martha E. Williams, "Analysis of Terminology in Various CAS Data Files as Access Points for Retrieval," *Journal of Chemical Information and Computer Sciences* 17 (1977): 16–20; Linda C. Smith, "Selected Artificial Intelligence Techniques in Information Retrieval Systems Research" (Ph.D. dissertation, Syracuse University, 1979); and McGill, *An Evaluation*.

18. Bella H. Weinberg, "Word Frequency and Automatic Indexing" (Ph.D. dissertation, Columbia University, 1981).

19. S. Artandi and E. H. Wolf, "The Effectiveness of Automatically Generated Weights and Links in Mechanical Indexing," *American Documentation* 20 (1969): 198–201; Miranda Lee Pao, "Automatic Text Analysis Based on Transition Phenomena of Word Occurrences," *Journal of the American Society for Information Science* 29 (May 1978): 121–124; Weinberg, "Word Frequency."

20. Salton, "Evaluation."

21. Fred J. Damerau, "An Experiment in Automatic Indexing," *American Documentation* 16 (1965): 283–289; John M. Carroll and Robert Roeloffs, "Computer Selection of Keywords Using Word-Frequency Analysis," *American Documentation* 20 (July 1969): 227–233.

22. Karen Sparck Jones, "Index Term Weighting," *Information Storage and Retrieval* 9 (November 1973): 619–633.

23. S. Artandi, "Computer Indexing of Medical Articles," *Journal of Documentation* 25 (1969): 214–223; Artandi and Wolf, "The Effectiveness"; G. Salton, *The SMART Retrieval System: Experiments in Automatic Document Processing* (Englewood Cliffs, N.J.: Prentice Hall, 1971); H. S. Heaps, *Information Retrieval: Computational and Theoretical Aspects* (New York: Academic Press, 1978), pp. 269–280; Pao, "Automatic Text"; and Wolfgang K. H. Sager and Peter C. Lockemann, "Classification of Ranking Algorithms," *International Forum on Information and Documentation* 1, No. 4 (1976): 12–25.

24. Kay Durkin et al., "An Experiment to Study the Online User of a Full Text Primary Journal Database," in *Proceedings of the 4th International Online Information Meeting, London, December 1980* (Oxford, England: Learned Information, Ltd., 1980), pp. 53–56; and Seldon W. Terrant, Lorrin R. Garson, and Barbara E. Meyers, "Online Searching Full Text of American Chemical Society Primary Journals," *Journal of Chemical Information and Computer Science* 24 (1984): 230–235.

25. J. Franklin, M. C. Buckingham, and J. Westwater, "Biomedical Journals in an Online Full Text Database: A Review of Reaction to ESPL," in *Proceedings of the 7th International Online Information Meeting, London, December 1983* (Oxford, England: Learned Information, Ltd., 1983), pp. 407–410.

26. Morris F. Collen and Charles D. Flagle, "Full-Text Medical Literature Retrieval by Computer," *Journal of the American Medical Association* 254, No. 19 (November 15, 1985): 2768–2774.

27. R. Pagell, "Searching Full-Text Periodicals: How Full Is Full?" *Database* 10 (October 1987): 33–38; and R. Pagell, "Searching IAC's Full-Text Files: It's Awfully Confusing," *Database* 10 (October 1987): 39–47.

28. Carol Tenopir, "Users and Uses of Full Text Databases," in *Proceedings of the International Online Meeting, London, December 1988* (Oxford, England: Learned Information, Ltd., 1988), pp. 263–270.

29. Richard P. Davis, "The LITE System," *Judge Advocate General Law Review* 8, No. 6 (November/December 1966): 6–10.

30. W. B. Eldridge, "An Appraisal of a Case Law Retrieval Project," in *Proceedings of the Computer and the Law Conference—1968,* ed. David Johnston (Kingston, Ontario: Faculty of the Law, Queen's University, 1968).

31. Colin Tapper, *Computer and the Law* (London: Weidenfeld and Nicolson, 1973).

32. Aaron M. Schreiber, "Computerized Storage and Retrieval of Case Law without Indexing: The Hebrew Responsa Project," *Law and Computer Technology* 2 (November 1969): 14–21.

33. Eberhard M. Fels, "Evaluation of the Performance of an Information Retrieval System by Modified Mooers Plan," *American Documentation* 14 (1963): 28–34.

34. This is an impractical statistical procedure suggested by Mooers to obtain absolute performance measures. The writer invents three questions that are "cru-

cial" (denoted by A), "relevant" (denoted by B), and "irrelevant" (denoted by C) to each of the test documents. Using the set of test documents sampled, the questions invented and relevance-values assigned to sampling units, overall performance of a retrieval system is evaluated in terms of Crucial-documents ratio, Relevant-documents ratio, and Irrelevant-documents ratio:

$$\text{Crucial-documents ratio} = \frac{\text{Number of sampling units retrieved with assignment "A"}}{\text{Total number of "A" entries in relevance-value matrix}}$$

$$\text{Relevant-document ratio} = \frac{\text{\# of sampling units retrieved with assignment "A" or "B"}}{\text{Total \# of "A" of "B" entries in relevance-value matrix}}$$

$$\text{Irrelevant-document ratio} = \frac{\text{\# of sampling units retrieved with assignment "C"}}{\text{Total \# of "C" entries in relevance-value matrix}}$$

35. D. C. Blair and M. E. Maron, "An Evaluation of Retrieval Effectiveness for a Full-Text Document-Retrieval System," *Communications of the ACM* 28, No. 3, (1985): 289–299.

36. Gerard Salton, "Another Look at Automatic Text-Retrieval Systems," *Communications of the ACM* 29, No. 7 (1986): 648–656.

37. Jung Soon Ro, "An Evaluation of the Applicability of Ranking Algorithms to Improve the Effectiveness of Full-text Retrieval. I. On the Effectiveness of Full-Text Retrieval," *Journal of the American Society for Information Science* 39 No. 2 (1988): 73–78.

38. David C. Blair, "Full Text Retrieval: Evaluation and Implications," *International Classification* 13, No. 1 (1986): 18–23.

39. Don Swanson, "Searching Natural Language Text by Computer," *Science* 132 (October 1960): 1099–1104.

40. G. Salton and M. E. Lesk, "Computer Evaluation of Indexing and Text Processing," *Journal of the Association of Computing Machinery* 25 (January 1968): 8–36.

41. David F. Hersey et al., "Free Text Word Retrieval and Scientist Indexing: Performance Profiles and Costs," *Journal of Documentation* 27 (September 1971): 167–183.

42. J. R. Rinewalt, "Evaluation of Selected Features of the EUREKA Full Text Information Retrieval System" (Ph.D dissertation, University of Illinois, 1976); and Idem, "Feature Evaluation of a Full Text Information Retrieval System," *Online Review* 1 (January 1977): 43–51.

43. Donald B. Cleveland, Ana D. Cleveland, and Olga B. Wise, "Less Than Full Text Indexing Using a Non-Boolean Searching Model," *Journal of the American Society for Information Science* 35 (January/February 1984): 19–28.

44. W. Goffman, "An Indirect Method of Information Retrieval," *Information Storage and Retrieval* 4 (December 1968): 361–373.

45. D. Stein et al., "Full Text Online Patent Searching: Results of a USPTO Experiment," in *Proceedings of the Online '82 Conference, Atlanta, November 1982* (Weston, Conn.: Online Inc., 1982), pp. 289–294.

46. Carol Tenopir, "Retrieval Performance in a Full Text Journal Article Database" (Ph.D. dissertation, University of Illinois, 1984).

47. John P. Abbott and Charles R. Smith, "Full-Text and Bibliographic ACS Databases: Rivals or Companions?" in *Proceedings of the 6th National Online Meeting, 1985* (Medford, N.J.: Learned Information, Inc., 1985), pp. 5–9.

48. Richard A. Love and Lorrin R. Garson, "Precision in Searching the Full-Text Database—ACS Journals Online," in *Proceedings of the 6th National Online Meeting, 1985* (Medford, N.J.: Learned Information, Inc., 1985), pp. 273–282.

49. R. Wagers, "The Decision to Search Databases Full Text," in *Proceedings of the 10th International Online Information Meeting, 1986* (Oxford, England: Learned Information, Ltd., 1986), pp. 93–107.

50. Carol Tenopir, "Search Strategies for Full Text Databases," in *Proceedings of the 51st Annual Meeting of the American Society for Information Science, Atlanta, GA, October 1988* (Medford, N.J.: Learned Information, 1988), pp. 80–86.

51. Carol Tenopir and Man Èvena Shu, "Magazines in Full Text: Uses and Search Strategies," *Online Review* 13, No. 2. (1989): 107–118.

52. Gary Marchionini, "Information-Seeking Strategies of Novices Using a Full-Text Electronic Encyclopedia," *Journal of the American Society for Information Science* 40, No. 1 (1989): 54–66.

53. Ibid., p. 65.

54. Jessica Milstead, "Indexing the News," in *Proceedings of the American Society for Information Science 43rd Annual Meeting, 1980* (White Plains, N.Y.: Knowledge Industry Publications, Inc., 1980), pp. 149–151.

55. Pauline Duckitt, "The Value of Controlled Indexing Systems in Online Full Text Databases," in *Proceedings of the 5th International Online Information Meeting, 1981* (Oxford, England: Learned Information, Ltd., 1981), pp. 447–453.

56. Ernest Perez, Text Enhancement: Controlled Vocabulary vs. Free Text, *Special Libraries* 73, No. 3 (July 1982): 183–192.

57. James A. Sprowl, "WESTLAW vs. LEXIS: Computer Assisted Legal Research Comes of Age," *Program* 15, No. 3 (July 1981): 132–141.

58. Dwight R. Tousignaut, "Indexing: Old Methods, New Concepts," *The Indexer* 15, No. 4 (1987): 197–204.

59. Lydia Jackson, "Searching Full-Text Databases," in *Proceedings of the 7th International Online Information Meeting, 1983* (Oxford, England: Learned Information, Ltd., 1983), pp. 419–425.

60. Connie Zuga, "Full Text Databases: Design Considerations for the Database Vendor," in *Proceedings of the 7th International Online Information Meeting, 1983* (Oxford, England: Learned Information, Ltd., 1983), pp. 427–434.

61. E. Judson Jennings, "Sam, You Made the Window too Small," in *Proceedings of the 8th National Online Meeting, New York, May 1987* (Medford, N.J.: Learned Information, Inc., 1987), 197–203.

62. Margaret M. Klinkroth, "Full-Text Databases in the Health Sciences," *Medical Reference Services Quarterly* 5, No. 3 (1986): 1–15.

63. Tenopir, "Retrieval"; Dolores P. Huth, "ASAP-Index Access to Full Text," in *Proceedings of the 6th National Online Meeting, 1985* (Medford, N.J.: Learned Information, Inc., 1985), pp. 227–232; and Love and Garson, "Precision."

64. Terry Noreault, Michael McGill, and Matthew B. Koll, "A Performance Evaluation of Similarity Measures, Document Term Weighting Schemes and Representation in a Boolean Environment," in *Information Retrieval Research*, ed. R. N. Oddy (London: Butterworth, 1981), pp. 57–76.

65. S. E. Robertson, C. J. Rijsbergen, and M. F. Porter, "Probabilistic Models of Indexing and Searching," in *Information Retrieval Research*, ed. R. N. Oddy (London: Butterworth, 1981), pp. 35–56.

66. Sager and Lockemann, "Classification."

67. Ibid., p. 23.

68. Jon Bing, "Text Retrieval in Norway," *Program* 15, No. 3 (July 1981): 150–162; and Jon Bing and Knut Selmer, *A Decade of Computer and Law* (Oslo, Norway: Norwegian University Press, 1980).

69. Jung Soon Ro, "An Evaluation of the Applicability of Ranking Algorithms to Improving the Effectiveness of Full Text Retrieval" (Ph.D. dissertation, Indiana University, 1985).

70. L. M. Bernstein and R. E. Williamson, "Testing of a Natural Language Retrieval System for a Full Text Knowledge Base," *Journal of the American Society for Information Science* 35, No. 4 (1984): 235–247.

71. Marry E. Rowbottom and Peter Willett, "The Effect of Subject Matter on the Automatic Indexing of Full Text," *Journal of the American Society for Information Science* 33, No. 3 (1983): 139–141.

72. G. Salton and M. J. McGill, *Introduction to Modern Information Retrieval* (New York: McGraw-Hill, 1983), p. 382.

73. William A. Benjamin, Kathleen C. Jamieson, and James P. Rutt, "The Design of a Full-Text Company Information Database for Multi-Vendor Delivery," in *Proceedings of the 4th National Online Meeting, 1983* (Medford, N.J.: Learned Information, Inc., 1983), pp. 33–37.

74. V. J. Geller and M. E. Lesk, "User Interfaces to Information Systems: Choice vs. Commands," in *Proceedings of the 6th Annual International ACM SIGIR Conference on Research and Development in Information Retrieval*, (ACM SIGIR, 1983), pp. 130–135.

75. G. V. Bochmann, J. Gecsei, and E. Lin, "Keyword Access in Telidon—an Experiment," in *Videotex 82: International Conference and Exhibition on Videotex, Viewdata and Teletext* (Northwood Hills, England: Online Conferences, 1982), pp. 345–357.

76. C. R. Watters et al., "Integration of Menu Retrieval and Boolean Retrieval from a Full-Text Database," *Online Review* 9, No. 5 (1985): 391–401.

77. Craig Stanfill and Brewster Kahle, " Parallel Free-Text Search on the Connection Machine System," *Communications of the ACM* 29, No. 12 (1986): 1229–1239.

78. Gerard Salton and Chris Buckley, "Parallel Text Search Methods," *Communications of the ACM* 31 No. 2 (1988): 202–215.

5

Retrieval Performance in Harvard Business Review

Many commentators have assumed that when full texts of journal articles are available for searching online, fields such as controlled vocabulary descriptors and abstracts become obsolete. Adding such value-added fields is indeed expensive and time-consuming for the database producer. Indexers and abstractors must be hired, new data must be input, and vocabularies must be kept up-to-date. Better retrieval performance from full text searching is assumed. No one disputes the value of full text search and retrieval, but experienced searchers often express the belief that controlled vocabulary descriptor terms offer benefit as well. A study by Tenopir tested these beliefs in one database by comparing full text searching with searching on controlled vocabulary descriptors and words or phrases from abstracts.[1] This study is summarized here.

HARVARD BUSINESS REVIEW ON BRS

All requisite fields must be available for the same articles, preferably in the same database, to be able to compare results from searching the full text of journal articles with searching of controlled vocabulary descriptors and abstracts. At the time the study reported here was conducted (1983–1984) the only commercially available database with full texts, controlled vocabulary descriptors, and abstracts was *Harvard Business Review* online (HBR/O), available now on BRS, NEXIS, and DIALOG and described in Chapter 2. Using a real database on a system that is widely used makes the results of this study more applicable to current searching situations. Chapter 8 discusses some of the implications for online searchers.

In September 1983, when the online searching portion of this study was conducted, HBR/O contained almost 900 full text records. In addition, it included bibliographic records for over 700 articles published from 1971 to 1975, some earlier "classic" articles, and 120 volumes of the HBR Library and Reprint series. All records prior to 1976 were excluded from this study.[2]

HBR/O records are indexed with two subject descriptor vocabularies. *Corporate Functions* and *Subject and Management Terms* are used to represent major subjects in each article. The Corporate Functions vocabulary includes seventeen broad and sixty-six narrow terms describing the functions of companies or areas of corporate responsibility. Each article is assigned at least one function, but not more than three or four.

The subject descriptor list includes approximately 800 descriptors in 1983. The terms are a combination of very broad subject terms assigned to articles prior to 1980 for the creation of printed indexes, general management terms, and specific subject terms added as articles are indexed. Terms reflecting "the way business people think and speak" are preferred. For example, a natural order term such as "corporate control" is preferred over an inverted form such as "control, corporate." Plurals are preferred over singulars. Indexers are instructed to use the most specific term possible and most articles are assigned two to a maximum of five descriptors.

All searches in this study were searched on the BRS search system to avoid lack of comparability due to differences in search software. BRS made HBR/O available in July 1982 and has several software features (described in Chapter 3) that made it especially appropriate for this study.

THE SEARCHES

The search topics used in this study are the business questions submitted to the online search service of the University of Illinois Labor and Industrial Relations Library from 1979 to 1982 and the University of Hawaii at Manoa Hamilton Library in 1982. (The University of Illinois Commerce Library did not do online searching until 1984, referring patrons instead to the Labor and Industrial Relations Library.) Both are large universities that offer undergraduate and graduate degrees in business. Search topics are listed in Table 5–1.

The researcher conducted all of the searches. This has the advantage of eliminating the variable of searcher experience and style, but has the potential disadvantage of the searcher learning about the database as searches are conducted. To guard against this, all search strategies were developed in advance and search strategies were not changed online (see Table 5–2). All results were printed out without being viewed online. This procedure does not fully use the interactive capabilities of the online system, but it

Table 5–1
Search Topics in Harvard Business Review Online

✓1. Specifically, I am looking for any material written on the interface of tourism and food service. Anything that might show any relationship between the two would be of assistance.

✗2. I am focusing on the fact that length of service or longevity in a given job situation produces complacency and agreement with the status quo, thus breeding low creativity and risk taking levels among workers.

✓3. I am interested in psychological aspects of women in management positions, including professional as well as business women.

✓4. Retirement planning, including pre-retirement planning, corporate and institutional guides, policies for planning for retirement, corporate retirement plans and policies of specific corporations.

5. I would like literature on cutback management or the process of transition management or administration.

6. Workaholism, workaholics, attitudes toward hard work.

7. Dale Carnegie courses in effective speaking and human development. Business students taking career writing skills course will share in the search for information on their research reports. Their goal is to mount an argument for or against company sponsorship in the 14-week Carnegie course. They would need to read not only Carnegie philosophy but as much as possible on the practical applied aspects of Carnegie speech training. They will need some idea of other confidence-building courses or training circumstances (Toastmasters, speech departments, offerings in professional and business speaking, etc.)

8. Any occupational stress studies specifically dealing with multi-ethnic situations.

9. U.S. exporting of manufactured goods to Asia.

10. I am trying to develop a psychographic and demographic profile of people who buy newly introduced products long before they become widely popular. According to diffusion theory, these early adopters will differ from the early majority, whom they will influence. The purposes of this study are to find out if there are such differences between the groups; to detail the differences; to be able to design advertising approaches on the basis of those differences.

✗11. The topic I am researching is the turnover and job satisfaction of female accountants.

12. Interactive computer-aided decision support service. We are investigating the commercial viability of a service.

13. How do working women cope with time pressures resulting from dual role responsibilities? What are the health effects of time pressure in general and with respect to sex? What are the health effects of perceived work overload?

✗14. Package or group tours and their restrictions.

15. Effect of diet and exercise programs on reduction of absenteeism and increase of productivity among corporate staffs and executives.

16. Scheduling of extended work hours. Computation of productivity and safety in relation to extended work hours. I am specifically interested in extended work hours over eight hours in relation to the above aspects.

17. Economics and law of compensation, especially for business or government damage to the environment and to human health. Also interested in mitigation of impacts from government projects, for example efforts to not kill fish at dams.

18. Job searching by dual-career couples.

Table 5–1 continued

_19_. Retraining workers for new jobs as an alternative to layoffs.

*X*20. Comparative studies of women's participation in the labor force in the U.S. and the U.S.S.R.

_21_. Experience with quality circles in the U.S.

_22_. Collective bargaining by women-dominated professions such as social workers, nurses, librarians, teachers.

_23_. Trade unions and guest workers (migrants, migrant workers, foreign workers) in Western Europe.

_24_. Personnel policies for spouses working in the same firm.

_25_. Impact of collective bargaining on the introduction of new technology.

_26_. Health education programs in industry.

_27_. Collective bargaining in colleges and universities.

*X*28. Social and economic impacts of teacher strikes on the community.

_29_. Technical and training assistance from the AFL-CIO and other trade unions in Africa.

_30_. Minorities in apprenticeship programs in both the public and the private sector.

_31_. Information retrieval systems for office files or personal collections.

✓32. Turnover and unemployment among food service workers.

_33_. Professional women's occupational mobility.

_34_. Women in labor unions.

_35_. In-plant recreational facilities.

_36_. Employer day-care centers.

_37_. Anything dealing with the concept of comparable worth.

_38_. Retirement planning by farmers or ranchers.

_39_. Productivity in Japan vs. productivity in the U.S.

_40_. Productivity with unions vs. productivity in nonunion companies

(✓ topics used in a pilot study; *X* topics with no documents retrieved)

would have been more difficult to control extraneous variables and searcher bias with a truly interactive procedure or with multiple searchers.

Four searches were conducted for each question: (1) a search of natural language words or phrases in the text of the article only, (2) a search of natural language words or phrases from the title only, (3) a search of natural language words or phrases from the abstract only, and (4) a search of controlled vocabulary index terms only. The combination of results from two to four above was also considered in the analysis.

Search strategies included either single words and multiword phrases in a concept as appropriate to the topic. In the free text searches on titles, abstracts, and full texts, the BRS adjacency operator (ADJ) or within the same sentence (WITH) were used as needed to make phrases. Boolean ORs and truncation were used as appropriate, but in an identical way for each free text search of a single topic. Each free text strategy was translated as directly as possible into controlled vocabulary terms.

Table 5–2
Search Strategies

QUESTION	STRATEGY
5 (Full text, abstract, title)	1. cutback$ or cut adj back$ or transition 2. manage$ or administ$ 3. 1 same 2
5 (controlled vocabulary)	1. crisis adj management.de. or management adj change.de. 2. organizational adj change.de. SAME management.de. 3. 1 OR 2
6 (Full text, abstract, title)	1. workahol$ 2. hard adj work 3. attitude$ or belief$ or feeling$ or believ$ 4. 1 OR (2 same 3)
6 (controlled vocabulary)	1. work adj ethic.de. 2. employees adj attitudes.de. or personality.de. 3. work adj environment.de. or quality adj work adj life.de. 4. 1 OR (2 SAME 3)
7 (Full text, abstract, title)	1. dale with carnegie 2. (speech$ or speak$) with public 3. toastmasters 4. confidence with build$ 5. human adj development 6. course$ or train$ or instruct$ or class$ or educat$ 7. (2 OR 4 OR 5) SAME 6 8. 1 OR 3 OR 7
7 (controlled vocabulary)	1. dale adj carnegie adj school.su. 2. continuing adj education.su. or business adj education.de. or employee adj training.de. 3. communication.de. 4. 1 OR (2 AND 3)
8 (Full text, abstract, title)	1. tension or stress 2. ethnic$ or minorit$ or racial 3. 1 SAME 2
8 (controlled vocabulary)	1. tension.de. or stress.de. 2. minority adj groups.de. or racial adj discrimination.de. 3. 1 SAME 2

Table 5–2 continued

QUESTION	STRATEGY
9 (Full text, abstract, title)	1. manufactur$ or fabricat$ 2. us or united adj states or u adj s 3. export$ 4. asia or bangladesh or burma or china or taiwan or hong adj kong or india or indonesia or japan or laos or malaysia or mongolia or nepal or korea or pakistan or philippines or singapore or thailand or vietnam 5.1 SAME 2 SAME 3 SAME 4
9 (controlled vocabulary)	1. export adj trade.de. 2. united adj states adj america.su. 3. machinery.pr. or manufacturing.su. 4. (countries listed above.su.) 5. 1 AND 2 AND 3 AND 4
1 0 (Full text, abstract, title)	1. early adj adopt$ 2. diffusion or adoption 3. consumer$ or advertis$ or product$ 4. 1 OR (2 SAME 3)
1 0 (controlled vocabulary)	1. new adj products.de. or product adj development.de. 2. advertising.de. or marketing.de. or consumers.de. or consumer adj behavior.de. 3. 1 SAME 2
1 2 (Full text, abstract, title)	1. decision with (support or making) 2. computer adj aided or information adj system$ 3. 1 SAME 2
1 2 (controlled vocabulary)	1. decision adj making.de or problem adj solving.de. or decision adj theory.de. 2. computer adj systems.de. or computer adj software.de. or information adj systems.de. or management adj information adj systems.de. 3. 1 SAME 2

Table 5–2 continued

QUESTION	STRATEGY

1 3
(Full text,
abstract,
title)
	1. woman or women or female or mother$
	2. dual adj role$
	3. work adj force or labor adj force or
	  career or working
	4. overwork or over adj work or work with
	  overload or pressure$ or stress or strain
	  or tension
	5. health or physical or medical or psychological
	  or mental
	6. 1 SAME 2
	7. 1 SAME 3 SAME 4
	8. 4 SAME 5
	9. 6 OR 7 OR 8

1 3
(controlled
vocabulary)
	1. women adj business.de. or women adj
	  executives.de. or women.de.
	2. stress.de. or tension.de. or time adj
	  management.de.
	3. physical adj fitness.de. or psychology.de.
	  or health adj care.de.
	4. 1 SAME 2
	5. 2 SAME 3
	6. 4 OR 5

1 5
(Full text,
abstract,
title)
	1. absentee$ or productivity or motivation
	2. executive$ or employee$ or worker$ or
	  personnel
	3. diet or exercise or health or
	  nutrition or physical adj fitness
	4. 1 SAME 2 SAME 3

1 5
(controlled
vocabulary)
	1. absenteeism.de. or productivity.de.
	  or motivation.de.
	2. personnel.de. or employees.de. or
	  employee adj attitudes.de. or executives.de.
	3. health adj care.de. or nutrition.de. or physical adj fitness.de.
	4. 1 SAME 2 SAME 3

1 6
(Full text,
abstract,
title)
	1. flexible adj hour$ or flex adj time or
	  flextime or overtime or four adj day adj
	  week or extended adj hour$
	2. schedul$ or productivity or safety
	3. 1 SAME 2

1 6
(controlled
vocabulary)
	1. flexible adj working adj hours.de. or
	  working adj hours.de.
	2. productivity.de. or scheduling.de. or
	  work adj environment.de.
	3. 1 SAME 2

Table 5–2 continued

QUESTION	STRATEGY
1 7 (Full text, abstract, title)	1. compensat$ or mitigat$ 2. harm or ruin or damage$ or effect$ or hazard$ 3. environment$ or health$ 4. pollut$ 5. 1 SAME 2 SAME 3 6. 1 SAME 4 7. 5 OR 6

1 7
(controlled
vocabulary)
	1. compensation adj administration.de.
	2. environmental adj protection.de. or
	   ecology.de. or pollution adj control.de.
	   or water adj pollution.de.
	3. 1 SAME 2

1 8 (Full text, abstract, title)	1. dual adj career or dual adj employment 2. nepotism or couple$ or married 3. employment or (job with (hunt$ or search$ or look$)) 4. 1 OR (2 SAME 3)

1 8
(controlled
vocabulary)
	1. nepotism.de. or marriage.de.
	2. career adj planning.de. or job adj mobility.de.
	   or recruiting adj employees.de. or
	   executive adj selection.de.
	3. 1 SAME 2

1 9 (Full text, abstract, title)	1. train$ or retrain$ 2. new with (skill$ or job or jobs) 3. layoff$ 4. 1 SAME (2 or 3)
1 9 (controlled vocabulary)	1. management adj training.de. or employee adj training.de. 2. layoffs.de. 3. 1 SAME 2
2 1 (Full text, abstract, title)	1. quality adj circle$ or theory adj z 2. us or u adj s or united adj states 3. 1 SAME 2
2 1 (controlled vocabulary)	1. united adj states adj america.su. 2. quality adj control.de. 3. 1 AND 2

Table 5–2 continued

QUESTION	STRATEGY

2 2
(Full text,
abstract,
title)
	1. librar$ or nurse$ or hospital$ or
	    social adj work$ or teacher$ or educator$
	2. woman or women or female
	3. occupation$ or job or jobs or profession$
	4. strike or strikes or union$ or
	    collective adj bargain$ or negotiat$
	5. 2 SAME 3
	6. (1 OR 5) SAME 4

2 2
(controlled
vocabulary)
	1. libraries adj information adj centers.pr.
	    or educational adj institutions.pr. or
	    social adj services.pr. or nursing adj care.pr.
	    women adj business.de.
	2. collective adj bargaining.de. or negotiation.de. or strikes.de. or
	    labor adj unions.de.
	3. 1 AND 2

2 3
(Full text,
abstract,
title)
	1. union$ or collective adj bargain$ or strike
	    or strikes or negotiat$
	2. (guest or foreign or migrant) with (labor$ or work$)
	3. europe$ or italy or germany or switzerland
	    or ireland or england or britain or
	    united adj kingdom or scandinavia$ or sweden
	    or finland or denmark or norway or netherlands
	    or holland or belgium
	4. 1 SAME 2 SAME 3

2 3
(controlled
vocabulary)
	1. labor adj unions.de. or collective adj
	    bargaining.de. or strikes.de. or negotiation.de.
	2. western adj europe.su. or appropriate countries
	    listed above.su.
	3. 1 AND 2

2 4
(Full text,
abstract,
title)
	1. nepotism or spouse$ or couple$ or
	    married or marriage
	2. personnel adj (management or policy or
	    policies or regulation$ or rule or rules)
	3. 1 SAME 2

2 4 (controlled vocabulary)	1. nepotism.de. or marriage.de. or family.de. 2. personnel adj management.de. or policy.de. 3. 1 SAME 2

Table 5–2 continued

QUESTION	STRATEGY

2 5
(Full text,
abstract,
title)
	1. collective adj bargain$ or strike$ or
	    union$ or negotiat$
	2. technolog$ or automat$ or robot$ or
	    computer$ or minicomputer$ or microcomputer$
	    or mechanization
	3. 1 SAME 2

2 5
(controlled
vocabulary)
	1. collective adj bargaining.de. or labor
	    adj unions.de. or strikes.de. or negotiation.de.
	2. technological adj change.de. or technology.de.
	    or high adj technology.de. or computers.de. or
	    computer adj systems.de. or minicomputers.de.
	    or computer-aided adj manufacturing.de. or
	    automation.de. or mechanization.de. or
	    industrial adj robots.pr.
	3. 1 AND 2

2 6 (Full text, abstract, title)	1. health or physical adj fitness or nutrition or medical 2. educat$ or train$ or class$ or course$ 3. 1 SAME 2

2 6
(controlled
vocabulary)
	1. health adj care.de. or nutrition.de
	2. employee adj training.de. or education.de.
	    or management adj training.de. or
	    handbooks.de. or continuing adj education.de.
	3. 1 SAME 2

2 7
(Full text,
abstract,
title)
	1. collective adj bargain$ or union$ or
	    strike or strikes or negotiat$
	2. college$ or universit$ or higher adj
	    education or professor$
	3. 1 SAME 2

2 7
(controlled
vocabulary)
	1. negotiation.de. or strikes.de. or
	    collective adj bargaining.de. or labor
	    unions.de.
	2. colleges adj universities.pr. or
	    educational adj institutions.pr. or
	    junior adj colleges.pr. or vocational
	    adj schools.pr. or business adj schools.pr.
	3. 1 AND 2

Table 5–2 continued

QUESTION	STRATEGY

29
(Full text,
abstract,
title)
	1. africa$ or algeria or angola or botswana
	   or cameroon or chad or congo or egypt or
	   gambia or ghana or ivory adj coast or kenya
	   or liberia or libya or niger$ or senegal
	   or sudan or swaziland or tanzania or uganda
	   or tunisia or volta or sahara or zaire or
	   zambia or zimbabwe or rhodesia
	2. (trade or labor) same union$
	3. afl adj cio or afl-cio
	4. 1 SAME (2 OR 3)

29 (controlled vocabulary)	1. appropriate countries listed above.su. 2. labor adj unions.de. or afl-cio.su. 3. 1 AND 2

30
(Full text,
abstract,
title)
	1. affirmative adj action or minorit$ or
	   oriental$ or blacks or negroes or asian$
	   or hispanic$ or latin$
	2. apprentice$ or (train$ with employee$)
	3 1 SAME 2

30
(controlled
vocabulary)
	1. employee adj training.de. or (personnel.de.
	   or employees.de.) with education.de.
	2. minority adj groups.de. or blacks.de. or
	   affirmative adj action.de.
	3. 1 SAME 2

31 (Full text, abstract, title)	1. information same (retrieval or system$) or database$ or data adj base$ 2. personal or private or office or inhouse 3. 1 SAME 2
31 (controlled vocabulary)	1. information adj system.de. or databases.de.
33 (Full text, abstract, title)	1. mobility with (occupation$ or job or jobs or profession$ 2. woman or women or female or sex 3. 1 SAME 2
33 (controlled vocabulary)	1. occupational adj mobility.de. 2. women.de. or women adj business.de. or women adj executives.de. 3. 1 SAME 2

Table 5–2 continued

QUESTION	STRATEGY
3 4 (Full text, abstract, title	1. woman or women or female or sex 2. union$ or collective adj bargain$ or strike or strikes 3. 1 SAME 2

3 4
(controlled
vocabulary
	1. labor adj unions.de. or collective adj
	    bargaining.de.
	2. women.de. or women adj business.de. or
	    sex adj discrimination.de.
	3. 1 SAME 2

3 5 (Full text, abstract, title)	1. recreation$ or tennis$ or baseball or sport$ 2. industr$ or manufactur$ or factories or plant or business$ or factory 3. employee$ adj benefit$ 4. 1 SAME (2 OR 3)
3 5 (controlled vocabulary)	1. employee adj benefits.de.
3 6 (Full text, abstract, title)	1. daycare or day adj care or childcare or child adj care
3 6 (controlled vocabulary)	1. day adj care.pr.
3 7 (Full text, abstract, title)	1. comparable adj worth or equal adj pay or discrimination same (pay or wages)
3 7 (controlled vocabulary)	1. equal adj employment adj opportunity.de. or sex adj discrimination.de. 2. income.de. or earnings.de. or wages.de. 3. 1 SAME 2
3 8 (Full text, abstract, title)	1. farm$ or ranch$ 2. retire$ 3. 1 SAME 2
3 8 (controlled vocabulary)	1. retirement.de.

Table 5–2 continued

QUESTION	STRATEGY
39 (Full text, abstract, title)	1. productivity 2. japan 3. united adj states or us or u adj s or america$ 4. 1 SAME 2 SAME 3
39 (controlled vocabulary)	1. productivity.de. 2. japan.su. 3. united adj states adj america.su. 4. 1 AND 2 AND 3

40
(Full text,
abstract,
 	
title)
	1. productivity
	2. union$ or collective adj bargain$ or strike
	   or strikes or open adj shop$ or nonunion or
	   non adj union
	3. 1 SAME 2

40 (controlled vocabulary)	1. productivity.de. 2. labor adj unions.de. 3. 1 SAME 2

(Note: Excludes questions used in the pilot study and those yielding zero postings. In each case searches were limited to January/February 1976 through July/August 1983 and for each search method terms were limited to the appropriate field. In BRS "$" is a truncation character, "adj" specifies words must be adjacent to each other, "with" specifies the same sentence, and "same" specifies the same paragraph.)

Searches on the full text were limited to the text field (with all subject paragraphs equally searchable), title searches were limited to the title field, abstract searches were limited to the abstract field, and index term searches included the appropriate controlled vocabulary field or fields. Full text searches used the paragraph proximity operator SAME rather than the Boolean AND, a strategy recommended in the HBR/O user's manual. SAME requires all concepts searched to be in the same paragraph and, since for all but the full text field, a paragraph is equivalent to a field, using SAME instead of AND when searching titles, abstracts, or descriptors makes no difference in the search. (When controlled terms were located in more than one controlled vocabulary, the AND operator had to be used.) The SAME operator is the recommended strategy for full text searching and does not affect results in other fields.

Relevance of each article to its search topic had to be judged in order to calculate recall and precision ratios, but the method of obtaining search questions precluded involvement of the requesters. Relevance was judged by a panel of three business experts from the University of Hawaii College of Business. A majority decision was used.

Retrieval results from each search method were pooled for each question to identify all unique articles. Photocopies were made of each article, and the appropriate accession number from the online search was written on the article. The researcher maintained a record of which search method or methods retrieved each article for each topic, but this was not indicated on the photocopy. Since past research has shown that the representation viewed may affect relevance judgments, the full text was used for relevance judging no matter what representation resulted in retrieval.[3]

RECALL, PRECISION, AND TOTAL DOCUMENTS

The goal of this study was to compare retrieval performance and search results from searching on the full text of journal articles with searching on different portions of the bibliographic records (document surrogates). Measures studied were recall, precision, total documents retrieved, overlap, and uniqueness, testing two hypotheses. The first hypothesis stated that searching on full text will result in higher recall, lower precision, and retrieve a greater number of documents than searching the document surrogates. The second stated that searching full text will retrieve a greater number of unique documents than searching the surrogates.

The total pool of search questions numbered forty originally, of which four were used in a pilot study to test the methodology. Search strategies were developed for the remaining thirty-six topics, from which thirty-one topics retrieved at least one document from at least one search method. (See Tables 5–1 and 5–2 for search topics and strategies.) The five topics that did not retrieve any documents were assumed to be inappropriate for the HBR/O database and are not considered in the analysis.

As shown in Table 5–3, total documents retrieved by the union of the full text, abstracts, and controlled vocabulary searches range from one to sixty-nine in the thirty-one searches. The bibliographic union was to be the union of documents retrieved by the abstract, controlled vocabulary and title fields—the fields normally available in a bibliographic database. Because only one search retrieved a document through the title field, titles are not considered in the quantitative analysis throughout. The bibliographic union is thus in reality the union of abstract results and controlled vocabulary results. Since these are the two most common value added fields that require intellectual effort and costs to producers to create, this revised bibliographic union is a meaningful field for comparison.

Half of the searches retrieved eleven or fewer documents, but due to several searches with a large number of retrieved documents there was a mean retrieval of more than twenty-one documents per topic (see Table 5–5). Table 5–4 shows that relevant documents retrieved range from zero to 23 (with a mean of 4.5 and a median of 2).

As hypothesized and as shown in Table 5–5, the full text generally re-

Table 5-3
Number of Documents Retrieved by Each Search Method in Rank Order by Union of All Search Methods

UNION	FULL TEXT	ABST	CONT VOCB	TITLE	BIB UNION	QUESTION #
69	65	11	0	0	11	25
67	61	7	9	0	15	13
64	61	5	1	0	6	26
58	53	6	9	1	13	5
54	34	8	24	0	29	31
47	32	1	15	0	16	35
38	36	7	1	0	7	40
33	25	3	6	0	9	10
30	29	2	0	0	2	19
27	26	2	0	0	2	22
18	15	4	4	0	8	39
17	17	0	0	0	0	27
15	12	4	0	0	4	34
11	9	1	1	0	2	12
11	0	1	10	0	11	23
11	10	3	2	0	3	37
10	10	0	0	0	0	15
9	7	0	2	0	2	6
9	7	2	2	0	4	16
9	9	1	0	0	1	36
8	7	0	1	0	1	18
7	5	3	0	0	3	30
7	1	0	6	0	6	38
7	6	2	1	0	3	9
5	5	0	0	0	0	7
5	5	0	0	0	0	17
3	3	0	0	0	0	29
3	1	0	2	0	2	21
2	1	0	1	0	1	24
1	0	1	0	0	1	8
1	0	1	0	0	1	33

trieved more total documents than any surrogate field or combination of fields. This might be explained by the greater number of words in the text as compared to other fields. Full texts in HBR/O average approximately 5,000 words; abstracts average approximately 200 words; controlled vocabulary fields appropriate to the thirty-one search topics in this study average ten words; and HBR article titles average approximately six words.

On the average, as can be extracted from Table 5–5, full text retrieved 7.4 times more total documents than did abstracts, 5.7 times more than controlled vocabulary, and 3.4 times more than the bibliographic union. The total number of relevant documents retrieved shows that the presence

Table 5–4
Number of Relevant Documents Retrieved by Each Search Method in Rank Order by Union of All Search Methods

UNION	FULL TEXT	ABST	CONT VOCB	TITLE	BIB UNION	QUESTION #
23	11	4	15	0	18	31
21	18	1	5	0	6	5
13	11	4	0	0	4	25
12	11	4	0	0	4	40
11	10	2	5	0	6	13
10	9	4	1	0	5	39
6	5	2	0	0	2	19
5	5	2	2	0	2	37
4	3	0	1	0	1	10
4	4	1	0	0	1	22
4	4	0	0	0	0	26
4	2	2	0	0	2	30
3	3	2	0	0	2	9
3	2	1	2	0	3	16
3	1	0	2	0	2	35
2	2	0	0	0	0	6
2	2	0	0	0	0	15
2	2	1	0	0	1	34
2	0	0	2	0	2	38
1	1	0	0	0	0	17
1	0	0	1	0	1	24
1	1	0	0	0	0	27
1	0	0	1	0	1	21
0	0	0	0	0	0	7
0	0	0	0	0	0	8
0	0	0	0	0	0	12
0	0	0	0	0	0	18
0	0	0	0	0	0	23
0	0	0	0	0	0	29
0	0	0	0	0	0	33
0	0	0	0	0	0	36

of the HBR journal article texts allowed relevant documents to be retrieved that would not have been found with any other available representation.

Relative recall as shown in Table 5–6 indicates what percentage of the total relevant documents retrieved was retrieved by each representation or by the full text. Relative recall for a search method can be viewed as the proportion of relevant documents a searcher would retrieve if only searching with that one method.

Table 5–6 indicates that searching the full text only in this study retrieved between 0 and 100 percent of the relevant documents for any given question. On average, for the questions searched in this study in the HBR/O database, when searching on the full text alone with no value-added fields,

Table 5–5
Mean of Relevant and Total Documents Retrieved by Each Search Method

SEARCH METHOD	MEAN # OF TOTAL DOCS.*	MEDIAN # OF TOTAL DOCS.	MEAN # OF REL DOCS.*	MEDIAN # OF REL. DOCS.	MEAN # OF WORDS
Union	21.2	11	4.5	2	(5210)
Full Text	17.8	9	3.5	2	5000
Abstract	2.4	1	1.0	0	200
Controlled Vocabulary	3.1	1	1.2	0	10
Bibliographic Union	5.3	3	2.0	1	(210)

* Significant difference at the .05 level (the Union is not included in the test of significance)

Source: Produced from "Full Text Database Retrieval Performance" by Carol Tenopir, *Online Review*, 9, no. 2 (1985) by permission of Learned Information, Inc., 143 Old Marlton Pike, Medford, NJ 08055.

almost three-quarters of all relevant documents were retrieved. Controlled vocabulary contributed on the average 28 percent and abstract searches 19.3 percent of the total relevant documents. Taken together (bibliographic union), that percentage increases to 44.9 percent.

Tables 5–5 and 5–6 show there was a significant difference between search methods for total documents retrieved, relevant documents retrieved, and recall at the .05 level. There was a difference in precision ratios but it was not significant at the .05 level. A Scheffé procedure was used in each instance where a significant difference was found. The analysis of variance procedure (ANOVA) used to test whether or not there is a significant difference does not identify which means differ significantly. The Scheffé procedure revealed what means are significantly different from what other means. For total documents retrieved, for relevant documents retrieved, and for recall the full text differs significantly from abstract, controlled vocabulary and bibliographic union, but the latter three are not significantly different from each other.

These results support hypothesis one and indicate the value of full text in the HBR/O database. They also suggest the value of combining free text searching of abstract words with controlled vocabulary descriptors in the bibliographic-only portion of the database. Still, on the average over 26 percent of the total relevant documents retrieved were not retrieved by any one search method or by the bibliographic union, showing that total reliance on one search method in HBR/O often precludes a comprehensive

Table 5–6
Relative Recall Ratios (in percents)

QUESTION #	FULL TEXT	ABSTRACT	CONTROLLED VOCABULARY	BIB UNION
5	85.7	4.8	23.8	28.6
6	100.0	0.0	0.0	0.0
7	- - -	- - -	- - -	- - -
8	- - -	- - -	- - -	- - -
9	100.0	66.7	0.0	66.7
10	75.0	0.0	25.0	25.0
12	- - -	- - -	- - -	- - -
13	90.9	18.2	45.5	54.5
15	100.0	0.0	0.0	0.0
16	66.7	33.3	66.7	100.0
17	100.0	0.0	0.0	0.0
18	- - -	- - -	- - -	- - -
19	83.3	33.3	0.0	33.3
21	0.0	0.0	100.0	100.0
22	100.0	25.0	0.0	25.0
23	- - -	- - -	- - -	- - -
24	0.0	0.0	100.0	100.0
25	84.6	30.8	0.0	30.8
26	100.0	0.0	0.0	0.0
27	100.0	0.0	0.0	0.0
29	- - -	- - -	- - -	- - -
30	50.0	50.0	0.0	50.0
31	47.8	17.4	65.2	78.3
33	- - -	- - -	- - -	- - -
34	100.0	50.0	0.0	50.0
35	33.3	0.0	66.7	66.7
36	- - -	- - -	- - -	- - -
37	100.0	40.0	40.0	40.0
38	0.0	0.0	100.0	100.0
39	90.0	40.0	10.0	50.0
40	91.7	33.3	0.0	33.3
MEAN*	73.9	19.3	28.0	44.9

* Significant difference at the .05 level.

search. In the twenty-three questions in which relevant documents were retrieved, the full text retrieved all the relevant documents in nine questions, the controlled vocabulary retrieved all in three questions, the bibliographic union retrieved all in four questions, and the abstract never retrieved all relevant documents. These results suggest that were the value added fields not included, some relevant documents would not be retrieved in some queries.

The precision ratio measures level-of-effort or "signal-to-noise" ratio because it indicates what proportion of irrelevant documents a user has to

Table 5–7
Precision Ratios (in percents)

QUESTION #	FULL TEXT	ABSTRACT	CONTROLLED VOCABULARY	BIB UNION
5	34.0	16.7	55.6	46.2
6	28.6	- - -	0.0	0.0
7	0.0	- - -	- - -	- - -
8	- - -	0.0	- - -	0.0
9	50.0	100.0	0.0	66.7
10	12.0	0.0	16.7	11.1
12	0.0	0.0	0.0	0.0
13	16.4	28.6	55.6	40.0
15	20.0	- - -	- - -	- - -
16	28.6	50.0	100.0	75.0
17	20.0	- - -	- - -	- - -
18	0.0	- - -	0.0	0.0
19	17.2	100.0	- - -	100.0
21	0.0	- - -	50.0	50.0
22	15.4	50.0	- - -	50.0
23	- - -	0.0	0.0	0.0
24	0.0	- - -	100.0	100.0
25	16.9	36.4	- - -	36.4
26	6.6	0.0	0.0	0.0
27	5.9	- - -	- - -	- - -
29	0.0	- - -	- - -	- - -
30	40.0	66.7	- - -	66.7
31	32.4	50.0	62.5	62.1
33	- - -	0.0	- - -	0.0
34	16.7	25.0	- - -	25.0
35	3.1	0.0	13.3	12.5
36	0.0	0.0	- - -	0.0
37	50.0	66.7	100.0	66.7
38	0.0	- - -	33.3	33.3
39	60.0	100.0	25.0	62.5
40	30.6	57.1	0.0	57.1
MEAN	18.0	35.6	34.0	37.0

view to find the relevant ones.[4] It is also useful as one measure of cost because all retrieved documents have a printing or viewing cost associated with them, whether or not they are relevant.

Table 5–7 shows that, as hypothesized, the full text searches have a lower precision ratio than do abstract or controlled vocabulary searches. The search strategies used in this test followed the recommendations in the HBR/O user's manual for increasing relevance in full text searching, yet full text still achieved an average precision ratio of only 18 percent. This is approximately half the precision of the other two search methods. Precision was low for almost all searches by any of the methods, reflecting perhaps the search strategies used. Because of the "fast batch" search

Table 5–8
Mean Asymmetric Overlap Values (for relevant and total documents retrieved)

MEASURE	RELEVANT*	TOTAL*
AOfa	.192	.076
AOaf	.769	.533
AOfc	.094	.028
AOcf	.288	.228
AOfb	.256	.091
AObf	.494	.330

f = full text, a = abstract, c = controlled vocabulary, b = bibliographic union
* significant difference at the .05 level.

strategies used, the comparison of precision between the search methods should be considered more important than the actual precision scores.

OVERLAP AND UNIQUENESS

Overlap of specific documents retrieved by each method was computed to test research hypothesis two. Three measures of overlap were adapted from a study of bibliographic surrogates conducted at Syracuse University.[5] Overlap measures compare how many of the specific documents are retrieved in common by two or more search methods and are similar to but go beyond recall and precision.

Asymmetric overlap is a pairwise measure giving the fraction of a set retrieved by one representation that is in common with a set retrieved by another representation. As defined in the Syracuse study: "For two representations i and j, this measure is computed by dividing the number of documents retrieved by both representations by the number retrieved by one of the representations."[6] This measure gives the fraction of a retrieved set that is common to both retrieved sets. If R_i and R_j are the sets of documents retrieved by representations i and j, then the asymmetric overlap measure can be given as:

$$AO_{ij} = (R_i * R_j)/R_i$$

where * is the intersection.

Table 5–8 presents asymmetric overlap means for all documents retrieved and for relevant documents retrieved.

Table 5–9
Mean Symmetric Overlap Values (for relevant and total documents retrieved)

MEASURE	RELEVANT*	TOTAL*
SOfa	.186	.064
SOfc	.066	.024

f = full text, a = abstract, c = controlled vocabulary
* significant difference at the .05 level.

Symmetric overlap is also a pairwise measure. It gives the fraction of documents that are common to both sets. It can be defined as: For two representations i and j, this measure is computed as "the number of retrieved documents in the intersection of the two representations divided by the union of those representations."[7]

$$SOij = (Ri * Rj)/(Ri + Rj)$$

Where * is the intersection and + is the union.

Table 5–9 presents symmetric overlap values for all documents retrieved and relevant documents retrieved.

In the asymmetric table, the higher the value, the greater the overlap or the lower the independent contribution of the first stated method of searching (for example, "a" in AOaf). This study shows the proportionately small contribution of abstracts, controlled vocabulary, and bibliographic union when compared to full text. This is especially dramatic for abstracts, where three-quarters of the relevant documents retrieved by the abstract searches overlap with the full text. An abstract might be considered a subset of the full text, as it summarizes the text content using similar words. Representations in the Syracuse study were more independent of each other and no representation pairs tested had such high asymmetric overlaps.

Symmetric overlap measures are closer to the Syracuse bibliographic database results. The numbers in Table 5–9 can be interpreted as: only 18.6 percent of the pooled set of relevant documents and 6.4 percent of the pooled set of total documents retrieved by both abstract and full text searches were found by both search methods. The controlled vocabulary/full text figures are lower—6.6 percent and 2.4 percent.

Combination overlap (Table 5–10) extends the symmetric overlap beyond pairwise overlaps to show what portion of documents retrieved by a given search method is common to those retrieved by the union of all other search methods. Combination overlap can be defined: For a representation

Table 5–10
Mean Combination Overlap Values (for relevant and total documents retrieved)

MEASURE	RELEVANT*	TOTAL*
COf	.188	.069
COa	.147	.057
COc	.063	.021

f = full text, a = abstract, c = controlled vocabulary
* significant difference at the .05 level.

i, this measure is computed by dividing the number of documents retrieved in common with that representation and the union of all other representations by the union of all representations. This measure gives the fraction of documents in set i that are common to the union of documents retrieved by all other methods.

$$COi = (Ri * [Rj + Rk + Rl])/(Ri + Rj + Rk + Rl)$$

where * is the intersection and + is the union.

Combination overlap is most meaningful when examined in conjunction with recall. If there is a large difference between a search method's average recall and its combination overlap for relevant documents, a greater percentage of the documents retrieved by the method are unique. This difference equals the combination uniqueness discussed below.

Uniqueness measures pertain more directly to research hypothesis two in that they measure the unique contribution of each search method. Uniqueness measures demonstrate clearly the value added by each field in terms of specific relevant documents contributed.

Table 5–11, 5–12, and 5–13 give the results from applying three uniqueness measures for relevant documents and all documents retrieved. Three uniqueness measures were used: two pairwise asymmetric measures and one combination uniqueness measure.

The first asymmetric uniqueness measure can be defined as: for two representations i and j, this measure is computed by dividing the number of documents retrieved in set i that are not also in set j by the number of documents in set i. This measure gives the fraction of set i that is unique.

$$AUij = (Ri - Rj)/Ri$$

where − is the complement. (This measure equals $1 - AOij$, where − is an arithmetic operator.)

Table 5–11
Mean Asymmetric Uniqueness Values (for relevant and total documents retrieved)

MEASURE	RELEVANT*	TOTAL*
AUfa	.808	.925
AUaf	.231	.467
AUfc	.906	.972
AUcf	.712	.772
AUfb	.744	.909
AUbf	.506	.670

f = full text, a = abstract, c = controlled vocabulary, b = bibliographic union
* significant difference at the .05 level.

Source: Produced from "Full Text Database Retrieval Performance" by Carol Tenopir, *Online Review*, 9, no. 2 (1985) by permission of Learned Information, Inc., 143 Old Marlton Pike, Medford, NJ 08055.

Table 5–12
Mean Second Method Asymmetric Uniqueness Values (for relevant and total documents retrieved)

MEASURE	RELEVANT*	TOTAL*
A2fa	.760	.801
A2af	.054	.135
A2fc	.717	.807
A2cf	.217	.169
A2bf	.261	.258

f = full text, a = abstract, c = controlled vocabulary, b = bibliographic union
* significant difference at the .05 level.

Source: Produced from "Full Text Database Retrieval Performance" by Carol Tenopir, *Online Review*, 9, no. 2 (1985) by permission of Learned Information, Inc., 143 Old Marlton Pike, Medford, NJ 08055.

The second asymmetric uniqueness measure is defined: For two representations i and j, this measure is computed by dividing the number of documents retrieved in set i that are not also in set j by the number of documents in the union of the two sets. This measure gives the fraction of the unique documents of the total retrieved set that are contributed by set i.

Table 5–13
Mean Combination Uniqueness Values (for relevant and total documents retrieved)

MEASURE	RELEVANT*	TOTAL*
CUf	.551	.673
CUa	.045	.104
Cuc	.216	.154

f = full text, a = abstract, c = controlled vocabulary
* significant difference at the .05 level.

Source: Produced from "Full Text Database Retrieval Performance" by Carol Tenopir, *Online Review*, 9, no. 2 (1985) by permission of Learned Information, Inc., 143 Old Marlton Pike, Medford, NJ 08055.

$$AU(2)ij = (Ri - Rj) / (Ri + Rj)$$
where − is the complement and + is the union.

The combination uniqueness is defined: For a representation i, this measure is computed by dividing the number of documents retrieved in set i that are not also contained in the union of the searches of the other representations by the union of all representations. This measure gives the fraction of the total documents retrieved that are unique to set i.

$$CUi = (Ri - [Rj + Rk + Rl])/(Ri + Rj + Rk + Rl)$$
where − is the complement and + is the union.

In all uniqueness measures the full text contributed a higher percent of unique articles than any other search method. These findings are consistent with the recall percentages and suggest a preferred search order of full text, controlled vocabulary, and abstract. The abstract combination uniqueness figure of .045 indicates that 95.5 percent of the relevant documents could be retrieved without searching the abstract field. Controlled vocabulary makes a much greater contribution of unique relevant documents in HBR/O (21.6 percent). The relative recall figures for these two fields were reasonably close; yet the abstracts contain a much lower percentage of unique documents and a much greater overlap with other fields. These overlap and uniqueness figures indicate that of the representations tested in this study, abstracts are of the least value for high recall.

These results also support the relative recall findings by indicating that, for the HBR/O database within the constraints of this study, the full text search alone would contribute almost three-quarters of the relevant documents (AUfb). To determine if the cost and effort to add the additional access points of abstract and controlled vocabulary are justified by the potential retrieval of the additional 25 percent of the relevant documents, the increased precision offered by these fields should be considered.

The results of an analysis of variance test in Tables 5–8 through 5–13 show that there is a significant difference at the .05 level for all measures of overlap and uniqueness except Combination Overlap for relevant documents.

COST PER RELEVANT CITATION

The recall, overlap, and uniqueness measures in this study all favor the full text. The low precision of full text must be taken into account, however, for there to be complete comparison with other search methods. Unit cost per relevant citation retrieved by each search method provides an indication of the level of effort a user "must expend to find each relevant item,"[8] and takes into consideration precision ratios as well as recall ratios.

Table 5–14 shows the estimated costs per relevant citation for full text, abstracts, and controlled vocabulary. The costs were calculated by combining the online search cost required for each method with the article duplication costs. Article duplication costs would be different in a real situation because searchers would probably first view online a shortened record of each retrieved document and then print or order the complete documents of only those judged to be relevant. The online costs would therefore be higher, but fewer documents would have to be duplicated.

Table 5–14 indicates that although full text retrieves a much greater percentage of unique items and has better recall than the other search methods tested, it also has a much greater cost per relevant citation. Full text searching is more expensive than abstract or controlled vocabulary searching. This indicates that the availability of full text without value-added fields will result in more time spent online and thus higher revenues to the database producer, but greater costs to the searcher.

CONTROLLED VOCABULARY

Controlled vocabulary results rely on the size and specificity of the vocabulary and the accuracy and consistency of the indexing. These results are therefore the least generalizable and most affected by idiosyncrasies of an individual database. The results of the controlled vocabulary searches were similar to abstract search results in recall, precision, and total documents retrieved, but made a much higher contribution of unique relevant documents. The controlled vocabulary searches were examined in more detail to try to explain these results and to examine variations among questions.

Size and specificity of the indexing vocabulary may contribute to the recall and precision results. Search strategies for controlled vocabulary

Table 5–14
Cost Effectiveness (unit cost per relevant item)

QUESTION #	FULL TEXT	ABSTRACT	CONTROLLED VOCABULARY
5	$ 3.07	$ 7.48	$ 2.11
6	$ 4.25	- - -	- - -
7	- - -	- - -	- - -
8	- - -	- - -	- - -
9	$ 4.06	$ 4.06	- - -
1 0	$ 8.94	- - -	$ 7.82
1 2	- - -	- - -	- - -
1 3	$ 6.70	$ 6.01	$ 2.38
1 5	$ 6.36	- - -	- - -
1 6	$ 5.23	$ 5.36	$ 2.79
1 7	$ 7.05	- - -	- - -
1 8	- - -	- - -	- - -
1 9	$ 6.18	$ 1.71	- - -
2 1	- - -	- - -	$ 2.43
2 2	$ 7.60	$ 5.95	- - -
2 3	- - -	- - -	- - -
2 4	- - -	- - -	$ 2.19
2 5	$ 6.25	$ 3.44	- - -
2 6	$ 15.96	- - -	- - -
2 7	$ 19.26	- - -	- - -
2 9	- - -	- - -	- - -
3 0	$ 3.62	$ 2.61	- - -
3 1	$ 3.32	$ 2.53	$ 1.67
3 3	- - -	- - -	- - -
3 4	$ 6.89	$ 5.64	- - -
3 5	$ 34.92	- - -	$ 7.83
3 6	- - -	- - -	$ 3.15
3 7	$ 2.31	$ 2.21	$ 1.71
3 8	- - -	- - -	- - -
3 9	$ 1.74	$ 1.36	$ 4.85
4 0	$ 3.49	$ 2.22	- - -
MEAN	$ 7.86	$ 3.89	$ 3.54

searches depend on how well the available terms match the search topic (and the documents). If terms in the vocabulary are too broad for a topic, the precision ratio can be expected to be relatively low; if terms are too narrow, the recall is likely to be low. Four of the questions required search strategies that were much too broad (questions 31, 35, 37 and 38). For the question on personal or office databases, for example, the only appropriate vocabulary terms were "information systems" or "databases." For retirement of farmers or ranchers, only the single descriptor "retirement" pertained. These broad searches had relatively high recall ratios, but precision ratios were also higher than average in two of the above four questions.

Terms in the HBR/O controlled vocabulary fields tend to be broad rather than narrow, although some concepts have very specific terms available. Finding terms in the vocabulary at the right level of specificity was usually possible, but the policy of assigning only five index terms resulted in low postings for most assigned terms. Searching broader terms when available, in addition to the more specific terms, may have increased recall without creating unacceptable precision ratios.

In nine questions relevant documents were retrieved by the controlled vocabulary that were not retrieved by any other search method. After examining these documents, there seem to be three major reasons why the controlled vocabulary resulted in retrieval while the full text did not: (1) variations or change in terminology, (2) specificity of terminology, (3) incomplete search strategy development by the searcher.

Terminology used in the texts of the articles in question varied from the more commonly used terms found in similar articles. A relevant article retrieved by controlled vocabulary only in question 10, for example, was a reprint of an article originally published in 1950. In 1950 the now common terms of "product diffusion" or "early adopters" were not in use. HBR's controlled vocabulary retained the older term "new products," use of which in the search strategy would have retrieved the 1950 reprint. In question 24 the controlled vocabulary term "family" retrieved a document relevant to personnel policies for spouses working in the same firm. Nowhere in this document were the terms nepotism, couple, marriage, married, or spouse found, but the terms family, wives, wife, or relatives would have resulted in retrieval by the full text. The author of the document assumed male-owned firms that were hiring relatives (including wives); the searcher failed to add the appropriate synonyms. In question 16 a relevant document retrieved by the descriptor "flexible working hours" was not retrieved by the full text search because only the term "flexitime" was used in the text of the article. The searcher used the alternate spelling "flextime" but failed to use "flexitime."

These three questions point out the need to use both modern and older forms of words and to use many synonyms to achieve complete full text retrieval. The constancy of controlled vocabulary terms for any concept as compared to the inconsistent and changing nature of text language often assists retrieval.

ABSTRACTS

The other value-added field, abstracts, did not contribute as many unique relevant documents as did the controlled vocabulary. The high overlap of abstracts with full text in a way shows the success of the HBR abstracters in summarizing the content of each article in the author's own words. Still, the relevant documents retrieved only by abstracts were examined to determine why they were not retrieved by any other method. There seem to be three main reasons why relevant articles were retrieved by abstract searching but not by full text: (1) words did not appear in the same text paragraphs, (2) language varies in texts, and (3) the searcher did not use all possible synonyms in the search strategy.

The most common reason for abstract-only retrieval resulted from using the SAME paragraph operator in the full text searches. Search terms from both facets of a search appeared somewhere in many of the texts of these documents but the terms did not appear in the same grammatical paragraphs. (Chapter 6 contrasts SAME paragraph searching of texts with Boolean AND.) In the abstract the important concepts were brought together into the same field (that is, paragraph). In question 25, for example, several articles about the effects of unions on the introduction of new technology were retrieved by the abstract because all the ramifications of unions were listed in the abstracts. The texts discussed each of these effects in turn without repeating the term "union." The same is true in question 19 in an article about second careers. The concept of training or retraining was not mentioned in the same text paragraphs as the concept of new jobs or layoffs, but these two concepts were brought together in the abstract. In the article that was retrieved for question 13 only the abstract is about the stressful role of corporate wives. A mention of them entering the work force was in a paragraph without other search terms, but all concepts were together in the abstract field.

Another reason for document retrieval by the abstract but not by the full text is language. In question 13, for example, " wives" or "wife" is used more frequently in the text than "woman" or "women." The abstract used "women." If the synonyms "wives" or "wife" were added to the full text search, this article would be retrieved. In question 30 an article about Sioux Indians does not refer to them as a "minority" group in the text, but the abstract uses this term.

As with controlled vocabulary, the abstracts in HBR/O sometimes compensate for the inconsistency of language and the necessity of many possible specific terms for the same concept. A comprehensive full text search requires listing many synonyms for each concept. Abstracts are also, of course, useful for judging relevance.

FULL TEXT

For many questions, full text searching retrieved many more unique relevant documents than either controlled vocabulary or abstract searching. One obvious contribution of the availability of full texts, therefore, is an increase in the number of documents retrieved. An examination of the relevant documents retrieved only by the full text revealed four major characteristics: (1) level of specificity can better match the question, (2) full text can compensate for deficiencies in the controlled vocabulary, (3) some concepts that are implied in the abstract but not mentioned explicitly are mentioned in the text, (4) full text sometimes uses more synonyms and can thus compensate for incomplete search strategies.

Articles that on the whole are broader in scope than the search request (that include the search topic as only a minor portion of the article) are the major reason for full text–only contributions. The abstractors and indexers attempt to match the depth or level of specificity of each article taken as a whole. Thus, an article on unionization of professional employees may list the specific professions in the text but not in the abstract or controlled vocabulary terms (see questions 22 and 27). For documents retrieved only by abstracts the opposite was sometimes found—terms in the abstract were broader than the text terms. In question 40 articles on the decline of productivity in the United States mentioned many reasons for this decline, including labor unions. The specific reasons are accessible only via the full text where they are listed or mentioned briefly. This variance in the level of specificity was the one major reason for many of the text-only retrievals.

Another contribution of the full text is that it compensates for deficiencies in the controlled vocabulary. Several topics did not have appropriate descriptors for a concept, so narrower or broader terms had to be used. For question 27, for example, there were no descriptors for colleges or universities. The product and services terms were used, but relevant articles discussed colleges and universities as a subject, not as a product or service. The same reason applies to question 22 with libraries, schools, and so on. HBR's policy of assigning only five descriptors means that only the major issues in an article are indexed. This, plus the policy of indexing and abstracting at the level of specificity of the article as a whole, results in many full text–only retrievals. All articles retrieved by the full text only seemed to have appropriate index terms within the constraints of the controlled vocabulary and the HBR indexing policy, however.

Compared to abstracts, full text facilitates retrieval of articles that mention a specific facet of a topic, but that are generally broader in scope than the search question. Full text also retrieved some articles where one facet was assumed but not explicitly mentioned in the abstract. For example, in question 35 the abstracts of some documents implied that recreational facilities provided to employees to reduce tension are benefits, but the term "benefit" was not explicitly used. In question 6 the concept of attitudes or feelings about hard work was implied.

Abstracts sometimes used jargon or a single term for a concept in the text while the full text stated it in several ways. For example, in question 30 the title and abstract of an article referred to "Mexicans." The text, however, used various synonyms such as "Hispanics," "Chicanos," and "Mexican-Americans." In question 19, "hard-to-employ" was the only

Table 5–15
Relevance of Documents Retrieved by More than One Search Method

SEARCH METHOD	# OF RELEVANT	# OF NON-RELEVANT	PRECISION RATIO
Controlled Vocabulary/ Full Text	1 1	3	78.57%
Abstract/Full Text	1 9	1 9	50.00%
Controlled Vocabulary/ Full Text/Abstract	4	3	57.14%

Source: Produced from "Full Text Database Retrieval Performance" by Carol Tenopir, *Online Review*, 9, no. 2 (1985) by permission of Learned Information, Inc., 143 Old Marlton Pike, Medford, NJ 08055.

term used in the abstract of one document to describe unemployed workers. Unemployment caused by layoffs was included in the article, but the term "layoff" was found only in the full text.

RELEVANCE JUDGING

Much of this analysis is based on relevance judging by a panel of three business experts. The majority opinion of the three was used to deem a document relevant or not relevant to the query. All judges agreed that a document was relevant or not for approximately two-thirds of the documents (68.7 percent). This falls within the range of relevance agreement by subject experts as reported by Saracevic.[9] The judges were more often consistent in judging a document not relevant because definite false drops seemed to be the easiest documents for all three to identify. Relevance is more prone to personal interpretations, and there was therefore less agreement.

WORD OCCURRENCE DATA

Although full text searching results in the highest recall on the average, the low precision results of the full text searches cause a high cost per relevant citation and a high level of user effort as they scan many irrelevant items to find the relevant ones. An accurate method of predicting relevance would be useful to searchers and could be incorporated into retrieval system design.

One factor found in this study that seems to be an accurate predictor of relevance is joint retrieval by both a full text search method and a controlled vocabulary search (see Table 5–15). This is consistent with results of a study reported by Neway and Lancaster.[10] Of those twenty-one items that were retrieved by both methods, fifteen (71 percent) were relevant, compared to an average precision ratio of 38.1 percent for controlled vocabulary alone. Joint retrieval by abstract and full text shows less dramatic results. Approximately 51 percent (twenty-three of forty-five) were relevant.

Other factors that might help to predict relevance in full text databases are (1) the number of times the search terms appear in the text, and (2) the number of paragraphs that contain search terms. The BRS Occurrence table feature (explained in Chapter 3) allows searchers to view this word placement information online.

As shown in Table 5–16, for relevant documents retrieved by full text, the search phrases occurred an average of 8.69 times per document. This compares with only 3.69 times in nonrelevant documents. A threshold for word occurrences, above which there would be a greater assurance of retrieving relevant documents, would be useful for searching, if one could be established. Table 5–17 presents the number of word occurrences per document in rank order for documents. In a document where the search words occur ten or more times there is a 58 percent chance that any document retrieved will be relevant. (This does not improve when that threshold is raised to twenty or more occurrences.)

Table 5–18 shows the average precision ratios for all questions listed in order of frequency of occurrence. This clearly demonstrates the relationship between word occurrence and precision and can be used as a searching guideline. When compared to the overall average precision ratio for full text this table is especially striking. By using word occurrence numbers as a guide to relevance, the searcher can increase the chances of viewing a relevant document.

Table 5–17 reveals some variations with individual search questions, however. Question 26 retrieved six documents with ten or more occurrences of the search words, none of which were relevant. Question 31, on the other hand, retrieved eight documents with ten or more word occurrences, seven of which were relevant. Relative frequency (frequency of a term in a document versus frequency in the database as a whole) was not examined in this study, but the study described in Chapter 6 examined word frequency ranking algorithms in detail.

Table 5–19 shows that on the average, relevant documents contained search phrases in approximately twice as many grammatical paragraphs as did nonrelevant documents. In the rank ordering for documents containing search phrases in four or more paragraphs (Table 5–20) it can be seen that documents having occurrences in four or more paragraphs have a 58 percent chance of being relevant. In documents where the search phrases occurred in only one paragraph, however, there is an almost 90 percent chance that the document will *not* be relevant (Table 5–21). This compares to an av-

Table 5–16
Word Occurrence Patterns for Relevant and Nonrelevant Documents (means of number of word occurrences)

QUESTION #	MEAN # OF OCCURRENCES (relevant)	MEAN # OF OCCURRENCES (nonrelevant)
5	3.78	5.03
6	3.00	2.00
7	- - -	4.00
8	- - -	- - -
9	13.67	5.33
10	4.67	2.77
12	- - -	3.89
13	12.45	4.86
15	7.00	4.88
16	10.00	3.00
17	3.00	4.50
18	- - -	2.00
19	7.80	4.92
21	- - -	2.00
22	15.75	3.32
23	- - -	- - -
24	- - -	3.00
25	5.70	4.64
26	5.00	5.37
27	25.00	2.44
29	- - -	5.67
30	4.50	4.33
31	13.36	4.43
33	- - -	- - -
34	9.00	2.90
35	3.00	3.90
36	- - -	2.78
37	12.00	1.80
38	- - -	2.00
39	9.78	3.40
40	5.27	4.24
MEAN	8.69	3.69

erage precision for full text of 18 percent. Table 5–22 summarizes the paragraph occurrence data. It shows that as the number of paragraphs with search phrases increases, the precision ratio generally increases.

SUMMARY

This study compared results from searching on free text words or phrases in the full text of *Harvard Business Review* journal articles with the results of searching the value-added fields of abstract and controlled vocabulary.

Table 5–17
Word Occurrences Per Document (in rank order)

NUMBER OF TIMES SEARCH WORDS OCCUR	RELEVANT/NOT RELEVANT	QUESTION #
70	N	26
45	N	5
40	R	37
38	N	25
30	N	26
29	N	13
29	R	13
29	R	31
25	R	27
24	N	13
24	R	25
24	R	39
23	R	13
23	N	26
22	R	5
22	R	31
21	R	13
21	N	19
21	R	40
20	R	22
20	N	31
19	R	9
19	N	35
18	R	5
18	R	13
18	R	22
17	R	22
17	R	31
16	N	5
16	N	25
16	R	31
15	R	19
15	R	34
14	N	5
14	R	9
14	N	25
14	R	39
13	R	31
13	N	40
12	N	13
12	R	13
12	R	16
12	R	19
12	N	26
12	R	31
11	N	13
11	N	22

Table 5–17 continued

NUMBER OF TIMES SEARCH WORDS OCCUR	RELEVANT/NOT RELEVANT	QUESTION #
1 1	N	2 6
1 1	R	3 1
1 1	N	3 5
1 1	R	3 7
1 0	N	1 3
1 0	R	1 5
1 0	N	2 5
1 0	R	2 5
1 0	N	2 6
1 0	N	3 6
1 0	R	3 9
1 0	R	3 9

20 or more = 57% relevant
10 or more = 58% relevant

Table 5–18
Mean Precision Ratios for Number of Times Search Words Occur

# OF TIMES WORDS OCCUR	MEAN OF ALL PRECISION RATIOS	# OF DOCUMENTS
1 - 5	12.6%	4 1 2
6 -10	29.2%	8 9
11 -15	55.0%	2 0
16 -20	66.7%	1 2
21 -25	72.7%	1 1
OVER 25	37.5%	8

These ratios were derived by pooling all retrieved documents from all search questions by number of times words occurred and computing a precision ratio without regard to individual questions.

Source: Produced from "Full Text Database Retrieval Performance" by Carol Tenopir, *Online Review*, 9, no. 2 (1985) by permission of Learned Information, Inc., 143 Old Marlton Pike, Medford, NJ 08055.

The results showed a significant difference at the .05 level between the full text searches and searches by other methods for total documents retrieved, relevant documents retrieved, recall ratio, and almost all measures of overlap and uniqueness. There was a difference between the precision ratios, but it was not found to be significant. Although full text searches retrieved significantly more documents and contributed a significantly greater num-

Table 5–19
Word Occurrence Patterns for Relevant and Nonrelevant Documents (means of number of paragraphs in which search phrases occur)

QUESTION #	MEAN # OF PARAGRAPHS (relevant)	MEAN # OF PARAGRAPHS (nonrelevant)
5	1.67	1.71
6	2.00	1.00
7	- - -	1.00
8	- - -	- - -
9	2.00	1.00
10	1.33	1.09
12	- - -	1.11
13	3.27	1.46
15	1.50	1.00
16	3.50	1.00
17	1.00	1.00
18	- - -	1.00
19	2.00	1.25
21	- - -	1.00
22	3.50	1.14
23	- - -	- - -
24	- - -	1.00
25	1.90	1.65
26	1.25	1.75
27	5.00	1.00
29	- - -	1.00
30	1.00	1.33
31	2.64	1.24
33	- - -	- - -
34	2.00	1.10
35	1.00	1.26
36	- - -	2.33
37	6.80	1.00
38	- - -	1.00
39	2.22	1.00
40	2.00	1.52
MEAN	2.38	1.21

ber of unique documents, the precision ratio was lower than all other methods and the cost per relevant document retrieved was twice that for full text.

Full text contributed the greatest number of uniquely relevant documents, but controlled vocabulary searching and, to a lesser degree, abstract searching contributed uniquely relevant documents as well. No one method was comprehensive.

Word occurrence patterns in the full text are an aid in improving the precision ratio of full text searching. If a search word occurs ten times or

Table 5–20
Full Text Paragraph Occurrences (four paragraphs or more per document)

NUMBER OF PARAGRAPHS	RELEVANT/NOT RELEVANT	QUESTION #
26	R	37
15	N	5
14	N	25
10	N	26
9	R	40
8	N	13
8	N	26
8	N	36
7	R	25
7	N	26
6	R	5
6	R	13
6	R	13
6	R	13
6	R	31
6	N	36
5	N	5
5	R	13
5	R	22
5	N	26
5	R	27
5	N	31
5	R	37
5	R	39
4	R	5
4	N	13
4	R	13
4	R	16
4	R	19
4	R	22
4	R	22
4	N	25
4	N	25
4	R	31
4	R	31
4	N	35
4	R	39
4	N	40

6 or more = 50% relevant
5 or more = 54% relevant
4 or more = 58% relevant

Table 5–21
Relevance of Documents with Only One Full Text Paragraph Occurrence

QUESTION #	RELEVANT	NOT RELEVANT
5	30.0%	70.0%
6	16.7	83.3
7	0.0	100.0
9	25.0	75.0
10	09.1	90.9
12	0.0	100.0
13	09.5	90.5
15	11.1	88.9
16	0.0	100.0
17	20.0	80.0
18	0.0	100.0
19	13.6	86.4
21	0.0	100.0
22	05.0	95.0
24	0.0	100.0
25	17.8	82.2
26	07.0	93.0
27	0.0	100.0
29	0.0	100.0
30	25.0	75.0
31	13.6	86.4
34	10.0	90.0
35	03.7	96.3
36	0.0	100.0
37	37.5	62.5
38	0.0	100.0
39	37.5	62.5
40	29.2	70.8
MEAN	11.5	88.5

more in a document, that document is three times more likely to be relevant than would be expected by the average precision for all documents retrieved. If a search term or phrase occurs in four or more textual paragraphs, that document is slightly more than four times as likely to be relevant than is a document in which the phrase occurs only once. Documents retrieved by both full text and controlled vocabulary searches are relevant an average 71 percent of the time.

NOTES

1. Carol Tenopir, "Retrieval Performance in a Full Text Journal Article Database" (Ph.D. dissertation, University of Illinois, 1984), summarized in Carol

Table 5–22
Precision Ratios for Number of Paragraphs in Which Search Phrases Occur

# OF PARAGRAPHS	PRECISION RATIO	# OF DOCUMENTS
1	13.4	417
2	27.9	68
3	34.5	29
4	64.3	14
5	62.5	8
6	83.3	6
7	50.0	2
8	0.0	3
9	100.0	1
10	0.0	1
OVER 10	33.3	3

Tenopir, "Full Text Database Retrieval Performance," *Online Review* 9, no. 2 (1985): 149–164.

2. See for more details: *HBR/Online: User Guide* (New York: John Wiley & Sons, Inc., Electronic Publishing Division, 1983).

3. Tefko Saracevic, "Comparative Effects of Titles, Abstracts, and Full Texts on Relevance Judgments," in *Cooperating Information Societies: Proceedings of the 32nd American Society for Information Science Annual Meeting; 1969 October 1–4, San Francisco* (Washington, D.C. ASIS, 1969), pp. 293–299.

4. F. Wilfred Lancaster, *Information Retrieval Systems: Characteristics, Testing, Evaluation*, 2d ed. (New York: John Wiley & Sons, 1979), p. 111.

5. Jeffrey Katzer et al., *A Study of the Impact of Representations in Information Retrieval Systems* (Syracuse, N.Y.: School of Information Studies, Syracuse University, 1982).

6. Ibid., p. 13.

7. Ibid.

8. F. Wilfred Lancaster, "The Cost-Effectiveness Analysis of Information Retrieval and Dissemination Systems," *Journal of the American Society for Information Science* 22 (January–February 1971): 14.

9. Tefko Saracevic, "RELEVANCE: A Review of and a Framework for the Thinking on the Notion in Information Science," *Journal of the American Society for Information Science* 26 (November–December 1975): 321–342.

10. Julie M. Neway and F. Wilfred Lancaster, "The Correlation Between Pertinence and Rate of Citation Duplication in Multidatabase Searches," *Journal of the American Society for Information Science* 34 (July 1983): 292–293.

6

Applicability of Ranking Algorithms to Full Text Retrieval

A study conducted by Ro builds on the study of *Harvard Business Review* online by Tenopir.[1] Ro's two experiments compare the effectiveness of full text retrieval with other approaches and evaluate the applicability of ranking algorithms to improve retrieval.

Tenopir's experimental data comparing full text searching with abstracts and controlled vocabularies (described in Chapter 5) was incorporated in Ro's study.[2] Since many documents are expected to be retrieved from full text searching, especially when using the Boolean AND operator instead of proximity operators only one judge was used to assess relevance in Ro's study. However, since relevance judgment by one judge was questioned in the previous research, Tenopir's data were used to check the reliability of relevance judgments assessed by one judge.[3] Using Tenopir's search strategy controls the variable of search strategy.

THE FIRST EXPERIMENT

From previous research and commentary, it was expected that searching with the SAME paragraph operator would achieve higher precision than searching with the Boolean AND operator. Experts suggest using the Boolean AND with caution when searching full text. The purpose of this experiment is to compare the Boolean AND searching in a full text journal database with SAME paragraph searching, which limits full text searches to the same grammatical paragraphs. Other retrieval approaches using abstracts or controlled vocabularies were also compared.

Tables 6-8 to 6-12, Figures 6-1 to 6-7 and portions of the text of this chapter have appeared in *The Journal of the American Society for Information Science* 39, Nos. 2 and 3 (1988). Copyright © 1988. Reprinted by permission of John Wiley & Sons, Inc.

Table 6–1
Descriptive Statistics on Full Texts of Articles

Total documents in the collection	448
Total words in the collection (collection length)	1,829,601
Number of word tokens: (document length)	
range	800- 13,891
mean word tokens per document	4,084

Experimental Design

Database. The database used for the study was a subset of *Harvard Business Review* online for the time period January 1979–August 1983. The descriptive characteristics of the collection of full texts of articles are given in Table 6–1.

Search Questions. Because of the enormous amount of time required to judge relevance of documents retrieved, only nine of Tenopir's thirty-one questions were used. In electing nine questions, two factors were considered. Tenopir used the SAME operator in intersecting two facets (in other words, her test searching was limited to paragraph searching) and she used ADJ and WITH in expressing a facet as a phrase. The first factor required was two or more facets (that is, at least one intersecting operator) in the search strategy so that the results of Boolean AND searching and proximity SAME searching could be compared. The second factor was important for the second experiment in which effectiveness of Boolean retrieval was compared with ranking algorithms. Since the ranking algorithms used in this study are based on individual word frequencies, only adjacent words were considered as phrases in applying weighting algorithms. Thus, search questions with the WITH operator in a facet were excluded. By considering these two factors, that is, eliminating questions without two or more facets or those with a WITH operator for phrases, twenty out of Tenopir's thirty-one questions remained, from which nine questions were selected randomly: Questions 5, 6, 15, 16, 22, 25, 38, 39, and 40. The nine questions were renumbered as shown in Table 6–2.

Search Strategy. The same search strategy used in Tenopir's paragraph searching was used, except for replacing the SAME operator with the Boolean AND. Thus "A AND B" instead of "A SAME B" retrieved documents in which concepts A and B appear not only within the same paragraph but also anywhere in a document.

Relevance Judgments. One doctoral student in the Department of Management, School of Business, Indiana University, assessed the relevance

Table 6–2
Search Topics

---

1. I would like literature on cutback management or the process of transition management or administration.
2. Workaholism, workaholics, attitudes toward hard work.
3. Effect of diet and exercise programs on reduction of absenteeism and increase of productivity among corporate staffs and executives.
4. Scheduling of extended work hours. Computation of productivity and safety in relation to extended work hours. I am specifically interested in extended work hours over eight hours in relation to the above aspects.
5. Collective bargaining by women-dominated professions such as social workers, nurses, librarians, and teachers.
6. Impact of collective bargaining on the introduction of new technology.
7. Retirement planning by farmers or ranchers.
8. Productivity in Japan vs. productivity in the U.S.
9. Productivity with unions vs. productivity in nonunion companies.

---

of documents retrieved both from full text retrieval and from other retrieval methods conducted by Tenopir. The knowledge of any Ph.D. student in the department was considered sufficient to judge the relevance of documents, since *Harvard Business Review* is a general, popular journal in the field of business. Recall and precision ratios associated with abstracts, descriptors, and paragraphs in Tenopir's study were recalculated using these new judgments. One judge has been found acceptable in previous research in legal full text retrieval in which questions were not submitted by the judge himself.[4] Nevertheless, the reliability of these judgments was investigated by computing the agreement of this judge with Tenopir's judges using both Holsti's coefficient of reliability and Scott's index of reliability (pi).[5]

Holsti's coefficient of reliability (C.R.) is a widely used measure, indicating the ratio of coding agreements to the total number of coding decisions: C.R. $= 2M/(M_1 + M_2)$, where M is the number of coding decisions on which the two judges are in agreement, and M_1 and M_2 refer to the number of coding decisions made by judges 1 and 2, respectively. However Holsti's C.R. has been criticized because "it does not take into account the extent of intercoder agreement which may result from chance."[6] Scott's index of agreement between two coders, Pi $= (Po - Pe)/(1 - Pe)$, takes into account both the observed proportion of agreement (Po) and the proportion that would be expected by chance (Pe). Compared with the agreement between the three judges in Tenopir's study (C.R. = 66 percent), the agreement between Ro's judge and Tenopir's judges was 87

Table 6–3
Number of Retrieved Documents from Each Search

QUESTION	FULL TEXT	PARAGRAPH	ABSTRACT	CONTROLLED
1	86	40	3	6
2	20	5	2	0
3	91	6	0	0
4	18	5	2	2
5	102	18	2	0
6	177	49	9	0
7	15	0	0	3
8	31	7	3	3
9	72	24	6	1
TOTAL	612	154	27	15
MEAN	68	17.1	3	1.7

percent. When considering the extent of interjudge agreement that may result from chance, Scott's index of reliability pi was 71 percent.

Findings

As shown in Table 6–3, based on the nine questions studied, the full text AND approach retrieved an average of sixty-eight documents, while SAME paragraph searching retrieved 17.1 documents, abstract retrieved 3 documents, and controlled vocabulary retrieved 1.7 documents. In Tenopir's experiments abstract searching retrieved fewer documents than did controlled vocabulary searching. The reason abstract searching retrieved more documents than controlled vocabulary in this study seems to be that questions 23, 31, and 35 were not considered. In Tenopir's study for those three questions, broad search techniques were used for natural language searches. For example, for Question 31, the broad concept "information system" was searched in the field of controlled vocabulary while a specific concept "personal information system" was used for abstract searching by intersecting the two concepts "information system" and "personal."

The number of relevant documents retrieved from each search is given in Table 6–4. On the average for nine questions, out of a total number of 8.9 relevant documents, full text searching retrieved 8.4 relevant documents while paragraph searching retrieved 5 documents, abstract retrieved 1.8, and controlled vocabulary retrieved 1 document. Full text searching retrieved 1.7 times more relevant documents than paragraph searching, 4.7 times more than abstracts, and 8.4 times more than controlled vocabularies. In Question 7 a relevant document retrieved by the descriptor "flexible working hours" was not retrieved by both paragraph and full text search

Table 6–4
Number of Relevant Documents from Each Search

QUESTION	UNION	FULL TEXT	PARAGRAPH	ABSTRACT	CONTROLLED
1	29	29	16	3	4
2	4	4	3	0	0
3	1	1	1	0	0
4	3	2	2	1	2
5	2	2	2	1	0
6	14	13	6	4	0
7	1	0	0	0	1
8	11	11	5	3	1
9	15	14	10	4	1
TOTAL	80	76	45	16	9
MEAN	8.9	8.4	5	1.9	1

Table 6–5
Relevance Degree of Relevant Documents Retrieved from Each Search

	FULL TEXT	PARAGRAPH	ABSTRACT	CONTROLLED
No. of relevant documents retrieved	76	45	16	9
No. of documents judged definitely relevant	43	29	14	9
No. of documents judged probably relevant	33	16	2	0
MEAN	3.566	3.644	3.875	4

because only the term "flexitime" was used in the text of the article. Tenopir mentions that she used the alternate spelling "flextime" but failed to use "flexitime."

The relevant documents retrieved from full texts or paragraphs had lower relevance value than that from controlled vocabularies or abstracts. Table 6–5 shows that the relevance degree of relevant documents retrieved by full text is an average of 3.566, compared with 3.644 for paragraphs, 3.875 for abstracts, and 4 for descriptors, when the weight of 4 is assigned to the documents judged "definitely relevant" to questions and the weight of 3 is assigned to the documents judged "probably relevant." All relevant documents retrieved by controlled vocabularies were definitely relevant.

Tables 6–6 and 6–7 translate the number of relevant documents retrieved from each search to relative recall and precision ratios. Relative recall was

Table 6–6
Relative Recall Ratio of Each Search

QUESTION	FULL TEXT	PARAGRAPH	ABSTRACT	CONTROLLED
1	100.00	55.17	10.35	13.79
2	100.00	75.00	0.00	0.00
3	100.00	100.00	0.00	0.00
4	66.67	66.67	33.33	66.67
5	100.00	100.00	50.00	0.00
6	92.86	42.86	26.67	0.00
7	0.00	0.00	0.00	100.00
8	100.00	45.45	20.00	6.67
9	93.33	66.67	25.00	6.25
MEAN	83.65	61.31	18.37	21.49

Table 6–7
Precision Ratio of Each Search

QUESTION	FULL TEXT	PARAGRAPH	ABSTRACT	CONTROLLED
1	33.72	40.00	100.00	67.67
2	20.00	60.00	0	- - -
3	1.10	16.67	- - -	- - -
4	11.11	40.00	50.00	100.00
5	1.96	11.11	50.00	- - -
6	7.34	12.24	44.44	- - -
7	0	- - -	- - -	33.33
8	35.48	71.43	100.00	33.33
9	19.44	41.67	66.67	100.00
MEAN	14.46	36.64	58.73	66.67

substituted for recall and defined as the number of relevant documents retrieved by a single search divided by the number of relevant documents in the union of sets retrieved by several searches on the same topic. Recall and precision ratios in Tables 6.6 and 6.7 are macroaveraged; a parameter (recall or precision) is calculated for each question and the average is then taken. Full texts had an average relative recall of 83.65 percent, much higher than paragraphs, abstracts, or controlled vocabularies. On the other hand, full texts achieved the lowest precision, an average of 14.46 percent, compared with 36.64 percent for paragraphs, 58.73 percent for abstracts, and 66.67 percent for controlled vocabularies. From the microaveraging viewpoint, which calculates totals over the set of questions, full texts achieved 95 percent of recall compared with 56.2 percent for paragraphs,

20 percent for abstracts, and 11.2 percent for controlled vocabularies. The precision of full text searching, by microaveraging, was 12.42 percent compared with 29.22 percent for paragraphs, 59.26 percent for abstracts, and 60 percent for controlled vocabularies.

As predicted, there was a significant difference between the full text search and searches by other methods. The hypothesis stated as a null was rejected using ANOVA at the significance level of .0001 for recall and at the level .0032 for precision ratio. That is, searching full text using the AND operator resulted in significantly higher recall and lower precision than searches by other methods. Scheffé and Tuckey HSD showed that the AND operator in full text differed significantly from abstract searching and controlled vocabulary searching, but did not differ significantly from SAME paragraph searching, for both recall and precision. The relevant documents retrieved from full text searching were judged less relevant than those from other searches.

THE SECOND EXPERIMENT

The second experiment examined how to improve the precision of full text retrieval with minimum decrease in recall and how document-term weighting algorithms affect full text retrieval. It was assumed that a good ranking algorithm will rank relevant documents higher than nonrelevant documents.

The Components of Ranking Algorithms

A ranking algorithm defines an ordering on a set of documents in terms of the similarity between each document and a query. It consists of three major components: (1) weighting of terms in the document, (2) weighting of terms in the query, and (3) similarity measures between query and document. Many possible ranking algorithms, in different combinations of these three components, have been suggested (see Table 6–8). This experiment tested the relative effectiveness of twenty-nine document-term weighting algorithms with binary query term weighting and an applied fuzzy-set theory for similarity measure.

Document-Term Weighting Algorithms. The document-term weighting algorithms used in this study are from the literature of both automatic extractive indexing and effectiveness of ranking algorithms in searching. Document-term weighting is based on the assumption that the degree of treatment of a subject in a document is reflected by the frequency of occurrence of a word naming that concept. This idea grows out of Zipf's laws of word distribution in text,[7] and Shannon and Weaver information theory, dealing with the frequency of linguistic symbols.[8] According to Luhn, the pioneer in automatic indexing based on word frequency, "the

Table 6–8
Ranking Algorithms

---

a. the frequency of term i in document n : f_{in} ,

b. the number of tokens in document n, i.e., document length: f_n ,

c. the number of documents in collection: **N** ,

d. the frequency of term i in collection: f_i ,

e. the number of tokens in collection, i.e., collection length **CL** ,

f. the number of documents in which term i occurs. i.e. posting : **p** and

WITHIN DOCUMENT TERM FREQUENCY

Formula (W_{in} =)	Reference
1. 1	binary weighting, i.e., full text search without algorithms
2. f_{in}	Luhn [9]
3. $\log f_{in}$	Sparck Jones[24]
4. $f_{in} / f_n = f$	Sparck Jones,[24] Weinberg[20]
5. $f_{in} / \log f_n$	Noreault[14]

6. $f_{in} / (f_n / 1000) = a$
    if a < = 1, then $W_{in} = 1$,
    if 1 < a < 3, then $W_{in} = 2$, and,
    if a >= 3, then $W_{in} = 3$
	Artandi[21]

Table 6–8 continued

WITHIN COLLECTION TERM FREQUENCY

7. $f_{in} \, / \, f_n \, - \, f_i \, / \, c_L \, = \, f_{-r}$ Edmondson & Willys, [10]
Damerau, Carroll, & Roeloffs

8. $(\, f_{in} \, / \, f_n) \, / \, (\, f_i \, / \, c_L) \, = \, f_{/r}$ Edmondson & Willys, [10]
Damerau, Carroll, & Roeloffs

9. $(\, f_{in} \, / \, f_n) \, / \, [(\, f_{in} \, / \, f_n)_+ (\, f_i \, / \, c_L)] \, = \, f_i \, f_{+r}$ Edmondson, Damerau[10]

10. $\log \, (\, f_{in} \, / \, f_n) \, - \, \log \, (\, f_i \, / \, c_L) \, = \, \log \, (\, f_{/r} \,)$ Edmondson[10]

11. $f_{-r} \, / \, r$ Carroll [10]

12. $f_{in} \, / \, f_i$ Sparck Jones [24]

13. $(\, f_{in} \, / \, f_n) \, \times \, (\, f_{in} \, / \, f_i)$ Sparck Jones [24]

14. $f_{in} \, \times \, \log \, (\, c_L \, / \, f_i \,)$ Noreault [14]

15. $f_{in} \, / \, \log \, f_i$ Noreault [14]

16. $f_{in} \, / \, f_n \cdot f_i$ Noreault [14]

17. $f_{in} \, / \, \log \, (\, f_n \cdot f_i \,)$ Noreault [14]

18. CL/EK   Dennis [22]

$$ EK = \left(\frac{f}{N} \right)^2 \, / \, \frac{[\, f - (\, f \, / \, N \,)]^2}{N-1} $$

Table 6–8 continued

WITHIN COLLECTION TERM FREQUENCY

19.
$$b = \frac{x\, e^{-m1}\, m1^{k}}{x\, e^{-m1}\, m1^{k} + (1-x)\, e^{-m2}\, m2^{k}} + \frac{m1 - m2}{m1 + m2} \qquad \text{Harter}[12]$$

20.
$$z = \frac{m1 - m2}{m1 + m2} \qquad \text{Harter}[12]\ \text{Robertson}[18]$$

21. $b\ \log(N/p)$ Robertson[18]

22. $z\ \log(N/p)$ Robertson[18]

23. $f_{in} \cdot b$

24. $f_{in} \cdot z$

DOCUMENT FREQUENCY

25. $1/p$ Noreault,[14] Sager[4]

26. $\log(N/p)$ Williams and Periens[23]
    $\log(N/p) + 1$ Sparck Jones[11]

27. $f_{in}(f_i / p)$ Sager,[4] Noreault[14]

28. $f_{in} \cdot p / (f_i - f_{in})$ Sager,[4] Noreault[14]

29. f_{in} / p Salton, Wu and Yu[19]

30. $f_{in}\ (\log N - \log p + 1)$ Salton & Yang[19]

justification of measuring word significance by use-frequency is based on the fact that a writer normally repeats certain words as he advances or varies his arguments and as he elaborates on an aspect of a subject."[9] On the other hand, relative frequency theories deal with the extent to which a document treats a subject as compared to other subjects treated in the same document or compared to other documents treating that subject.[10] Sparck Jones's inverse document frequency theory is that the information value of rare words in a document collection is greater than that of frequent ones.[11] This idea is based on the specificity of indexing language, that is, the less specific the index term, the greater the frequency. Probabilistic theory hypothesized that words possessing little potential utility for indexing purposes would be likely to be distributed at random in the document collection, while words not distributed randomly would be good index words.[12]

Algorithms examined in this experiment were limited to those proposed to select single keywords from documents. Thus, algorithms for constructing phrases as index words by statistical association were excluded. Impractical weighting algorithms such as term precision or term utility weighting algorithms, which require the knowledge of all relevant and nonrelevant documents in a database in advance for all queries, were also excluded. The algorithms for single words were applied to weight adjacent words. Heaps's relative frequency algorithm was excluded, since Kucera and Francies q_i values are not available for adjacent words.[13] Table 6–8 lists the 29 algorithms examined in this study.

Query Term Weighting. Only binary weighting was applied to the queries.

Similarity Measure. Boolean similarity measures such as those introduced by Sager and Lockemann, or Noreault, McGill, and Koll were not used in this study.[14] Ranking algorithms with a Boolean environment have been also discussed by Angione, Bookstein, and others.[15] This study employed a ranking approach used in fuzzy-set retrieval, outlined by Kaufmann, Bookstein, and others, where the weight of a document in the intersection of sets A AND B is the minimum of its weight in A and its weight B.[16] The weight with which a document is in the Boolean union to two sets, A OR B, is the maximum of its weights in A and B. Complement was not considered in this study, since the operator NOT was not used in any search strategy.

Experimental Design

To test the applicability of ranking algorithms to improving the effectiveness of full text retrieval, full text searching with ranking algorithms was compared with the unranked Boolean searching from the first experiment. The same database, questions, search strategies, and relevance judgments used in the first experiment were used for the second.

Question 7 was not used in the second experiment because it did not

Table 6–9
Number of Documents Retrieved from Each Search to Get the Same Number of Relevant Documents as Paragraph Searching

QUESTION	CUT-OFF POINT	PARAGRAPH	FULL TEXT	FULL TEXT SEARCH WITH ALGORITHM							
				2	3	4	5	6	7	8	9
1	16	40	47.5	40.2	40.2	43	44	39.5	32	37	37
2	3	5	15	10.3	10.3	6	7	10.5	6	4	4
3	1	6	91	72	72	41	43	91	6	3	3
4	2	5	18	2	2	3	2	3	2	4	4
5	2	18	102	7	7	8	6	102	10	4	4
6	6	49	81.7	21	21	26	20	74.6	41	33	33
8	5	7	14.1	6	6	6	6	8.7	6	7	7
9	10	44	51.4	40	40	32	29	44	39	36	36
MEAN	16	5.63	21.75	52.59	24.8	24.8	20.6	19.6	46.7	17.8	16

FULL TEXT SEARCH WITH ALGORITHM

QUESTION	10	11	12	13	14	15	16	17	18	19	20
1	37	32	35	32	42	42	36	44	36.8	40	42.2
2	4	4	4	4	5	4	4	5	4	4	4
3	3	1	4	2	24	22	3	22	75	42	42
4	4	3	3	3	2	2	4	2	8	2	15
5	4	8	4	7	7	8	4	10	25	53	73
6	33	31	30	26	22	19	33	20	38	20	69.8
8	7	7	5	6	6	6	7	6	13.2	6	14.1
9	36	37	37	33	33	33	36	29	51.4	43	64
MEAN	16	15.4	15.3	14.1	17.6	17	15.9	17.3	31.4	26.3	40.5

FULL TEXT SEARCH WITH ALGORITHM

QUESTION	21	22	23	24	25	26	27	28	29	30	MEAN
1	35	30.2	46	40.9	35.8	35.8	39	44.8	41	38	38.57
2	4	4	5	4	4	4	4	12	4	5	5.31
3	46	43	45	45	15	15	24	7	3	24	28.90
4	6	13	2	2	9	9	2	2	4	2	4.24
5	32	56	8	8	13	13	9	7	7	5	17.55
6	39	64	18	19	24.5	24.25	17	25	21	18	30.39
8	8	13.5	6	7.5	12.3	12.3	6	6	6	6	7.57
9	43	51.4	40	40	51.4	51.4	39	34	43	43	40.16
MEAN	26.6	34.4	21.3	20.8	20.6	20.6	17.5	17.2	16.1	17.6	21.58

retrieve any relevant documents from full text searching. It is necessary to have at least one relevant and one nonrelevant document retrieved from a question in order to test an assumption that weighting algorithms rank relevant documents higher than nonrelevant documents.

The full text of each HBR article of the time period January 1979–August 1983 was obtained from BRS in machine readable form. A series of computer programs was written in Pascal to process the text data, to calculate the number of tokens of a word in each document, the total number of tokens of a word in the document collection, the total number of word tokens in a document and in the document collection, and the number of documents in which a word occurs, to compute the two-Poisson parameters of m1, m2, and x of each word in each document of the collection, and to weight words using algorithms. In computing the algorithms, the three parameters x, m1, and m2 for two-Poisson were computed using the methods of Harter.[17]

Processing the Text

All characters bounded by two spaces were considered a single word. Text was converted to upper case. Basic punctuation marks were set to null and converted to spaces except the period and the comma if followed by a nonblank character. Thus the number "23,438" or "23.6" was counted as one word, and the word "Women," or "women." or "Women" was counted as the same word. Words were not stemmed, since most of the words in the search strategy were truncated. Thus the frequency of the truncated search word " manage$" was the total frequency of words like "management," "managers," "manage," "managemental," and so on, but not "managing." No stopwords were designated.

Several misspelled words were found in the HBR/O text. However, misspellings were excluded in counting the occurrence frequency of a word in a document, since the misspelled words were not retrieved by the full text searching in the first experiment. It is believed that misspellings were not sufficient in number to alter significantly the effectiveness of weighting algorithms.

Cut-off Point

The cut-off point used in this study was the number of relevant documents retrieved from the SAME paragraph search. Thus the recall for each approach is the same, and the precision could be compared. It was also possible to compare ranking algorithms. The precision measured at this cut-off point was tested for statistical significance. However, the effectiveness of full text searching with ranking algorithms was examined and compared to that without at both the highest and lowest levels of recall achieved from the full text search.

If more than one document ranked the same, the average rank was taken. For example, suppose that two documents ranked first, one of which is relevant, and five documents rank second, of which two are relevant. When the cut-off point is one, the number of documents retrieved to get one relevant document is two. If the cut-off point is two, the number of documents retrieved to get two relevant documents is calculated as 4.5 (= 2 + 5/2). The number of documents retrieved to get three relevant documents is 7 (= 2 + 5).

Results

Precision Using Ranking Algorithms at Fixed Levels of Recall. Table 6–9 shows the number of documents retrieved from full text searching with and without weighting algorithms in order to achieve the same number of relevant documents retrieved from paragraph searching. To retrieve an average of 5.63 *relevant* documents, paragraph searching required retrieving an average of 21.75 documents, full text searching required 52.59 documents, and ranking algorithms required an average of 21.58 documents. Table 6–10 translates these numbers to precision ratios. The mean value of precision obtained from the twenty-nine weighting algorithms was 42.02 percent compared with a mean precision of 16.27 percent for non-ranked Boolean full text searching and 36.64 percent for paragraph searching, at the recall level of 69.0 percent. The significance test using ANOVA showed a significant difference between full text with and without algorithms at the significance level of .0290. Twenty-two of the twenty-nine ranking algorithms improved the precision of full text retrieval more than that of paragraph searching although these results were not statistically significant. There was no significant difference between algorithms at the .05 level, although the precision of the twenty-nine algorithms varied from 23.90 percent for algorithm 20 to 54.31 percent for algorithm 11.

Tables 6–11 and 6–12 show the precision of full text retrieval using ranking algorithms in order to get only one relevant document and all relevant documents to each question, that is, at the lowest and highest levels of recall, respectively. On average, weighted retrieval resulted in 31.84 percent precision at the highest recall level of 94.11 percent, and 66.85 percent precision with the lowest recall ratio of 29.34 percent. That is, the algorithms improved the precision of full text retrieval by a factor of 2 at the highest level of recall, 2.6 times better at the middle level of recall, and 4.1 times better at the lowest level of recall.

The algorithms that assigned the same value to a word type regardless of the occurrence frequency of the term in each document performed worst (that is, algorithms 18, 20, 22, 25, and 26). Algorithms 25 and 26, algorithms

Table 6–10
Precision Ratio for Each Search (at the 69% of recall ratio)

QUESTION

		1	2	3	4	5	6	8	9	MEAN
Recall		55.17	75.00	100.00	66.67	100.00	42.86	45.45	66.67	69.00
Paragraph		40.00	60.00	16.67	40.00	11.11	12.24	71.43	41.67	36.64
Full Text		33.72	20.00	1.10	11.11	1.96	7.34	35.48	19.44	16.27

RANK ALGORITHM

		1	2	3	4	5	6	8	9	MEAN
1	11	50.00	75.00	100.00	66.67	25.00	19.35	71.43	27.03	54.31
2	12	45.71	75.00	25.00	66.67	50.00	20.00	100.00	27.03	51.18
3	13	50.00	75.00	50.00	66.67	28.57	23.08	83.33	30.30	50.87
4	15	38.10	75.00	4.55	100.00	25.00	30.77	83.33	30.30	48.38
5	27	41.03	75.00	4.17	100.00	22.22	35.29	83.33	25.64	48.34
6	30	42.11	60.00	4.17	100.00	40.00	33.33	83.33	23.26	48.28
7	14	38.10	60.00	4.17	100.00	28.57	27.27	83.33	30.30	46.47
8	16	44.44	75.00	33.33	50.00	50.00	18.18	71.43	27.78	46.27
9	8	43.24	75.00	33.33	50.00	50.00	18.18	71.43	27.78	46.12
9	9	43.24	75.00	33.33	50.00	50.00	18.18	71.43	27.78	46.12
9	10	43.24	75.00	33.33	50.00	50.00	18.18	71.43	27.78	46.12
12	17	36.36	60.00	4.55	100.00	20.00	30.00	83.33	34.38	46.09
13	24	39.10	75.00	2.22	100.00	25.00	31.58	66.67	25.00	45.57
14	23	34.78	60.00	2.22	100.00	25.00	33.33	83.33	25.00	45.46
15	5	36.36	42.86	2.33	100.00	33.33	30.00	83.33	34.48	45.34
16	29	39.02	75.00	33.33	50.00	28.57	28.57	83.33	23.26	45.14
17	7	50.00	50.00	16.67	100.00	20.00	14.63	83.33	25.64	45.03
18	19	40.00	75.00	2.38	100.00	3.78	30.00	83.33	23.26	44.72
19	28	35.71	25.00	14.29	100.00	28.57	24.00	83.33	29.41	42.54
20	2	39.82	29.01	1.39	100.00	28.57	28.57	83.33	25.00	41.96
20	3	39.82	29.01	1.39	100.00	28.57	28.57	83.33	25.00	41.96
22	4	37.21	50.00	2.44	66.67	25.00	23.08	83.33	31.25	39.87
23	21	45.71	75.00	2.17	33.33	6.25	15.38	62.50	23.26	32.95
24	25	44.68	75.00	6.67	22.22	15.39	24.49	40.75	19.55	31.09
24	26	44.68	75.00	6.67	22.22	15.39	24.49	40.75	19.55	31.09
26	6	40.53	28.57	1.10	66.67	1.96	8.05	57.38	22.73	28.37
27	18	43.48	75.00	1.33	25.00	8.00	15.79	37.94	38.46	28.26
28	22	52.92	75.00	2.33	15.38	3.57	9.38	37.04	13.89	26.90
29	20	37.93	75.00	2.38	13.33	2.74	8.60	35.55	15.63	23.90
MEAN		41.98	63.60	14.87	69.48	25.48	23.11	71.92	25.74	42.02

2 and 3, and algorithms 8 and 10 had the same performance, respectively. Logarithms were introduced to diminish the impact of document length; this did not affect the rank of documents although the weight of words is reduced. N also did not affect the rank of documents, since it is a constant.

The effectiveness between probability weighting algorithms in this study was different from that of the Cambridge study, that used a different similarity measure on a document collection of titles and abstracts. The Cambridge study reported that Algorithm 19 (b) had the poorest performance among the probabilistic algorithms.[18] The precision of these algo-

Table 6–11
Precision of Each Algorithm at the Lowest Level of Recall

QUESTION	RECALL	WEIGHTING ALGORITHMS					
		2	3	4	5	6	7
1	3.45	100.00	100.00	100.00	100.00	100.00	100.00
2	25.99	100.00	100.00	100.00	100.00	28.57	100.00
3	100.00	1.39	1.39	2.44	2.33	1.10	15.57
4	33.33	100.00	100.00	100.00	100.00	66.67	100.00
5	50.00	50.00	50.00	20.00	50.00	20.00	50.00
6	7.14	25.00	25.00	20.00	25.00	11.76	20.00
8	9.09	100.00	100.00	100.00	100.00	80.00	100.00
9	6.67	100.00	100.00	100.00	100.00	55.56	100.00
MEAN		29.34	72.05	72.05	67.81	72.17	45.46
73.20							

QUESTION		FULL TEXT WITH ALGORITHMS						
	8	9	1 0	1 1	1 2	1 3	1 4	
1	100.00	100.00	100.00	100.00	100.00	100.00	100.00	
2	100.00	100.00	100.00	100.00	100.00	100.00	100.00	
3	33.33	33.33	33.33	100.00	25.00	50.00	4.17	
4	100.00	100.00	100.00	100.00	100.00	100.00	100.00	
5	100.00	100.00	100.00	100.00	100.00	100.00	50.00	
6	100.00	100.00	100.00	16.67	33.33	20.00	24.00	
8	100.00	100.00	100.00	100.00	100.00	100.00	100.00	
9	50.00	50.00	50.00	100.00	50.00	100.00	100.00	
MEAN		85.42	85.42	85.42	89.58	76.04	83.75	
72.27								

QUESTION		FULL TEXT WITH ALGORITHMS						
	1 5	1 6	1 7	1 8	1 9	2 0	2 1	2 2
1	100.00	100.00	100.00	43.48	100.00	37.93	100.00	52.94
2	100.00	100.00	75.00	100.00	100.00	75.00	100.00	75.00
3	4.55	33.33	4.55	1.33	2.44	2.44	2.17	2.33
4	100.00	100.00	100.00	25.00	100.00	13.33	33.33	15.38
5	33.33	100.00	20.00	4.55	50.00	3.57	50.00	2.00
6	25.00	100.00	25.00	36.36	50.00	8.60	100.00	18.18
8	100.00	100.00	100.00	37.93	100.00	35.46	100.00	37.04
9	100.00	50.00	100.00	19.44	100.00	100.00	100.00	19.44
MEAN		70.36	85.42	68.69	30.39	75.31	34.54	73.19
27.79								

Table 6–11 continued

QUESTION	FULL TEXT WITH ALGORITHMS							
	2 3	2 4	2 5	2 6	2 7	2 8	2 9	3 0
1	100.00	100.00	44.68	44.68	100.00	100.00	100.00	100.00
2	100.00	100.00	75.00	75.00	100.00	100.00	100.00	100.00
3	2.22	2.22	6.67	6.67	4.17	14.29	33.33	4.17
4	100.00	100.00	22.22	22.22	100.00	100.00	100.00	100.00
5	33.33	20.00	50.00	50.00	33.33	33.33	100.00	50.00
6	33.33	33.33	50.00	50.00	33.33	50.00	20.00	20.00
8	100.00	100.00	40.82	40.82	100.00	100.00	100.00	100.00
9	50.00	50.00	19.44	19.44	50.00	100.00	50.00	100.00
MEAN		64.86	63.19	38.60	38.60	65.10	74.70	75.42
71.77								

MEAN OF 29 ALGORITHMS = 66.85%

rithms in this study was found that $Z \log(N/P) < Z < \log(N/P) < b \log(N/P) < b$. As reported by Harter, algorithm 19 (b) was better than algorithm 20 (Z) and also better than algorithm 2 (f_{in}).

From the overall point of view observed at the three levels of recall, the algorithms based on relative frequency theories were better than algorithms based on absolute frequency theories or inverse document frequency theories. Algorithm 11 ($f - r/\sqrt{r}$), algorithm 12 (f_{in}/f_i), algorithm 15 ($f_{in}/\log f_i$), and algorithm 13 ($f_{in}/f_n * f_{in}/f_i$) based on relative frequency theories are the four algorithms which resulted in best precisions. Algorithm 2 (f_{in}) and 3 (log f_{in}) based on absolute frequency theories ranked twentieth. Algorithm 25 (1/P) and 26 (log (N/P)), based on reverse document frequency theories, ranked twenty-fifth. The absolute frequency theories and the inverse document frequency theories resulted in better precision when these two theories were combined like algorithm 27 ($f_{in}(f_i/p)$) and algorithm 30 ($f_{in} * (\log (N/P) + 1)$). As suggested by Salton and Sager, words that have a low document frequency (posting) in a collection but high frequency in a document have more value as content words in the fuzzy similarity measure.[19]

Overall Effectiveness of Seven Algorithms. The overall effectiveness of seven representative algorithms is presented in recall and precision graphs, Figures 6–1 to 6–7. In order to compare precision ratios of algorithms at all levels of recall, only seven representative algorithms were considered because several algorithms produced similar effectiveness. The absolute frequency theory, algorithm 2, was selected, since it is basic to a theory of automatic extractive indexing based on word frequency. The relative frequency theory, algorithm 11, was selected because it ranked first on the significance test. To examine the superiority of the algorithm ranked first, another relative frequency theory, algorithm 12, which ranked second, was

Table 6–12
Precision of Each Algorithm at the Highest Level of Recall

QUESTION	RECALL	WEIGHTING ALGORITHMS					
		2	3	4	5	6	7
1	100.00	34.94	34.94	34.80	35.37	34.94	35.80
2	100.00	28.57	28.57	28.57	28.57	28.57	23.08
3	100.00	1.39	1.39	2.44	2.33	1.10	16.67
4	66.67	100.00	100.00	66.67	100.00	66.67	100.00
5	100.00	28.57	28.57	25.00	33.33	1.96	20.00
6	92.86	7.34	7.34	7.96	7.98	7.34	7.60
8	100.00	35.48	35.48	45.88	45.83	35.48	40.74
9	93.33	19.44	19.44	21.21	21.21	19.44	22.22
MEAN 33.14		94.11	31.97	31.97	34.38	34.33	24.44

QUESTION	FULL TEXT WITH ALGORITHMS						
	8	9	10	11	12	13	14
1	35.80	35.80	35.80	35.80	36.71	37.66	35.80
2	80.00	80.00	80.00	33.33	80.00	23.08	28.57
3	33.33	33.33	33.33	100.00	25.00	50.00	4.17
4	50.00	50.00	50.00	66.67	66.67	66.67	100.00
5	50.00	50.00	50.00	25.00	50.00	28.57	28.57
6	7.65	7.65	7.65	7.56	7.34	7.56	7.34
8	40.74	40.74	40.74	45.83	36.67	40.74	35.48
9	21.21	21.21	21.21	21.54	21.88	21.21	21.88
MEAN 32.73		39.84	39.84	39.84	41.97	40.53	34.44

QUESTION	FULL TEXT WITH ALGORITHMS						
	15	16	17	18	19	20	21	22
1	35.80	36.25	36.71	34.94	34.94	34.94	36.71	34.94
2	23.08	80.00	28.57	23.08	28.57	28.57	28.57	28.57
3	4.55	33.33	4.55	1.33	2.38	2.38	2.17	2.33
4.	100.00	50.00	100.00	25.00	100.00	13.33	33.33	15.38
5.	25.00	50.00	20.00	8.00	3.78	2.74	6.25	3.57
6	7.34	7.56	7.65	7.34	7.51	7.34	7.98	7.51
8	35.48	40.74	40.74	37.93	45.83	35.48	36.67	35.48
9	21.88	21.21	21.21	19.44	22.22	21.88	20.00	19.44
MEAN 18.40		31.64	39.89	32.43	19.63	30.65	18.33	21.46

Table 6–12 (continued)

QUESTION			FULL TEXT WITH ALGORITHMS					
	2 3	2 4	2 5	2 6	2 7	2 8	2 9	3 0
1	34.94	34.94	34.94	34.94	34.94	37.18	38.16	36.71
2	28.57	28.57	50.00	50.00	28.57	28.57	50.00	23.08
3	2.22	2.22	6.67	6.67	4.17	14.29	33.33	4.17
4	100.00	100.00	22.22	22.22	100.00	100.00	50.00	100.00
5	25.00	25.00	15.39	15.39	22.22	28.57	28.57	40.00
6	11.40	7.51	7.34	7.34	8.07	7.34	7.34	7.34
8	50.00	52.38	40.74	40.74	52.38	35.48	36.67	35.48
9	20.59	20.59	19.44	19.44	21.54	21.88	19.44	19.44
MEAN	33.28	34.09	33.90	24.59	24.59	33.99	34.16	32.94

MEAN OF 29 ALGORITHMS = 31.84%

also selected. From the middle group of the ranking, the original probability theory, two-Poisson algorithm 19, was selected, and a modified algorithm, algorithm 23, was also selected because it resulted in better precision than the original. Two algorithms, algorithms 27 and 39 where the inverse documents frequency theory is applied to the absolute frequency theory, also were selected in order to compare the superiority among the absolute, relative, probabilistic, and applied inverse document-frequency theories. Figures 6–1 to 6–7 present the effectiveness of weighting algorithms performed by questions 1 to 9, respectively. Effectiveness of the selected algorithms is examined question by question.

As shown in Figures 6–1 to 6–7, from the overall view, effectiveness of algorithms seemed to depend on the search strategy and level of recall. Questions 1, 3, 4, 8, and 9 were stated in terms of the Boolean intersection, A AND B, where the weight of A or B is the maximum of the weights of words in group A or B. In this strategy the weights of documents always depend on the lowest weight of words A and B, so that any algorithms which gave high value to common words and low value to rare words resulted in high precision at low levels of recall. The rank of documents depended on the weight of rare words. On the other hand, in a Boolean union (e.g., question 2), A OR B, algorithms that gave high value to rare words and low value to common words performed better. Since the weight of a document in the strategy depends on the maximum weight of words A and B, when rare words have a maximum weight and the documents retrieved from this strategy are ranked in order of weight of the rare word in each document, better precision resulted.

Probabilistic algorithm 19, two-Poisson, gave high beta (b) value to

Figure 6–1
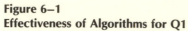
Effectiveness of Algorithms for Q1

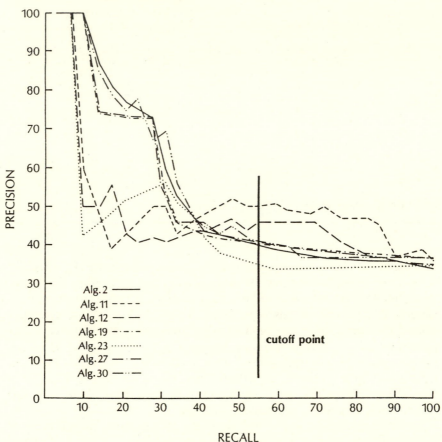

common words and low b value to rare words in the full texts of documents. The b value of a type of word did not vary on the frequency data of the word in a particular document. The performance of the two-Poisson was improved, especially at high levels of recall, when the frequency data of a word in each document was involved by multiplying b value by the frequency data of a word in a document like algorithm 23.

The absolute frequency algorithm worked very well at a low level of recall ratio because of the pyramidal structure of its frequency data, in other words, the lower the occurrence value, the greater the document frequency value. For example, in question 1, in one document the word "transition" occurred twenty-two times, in one document ten times, in eleven documents two times, and in thirty-five documents it occurred one time. Thus for low recall, that is, to retrieve only the top three or five

Figure 6–2
Effectiveness of Algorithms for Q 2

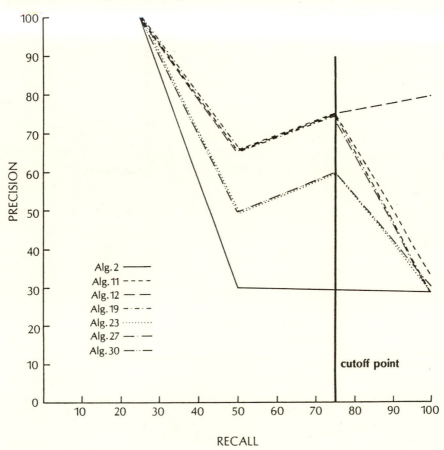

documents, this algorithm seemed to work well compared with the overall effectiveness of other algorithms.

Algorithm 11, reported best in the significance test, resulted in the best precision only at a certain level of recall. Overall, algorithm 11 performed worst in questions 1, 4, 6, and 8. The reason it has highest precision in the first experiment is its effectiveness in question 3, in which the precision ratios range from 1.30 to 100. The algorithm resulted in 100 percent precision in this question. But since only one out of the ninety-one documents retrieved in total is relevant to the question, it is difficult to generalize the effectiveness of ranking algorithms based on this question. The performance of algorithms did not vary much at high levels of recall.

Effect of the Parsing Rules for Stopwords and Punctuation Marks on Full Text Retrieval. A negative effect of stopwords on full text retrieval was

Figure 6–3
Effectiveness of Algorithms for Q 4

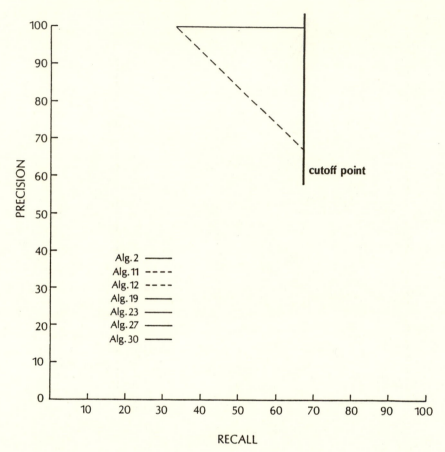

also found in this study. As mentioned, this experiment did not designate any stopwords. However, BRS assigns seventy-one stopwords. Thus the effect of stopwords on full text retrieval was examined by comparing the documents retrieved through BRS in the first experiment with the documents retrieved in the second experiments. On the BRS System, although stopwords have been omitted from the inverted index, they are not counted when each word is assigned a sequential number during the preparation of the inverted index. Because of this parsing rule for stopwords on BRS, documents with phrases such as "executives hard at work," "if you try hard and work diligently," "is hard at work," and so on were retrieved for the search term "hard work" in question 2. The sentence "may not cut the backlog" was retrieved for the search word "cut back$" in question 1. All six documents retrieved because of ignoring the noncontent word be-

Figure 6–4
Effectiveness of Algorithms for Q 5

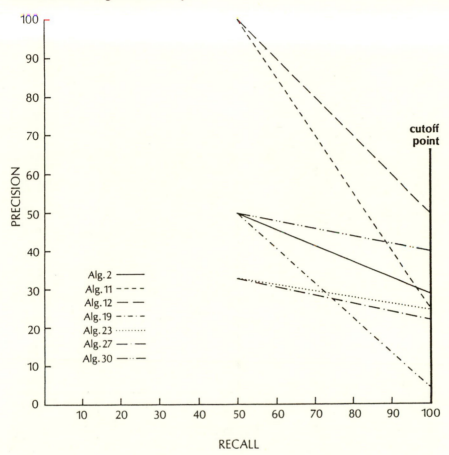

tween two words "hard" and "work" were judged nonrelevant to question 2. All three documents retrieved from question 1 because of the stopwords between two words "cut" and "back$" were also judged nonrelevant to question 1. Thus, question 2 retrieved a total of fourteen documents, of which four are relevant, in this experiment with weighting algorithms, while twenty documents were retrieved from the full text Boolean search. For question 1, eighty-three documents were retrieved from the experimental system with weighting algorithms. On the other hand, a total of eighty-six documents were retrieved from the full text search through BRS. That is, the way in which stopwords are processed by BRS results in increasing the number of nonrelevant documents retrieved.

The parsing rules for punctuation on BRS were also found to result in the increased number of nonrelevant documents from full texts. BRS ig-

Figure 6–5
Effectiveness of Algorithms for Q 6

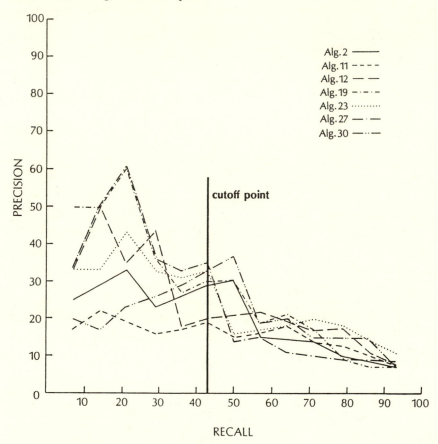

nores the period for abbreviation of words. Thus the search word "US"
retrieved the words "U.S." and also "us," the objective case of "We."

SUMMARY AND CONCLUSIONS

Using a journal document collection, this study attempted to measure
the effectiveness of full text retrieval and to find a solution to improving
the low precision of full text searching with a minimum decrease in recall.

In the first experiment, full text searches using the Boolean AND operator resulted in significantly higher recall but lower precision compared
with that of searches on paragraphs (SAME paragraph search), abstracts,
and controlled vocabularies. A larger percentage of documents retrieved
from full text searching were judged to be *probably*, rather than *definitely*
relevant than those from abstracts or controlled vocabularies.

Figure 6–6
Effectiveness of Algorithms for Q 8

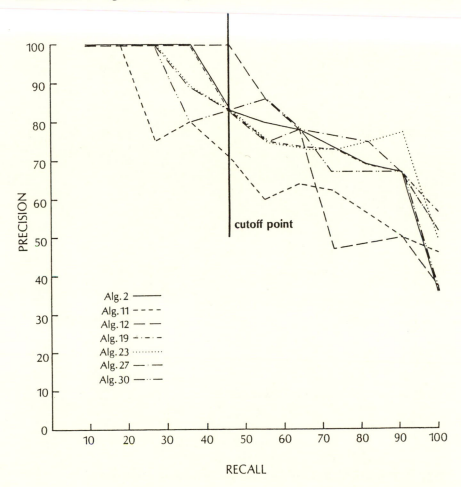

In the second experiment, the precision of full text retrieval was reported to have improved when ranking algorithms were applied to full text retrieval. There was no significant difference between algorithms at the .05 level and the relative effectiveness of algorithms seemed to depend on the Boolean strategy employed as well as the level of recall. An algorithm that gave high weights to common words and low weights to rare words in the Boolean intersection performed well at low levels of recall. The performance of algorithms did not vary much at high levels of recall. The processing of stopwords by BRS resulted in increasing the number of nonrelevant documents retrieved from full text searching, especially for

Figure 6–7
Effectiveness of Algorithms for Q 9

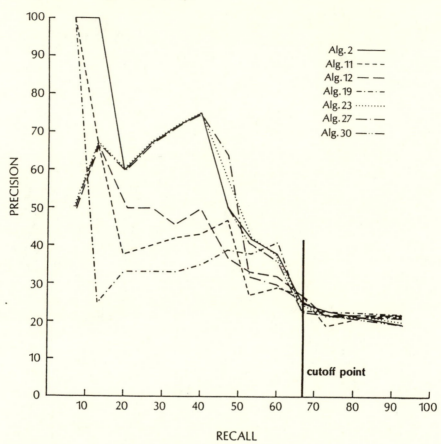

searching adjacent word phrases. The processing of punctuation on BRS was also found to impact the increased number of nonrelevant documents.

NOTES

1. Jung Soon Ro, "An Evaluation of the Applicability of Ranking Algorithms to Improving the Effectiveness of Full Text Retrieval" (Ph.D. dissertation, Indiana University, 1985); Idem, "An Evaluation of the Applicability of Ranking Algorithms to Improve the Effectiveness of Full-Text Retrieval. I. On the Effectiveness of Full-Text Retrieval," *Journal of the American Society for Information Science* 39, No. 2 (1988): 73–78; Idem, "An Evaluation of the Applicability of Ranking Algorithms to Improve the Effectiveness of Full-Text Retrieval. II. On the Effectiveness of Ranking Algorithms on Full-Text Retrieval," *Journal of the American Society for Information Science* 39, No. 3 (1988): 147–160.

2. Carol Tenopir, "Retrieval Performance in a Full Text Journal Article Database" (Ph.D. dissertation, University of Illinois, 1984).

3. Tefko Saracevic, "RELEVANCE: A Review of and a Framework for the Thinking on the Notion in Information Science," *Journal of the American Society for Information Science* 26 (1975): 321–343.

4. Wolfgang K. H. Sager and Peter C. Lockemann, "Classification of Ranking Algorithms," *International Forum on Information and Documentation* 1, No. 4 (1976): 12–25.

5. R. Holsti, *Content Analysis for the Social Sciences and Humanities* (Reading, Mass.: Addison-Wesley, 1969), and William A. Scott, "Reliability of Content Analysis: The Case of Nominal Scale Coding," *Public Opinion Quarterly* 19 (1955): 321–325.

6. Holsti, *Content Analysis*.

7. G. Zipf, *Human Behavior and the Principle of Least Effort* (New York: Addison-Wesley, 1949).

8. Claude E. Shannon and Warren Weaver, *The Mathematical Theory of Communication* (Urbana: University of Illinois Press, 1964).

9. H. P. Luhn, "A Statistical Approach to Mechanized Encoding and Searching of Literary Information," *IBM Journal of Research and Development* 1 (1957): 309–317.

10. H. P. Edmundson and R. E. Wyllys, "Automatic Abstracting and Indexing—Survey and Recommendation," *Communication of the Association for Computing Machinery* 4 (1961): 226–234; Fred J. Damerau, "An Experiment in Automatic Indexing," *American Documentation* 16 (1965): 283–289; and John M. Carroll and Robert Roeloffs, "Computer Selection of Keywords Using Word Frequency Analysis," *American Documentation* 20 (1969): 227–233.

11. Karen Sparck Jones, "A Statistical Interpretation of Term Specificity and its Application in Retrieval," *Journal of Documentation* 28 (1972): 11–21.

12. Stephen Harter, "A Probabilistic Approach to Automatic Keyword Indexing" (Ph.D. dissertation, University of Chicago, 1974); and Abraham Bookstein and Don R. Swanson, "Probabilistic Models for Automatic Indexing," *Journal of the American Society for Information Science* 25 (1975): 312–318.

13. H. S. Heaps, *Information Retrieval: Computational and Theoretical Aspects* (New York: Academic Press, 1978); H. Kucera and W. N. Francis, *Computational Analysis of Present-day American English* (Providence, R.I.: Brown University Press, 1967).

14. Sager and Lockemann, "Classification"; Terry Noreault, Michael McGill, and Matthew B. Koll, "A Performance Evaluation of Similarity Measures, Document Term Weighting Schemes and Representation in a Boolean Environment," in *Information Retrieval Research*, ed. R. N. Oddy (London: Butterworth, 1981), pp. 57–76.

15. Pauline V. Angione, "On the Equivalence of Boolean and Weighted Searching Based on the Convertibility of Query Forms," *Journal of the American Society for Information Science* 26 (1975): 112–124; and Abraham Bookstein, "Perils of Merging between Boolean and Weighted Retrieval Systems," *Journal of the American Society for Information Science* 29 (1978): 156–157.

16. Arnold Kaufmann, *Introduction to the Theory of Fuzzy Subsets* (New York: Academic Press, 1975); Abraham Bookstein, "Probability and Fuzzy-set Appli-

cations to Information Retrieval," *Annual Review of Information Science and Technology* 20 (1985): 117–151.

17. Harter, "A Probabilistic Approach"; and Bookstein and Swanson, "Probabilistic Models."

18. S. E. Robertson, C. J. Rijsbergen, and M. F. Porter, "Probabilistic Models of Indexing and Searching," in *Information Retrieval Research*, ed. R. N. Oddy (London: Butterworth, 1981), pp. 35–56.

19. G. Salton and C. S. Yang, "On the Specification of Term Values in Automatic Indexing," *Journal of Documentation* 29 (1973): 351–371; G. Salton, H. Wu, and C. T. Yu, "The Measurement of Term Importance in Automatic Indexing," *Journal of the American Society for Information Science* 32, No. 3 (1981): 175–186; Sager and Lockemann, "Classification."

7

Research on Full Text Magazines

The studies described in Chapters 5 and 6 both examined the *Harvard Business Review* online database on the BRS search system. Using a single-title database means that the results must be interpreted with caution—within the limitations of the writing style, controlled vocabulary, and editorial idiosyncracies of one journal. Studying a single journal does not allow variations in writing style to be studied, nor does it allow for a variety of topics to be searched. Even when not limited to a single journal, most of the other studies of retrieval performance described in Chapter 4 were limited to a database that covered a narrow range of documents in a certain subject area. While such studies are easier to control, it is difficult to make generalizations or to recommend optimal search techniques when the variables of type of literature, nature of the queries or uses, and writing style cannot be taken into account. In 1988 and 1989 Tenopir began to examine some of these variables in a series of studies on multititle full text magazine databases.[1]

Two of the studies described here were conducted on the Magazine ASAP (MASAP) database on DIALOG. MASAP, produced by Information Access Company, is described in more detail in Chapter 2. The DIALOG version includes nearly 170,000 articles from over 100 different magazines. As mentioned in Chapter 2, feature articles, editorials, reviews, columns, product evaluations, and recipes are included, while items such as letters to the editor, short news notes, and advertisements are not. Still, the records range in length from a few lines to many pages.

Figure 1–2 shows a record from MASAP. Note that in addition to the text, each record contains full bibliographic information, descriptors, and picture captions. Some records contain other value-added fields such as

SIC codes, named persons, a special features designation (for example, photographs or illustrations present in print version), or a letter grade for reviews. Journal names are searchable, so that a search can be limited to a specific title if desired; otherwise articles from all 100 journals are searched together.

Because MASAP represents a mixture from such a variety of source magazines, it is probably one of the most interesting and challenging full text databases to study. Its variety makes any search results difficult to generalize because they are subject to such a range of variables. It is quite the opposite problem of *Harvard Business Review* where tight editorial control over writing style may impose a consistency on the text that directly impacts retrieval. In MASAP sources such as *Time, Newsweek,* and *Forbes* are mixed with the *Department of State Bulletin, Science,* and *Playboy.* Any search may retrieve articles from all of these. False drops can be especially dramatic (and sometimes entertaining).

A third research project described in this chapter studied Trade & Industry ASAP (T&IASAP), a companion database to MASAP described in more detail in Chapter 2. T&IASAP is also produced by Information Access Company and also mixes a variety of types and styles of magazines. Although it is more narrowly focused on business sources, within this broad subject designation there is much diversity. T&IASAP includes over 500,000 articles from 1983 to the present from approximately eighty-five journals plus full text of the PR Newswire. Coverage includes full texts of articles, trade news, reviews, new product announcements, editorials, and columns from sources such as *Automotive Industry, Datamation, Dallas-Fort Worth Business, Fortune, Monthly Labor Review,* and *PC Week.* There is some overlap with MASAP.

As mentioned in Chapter 2, there are differences in the versions of these two databases available on different search systems.[2] (Both are available on DIALOG, BRS, and NEXIS.) The two studies on MASAP reported here used only DIALOG; the study of T&IASAP compared full text search features and differences in the database on DIALOG and BRS.

RETRIEVAL PERFORMANCE

Part of Ro's study described in Chapter 6 compared results when searching full text using the Boolean AND operator with using the BRS SAME paragraph proximity operator. Using a question array technique allowed her to average the results of several searches and make some generalizations about the retrieval results of the two different methods of linking concepts. Retrieval performance for MASAP, including differences among several search techniques, was studied using the same question array methodology.[3]

In this later study eight queries were searched in turn on the MASAP database on DIALOG. The queries were generated from questions asked at the reference desks of a university undergraduate library and a public library and were mostly current event topics from students who were writing term papers or preparing class presentations. Table 7–1 lists the queries and the strategies used online.

As can be seen in Table 7–1, each question was searched four different ways in order to test a variety of search techniques offered by DIALOG. Concepts were linked in the texts in the following four ways in turn: (1) Boolean AND, (2) within the same grammatical paragraph (the (S) operator on DIALOG), (3) within ten words in either order ((10N) on DIALOG), and (4) within five words in either order ((5N) on DIALOG). Ten intervening words were chosen because an average sentence probably has about ten words (although (10N) does not take sentence punctuation marks into account). Five N was expected to achieve lower recall and higher precision than (10N), but is otherwise a purely arbitrary choice. As described in Chapter 3, DIALOG allows a user to specify a selected number of intervening words with the near (N) operator.

Search methods go from broadest to narrowest, with the broader strategies almost always including all of the records retrieved by the narrower. (The only exception is some documents may be retrieved by (10N) or (5N) that were not retrieved by (S) if the words occurred close to each other but in separate paragraphs.) The broadest strategy, AND, includes all documents retrieved by the other methods. Recall cannot be measured in this study, but if the results of AND searching are defined as 100 percent recall, relative recall can be calculated for the other search techniques.[4] Relative recall was expected to decrease and precision was expected to increase as the search methods narrowed.

All searches were formulated and conducted by the author. The same words or phrases were used for each of the four methods searched in each question; only the linking operator was changed. The patrons who asked the questions originally were not involved in the study, and no question required subject expertise, so the searcher judged relevance.

Earlier studies encountered a problem with relevance judging of full texts because a binary relevant–not relevant decision was difficult to make. In the *Harvard Business Review* studies no value for partial relevance was established. In this study of MASAP a three-value scale of relevance was used. Documents were assigned to one of three categories: (1) not relevant at all, (2) partially relevant (defined for this study as ten lines or fewer of relevant information), and (3) relevant (entire article or more than ten relevant lines).

Table 7–2 shows for each question and each search method how many documents were retrieved, how many relevant documents or partially relevant documents were retrieved, relative recall, and precision.[5] Average values for all eight questions are presented in Table 7–3.

Table 7–1
Queries and Search Strategies on MASAP

1. How do liquor laws affect the liquor industry?

  liquor(w)industry/tx **AND** (laws or legislation)/tx
      (S)
      (10N)
      (5N)

2. Is abortion discussed in sex education programs? Does sex education have any affect
  on the abortion rate (increase or decrease)?

  sex(w)education/tx **AND** abortion/tx
      (S)
      (10N)
      (5N)

3. How does attitude toward death vary by religion?

  (death or dying)/tx **AND** religio?/tx **AND** (belief? or attitude?)/tx
      (S)   (S)
      (10N)   (10N)
      (5N)   (5N)

4. Is plagiarism in politicians' speeches or writings new? Is it common?

  plagiarism/tx **AND** politic?/tx
      (S)
      (10N)
      (5N)

5. How have microcomputers been used with preschool children?

  (microcomputer? or micro(w)computer?)/tx **AND** (preschool? or
  nursery(w)school?)/tx   (S)
              (10N)
              (5N)

6. Find me information about the morals or ethics of tv evangelists.

  (((T V or t(w)v or television)/tx **AND** evangelis?/tx) or televangelis?)/tx
  AND (ethic? or moral?)/tx (S)
  (S)   (10N)
  (10N)   (5 N)
  (5 N)

7. I need information on the fishing rights that were granted to the Soviet Union by
  Pacific nations such as Kiribati and Vanuatu.

  (kiribati or new(w)hebrides or vanuatu or Pacific)/tx **AND**
  fish?/tx(2n)right?/tx **AND** soviet/tx   (S)
      (S)   (10N)
      (10N)   (5N)
      (5N)

Table 7–1 continued

8. Can you get AIDS from mosquitoes?

```
(aids or acquired(w)immun?(1w)syndrome)/tx  AND  mosquito?/tx
                                     (S)
                                     (10N)
                                     (5N)
```

Source: Produced from "Magazines in Full Text: Uses and Search Strategies," by Carol Tenopir and Man Evene Shu, *Online Review*, 13, no. 2 (1989) by permission of Learned Information, Inc., 143 Old Marlton Pike, Medford, NJ 08055.

As expected, Boolean AND searching usually retrieved many more documents, including more false drops, than did the other techniques. Precision averaged almost 50 percent with AND, ranging from a low of 19 percent to a high of 86 percent. Only questions 3 and 6 retrieved an unmanageable total number of articles with the AND operator.

A finding that may be surprising is that AND was particularly useful for retrieving partially relevant documents that were not found by other search techniques. These articles typically had several sentences that were relevant to the topic, but words for every concept did not appear in the same paragraph. For example, an article about AIDS contained the important relevant line " mosquitoes do not carry the disease" without repeating the term AIDS in the same paragraph. Some articles about TV evangelists contained sections that described specific kinds of moral or immoral behavior, but did not repeat the evangelist concept in those paragraphs. Discussions of liquor laws did not always mention they concerned the liquor industry. In Question 5 (microcomputer use with preschool children) AND was the only technique that retrieved relevant information. Relevant sentences or paragraphs were in the texts, but they were parts of larger themes.

This finding goes against conventional wisdom. It suggests that for partial document retrieval or retrieval of relevant lines, sentences, or paragraphs the AND operator is better on the average than same paragraph or intervening word searching. This seems to result from authors' elimination of redundancy by not repeating an overall theme of their article ("preschool children," "liquor industry," "AIDS") in each paragraph. When we search using proximity operators that isolate parts of the whole, we forget these subtleties of writing style. Overall implied or understood concepts are missed in systems that demand that all parts of a search query must be present in order to retrieve a document. The value of probabilistic retrieval or fuzzy sets is briefly mentioned in Chapter 4.[6] Word frequency algorithms are useful in predicting relevance of entire documents, but they do not solve the partial document retrieval problem, because often the important words are mentioned only once in the document.

When fully relevant documents are required, the same paragraph (S) operator achieved the best balance between recall and precision. As ex-

Table 7–2
Documents Retrieved by Search Techniques in MASAP

QUESTION #	SEARCH STRATEGY	DOCUMENTS RETRIEVED	RELEVANT RETRIEVED			PRECISION	RELATIVE RECALL
			All	Part	False		
1	AND	7	3	3	1	86%	
	(S)	5	2	2	1	80	67
	(10N)	2	1	1	0	100	33
	(5N)	1	1	0	0	100	17
2	AND	57	3	14	40	30	
	(S)	22	2	7	13	41	53
	(10N)	12	2	2	8	33	24
	(5N)	8	0	2	6	25	12
3	AND	412*	20	60	332	19	
	(S)	9	2	3	4	56	- - -
	(10N)	1	1	0	0	100	- - -
	(5N)	0	0	0	0	- - -	- - -
4	AND	30	2	14	14	53	
	(S)	7	2	4	1	86	38
	(10N)	1	0	0	1	0	0
	(5N)	1	0	0	1	0	0
5	AND	25	0	16	9	64	
	(S)	1	0	0	1	0	0
	(10N)	1	0	0	1	0	0
	(5N)	0	0	0	0	- - -	0
6	AND	97	11	16	70	28	
	(S)	12	4	3	5	58	26
	(10N)	0	0	0	0	- - -	0
	(5N)	0	0	0	0	- - -	0
7	AND	7	2	2	3	57	
	(S)	4	2	2	0	100	100
	(10N)	2	1	1	0	100	50
	(5N)	1	1	0	0	100	25
8	AND	28	5	11	12	57	
	(S)	14	5	8	1	93	81
	(10N)	10	5	4	1	90	56
	(5N)	8	4	3	1	88	44

* Relevance judging for question 3 was done by sampling

Source: Produced from "Magazines in Full Text: Uses and Search Strategies," by Carol Tenopir and Man Evene Shu, *Online Review*, 13, no. 2 (1989) by permission of Learned Information, Inc., 143 Old Marlton Pike, Medford, NJ 08055.

Table 7–3
Average Values for All Questions for MASAP

SEARCH TECHNIQUE	TOTAL RETRIEVED	RELEVANT RETRIEVED			PRECISION RETRIEVED	RELATIVE RECALL
		All	Part	False		
AND	82.9	5.8	17.0	60.0	49.3%	---
(S)	9.3	2.4	3.6	3.3	64.3	52.1%
(10N)	3.6	1.3	1.0	1.4	60.4	23.3
(5N)	2.4	.8	.6	1.0	62.6	14.0

Source: Produced from "Magazines in Full Text: Uses and Search Strategies," by Carol Tenopir and Man Evene Shu, *Online Review*, 13, no. 2 (1989) by permission of Learned Information, Inc., 143 Old Marlton Pike, Medford, NJ 08055.

pected, same paragraph searches achieved much better recall than (10N) or (5N), but unexpectedly the precision was slightly better as well. Often the (10N) and (5N) techniques eliminated relevant documents while retaining some of the false drops. The (5N) technique even had a lower precision score than (10N) and (S) in some questions.

Reasons for these precision scores varied. One cause of false drops for all search techniques and low precision scores for (5N) was news summary stories. Such stories often list all events of a week or all issues discussed by a presidential candidate, making a string of unrelated topics separated by commas. Some false drops in the question on how sex education in schools affects abortion rates described all the things a certain candidate opposed, including sex education, abortion, and restriction of prayers in schools. The false drops were the only articles retrieved by the (5N) search technique. Major commercial search services ignore commas and most other punctuation marks when text words are extracted for creation of the inverted indexes. Punctuation cannot therefore be used to modify search strategy.

The mixture of different types of magazines and different types of articles in this database resulted in many of the false drops. Magazine ASAP does have an Article Type field that broadly categorizes each record. Eliminating news stories with a Boolean NOT would eliminate many of the false drops described above, but "news stories" is not one of the article types. Book or movie reviews were another predicable source of false drops, and there is a Review category that could be NOTed out to improve precision. This value-added field is clearly useful if the categories were reexamined in the light of actual searches.

The magazines themselves were a predictor of false drops to a certain degree. In the question on AIDS, for example, relevant documents came from *Science, Science News*, and *Time*. False drops with no relevant documents came from titles such as *Flying, Datamation, Fortune*, and *Cycle*. Precision could be improved if searchers could select or eliminate types of magazines, perhaps in preselected categories as with the Article Type designators. False drops seem to be an inherent danger in a mixed-article database such as MASAP, but, on the positive side, it provides access to sources that might not otherwise be considered.

Often the false drops retrieved with full text searching were attributable to the peculiarities of the English language. This was studied in more detail in a later project, but this first study found some examples where figurative language clearly caused false drops. For example, a false drop in the question on AIDS and mosquitoes had the sentence "You can't fight attack helicopters piloted by Cubans with band-aids and mosquito nets." In the question about microcomputer use by preschool children, a false drop included the sentence "warns that the computerization of the home via cable TV, microcomputers, and other interactive systems will enable organizations to construct master profiles of citizens that make today's data collection seem like nursery school activities."

Solutions for these false drops already exist in experimental information retrieval systems and in theory. Term frequency occurrence data and ranking algorithms as explored by Ro and discussed in Chapter 6 would help predict the kind of false drops mentioned above. As mentioned earlier, the negative side of such techniques is that some additional partially relevant documents would be eliminated with these false drops. Grammar, punctuation, and word parsing decisions might also affect search results with the type of false drops mentioned above.

PROXIMITY OPERATORS ON BRS AND DIALOG

The differences between the ways that two search systems treat the same full text database and the full text search or display features offered may affect search results. A follow-up study by Shu compared results from searching the same questions on the DIALOG and BRS versions of Trade & Industry ASAP.[7]

The four questions shown in Table 7–4 were each searched a total of four times: twice on the DIALOG version of T&IASAP and twice on the BRS version. As shown in Table 7–4, on DIALOG the (10N) and (S) proximity operators were used to link concepts and in BRS the WITH (within the same sentence) and SAME paragraph were used. It was assumed that the use of (S) in DIALOG and SAME in BRS would retrieve the same records if the records were available in both versions of the database. DIALOG's (10N) and BRS's WITH are not exact equivalents because WITH uses sentence punctuation and (10N) does not. DIALOG's (10N) will retrieve records where words occur within 10 words of each other, in either order, and regardless of sentence structure. WITH requires

Table 7–4
Queries and Search Strategies for T&IASAP

1. How is FAX and Teletext being applied in business communication?

DIALOG:

> business(w)communication?/tx (S) (facsimile? or fax or teletext?)/tx
> (10N)

BRS:

> business **adj** communications$.tx. SAME (facsimile$ or fax$ or teletext$)/tx
> WITH

2. How do liquor laws affect the liquor industry?

DIALOG:

> liquor(w)industr???/tx (S) (law? ? or legislat??? or regulation? ?)/tx
> (10N)

BRS:
> liquor **adj** industr$3.tx. SAME (law$1 or legislat$3 or regulation$1).tx.
> WITH

3. What is the interface between tourism and the food services?

DIALOG:

> (food(w)service? ?)/tx (S) (touri?? or travel(w)industr??? or hotel? ?
> (10N)
> or transportation? ?)/tx

BRS:

> (food **adj** service$1).tx. SAME (touri$2 or travel **adj** industr$3 or hotel$1
> WITH
> or transportation$1).tx.

4. How is atificial intelligence being applied in management information systems?

DIALOG:

> (mis or management(w)information(w)system? ?)/tx (S)
> (10N)
> (expert(w)system? ? or artificial(w)intelligence)/tx

BRS:

> (mis or management **adj** information **adj** system$1).tx. SAME (expert **adj**
> system$1 or artificial **adj** intelligence).tx.   WITH

Source: Produced from "Magazines in Full Text: Uses and Search Strategies," by Carol Tenopir
        and Man Evene Shu, *Online Review*, 13, no. 2 (1989) by permission of Learned
        Information, Inc., 143 Old Marlton Pike, Medford, NJ 08055.

Table 7–5
Documents Retrieved by Search Techniques in T&IASAP

	DIALOG				BRS			
QUESTION #	(10N)		(S)		WITH		SAME	
	Total Ret.	Relevant Ret.	Total Ret.	Relevant Ret.	Total Ret.	Relevant Ret.	Total Ret.	Relevant Ret.
1.	9	6	13	7	3	2	9	6
2.	1	1	1	1	1	1	1	1
3.	31	8	51	13	26	10	32	13
4.	11	9	16	13	10	9	19	11
TOTAL #	52		81		50		61	
AVERAGE	13		20		10		15	
AVERAGE PRECISION	68.6%		65.2%		73.8%		66.3%	

Source: Produced from "Magazines in Full Text: Uses and Search Strategies," by Carol Tenopir and Man Evene Shu, *Online Review*, 13, no. 2 (1989) by permission of Learned Information, Inc., 143 Old Marlton Pike, Medford, NJ 08055.

both concepts to be in the same grammatical sentence in either order. A sampling of the articles in the database showed an average sentence length of approximately ten words, hence the use of (10N). Searches were limited to articles published in 1987 or 1988.

All searches were formulated and conducted by a single searcher. The searcher also judged relevance. There was no division made between totally relevant and partially relevant; if even a single line of an article was relevant, that document was judged to be relevant. As in the previous study on MASAP, no end users were directly involved in this study, and the questions were not necessarily originally searched online by the reference librarians who received them.

Table 7–5 shows the total number of articles retrieved and relevant documents retrieved by each of the search methods for each question. (Actual numbers are low because of the publication year restriction.) Average precision ratio is calculated by averaging the precision ratios for each question. Table 7–6 shows how many unique documents were retrieved by each. Every article that was uniquely retrieved in one system was verified in the other by a title search. The analysis could thus determine exactly why the articles were not retrieved.

The (10N) technique on DIALOG retrieved on the average three more records per question than did WITH on BRS. Punctuation and format account for most of the unique retrievals on DIALOG. For example, in question 4 about Management Information Systems and Artificial Intelli-

Table 7–6
Unique Documents Retrieved by Search Techniques for T&IASAP

QUESTION #	DIALOG (1 0 N)	DIALOG (S)	BRS WITH	BRS SAME
1.	6	1	0	0
2.	0	0	0	0
3.	14	11	2	2
4.	4	4	2	3
TOTAL #	24	16	4	8
AVERAGE	6	4	1	2

gence, all the unique records were retrieved because two search terms occurred in separate sentences or separate paragraphs but within ten words of each other. The two search terms were separated by a period ("."), the delimiting factor for WITH on BRS. (For example, DIALOG uniquely retrieved an article with the phrase "artificial intelligence zealots can help here. MIS must also be more responsive.")

Another factor affecting retrieval is the portions of the full text that two systems choose to include. Only DIALOG included a photo caption for a record uniquely retrieved in question 4. In the (S) and SAME paragraph searches, a unique record in DIALOG was retrieved because only DIALOG included a special advertising supplement. Other unique retrievals came from directories that were included only in the DIALOG version. Such record-loading decisions have a great impact not only on free-text searching, but on the ability to locate special things, such as a specific illustration or photograph.

As expected, there was more uniformity in the number of documents retrieved with (S) in DIALOG and SAME in BRS. Still, DIALOG retrieved some unique records. In at least one case this was due to the parsing rules used by the two systems. DIALOG parses "MIS's" as two words (MIS and S), because it treats all punctuation as blanks when word parsing. On the other hand, BRS employs some text editing features that treat an apostrophe differently from other punctuation. BRS strips out the apostrophe and parses MIS's as one word—MISs. Because the searcher did not truncate MIS, the BRS record was missed.

It is important to remember that the DIALOG version of T&IASAP includes more journal titles than does the BRS version.[8] In addition, as mentioned above, DIALOG sometimes includes peripheral materials such as advertising supplements and directories that are not in the BRS version. Update schedules may also vary with the two systems.

Shu viewed records with the DIALOG KWIC display and BRS HITS feature as described in Chapter 3. She found KWIC useful mainly for browsing and deciding whether to view an entire document because it shows a 2- 50-word window of text, often with ellipses to show where words are left out. The BRS HITS feature displays entire paragraphs, making it easier to read and easier to use for fact retrieval or full paragraph retrieval. She felt that relevance is also easier to judge with HITS.

Both systems offer highlighting of search terms, but the implementation of this feature varies with the system as well. BRS highlights individual words used as part of a phrase specified with adjacency (that is, when searching Management Information System each of the three individual words are highlighted in the text in addition to the phrase). DIALOG highlights only the desired phrase.

Shu made several recommendations to improve scanning or browsing in full texts. She recommends better background shading, line counts on the margin so that a searcher can estimate the time to be spent on printing, the ability to scroll forwards and backwards (this is often part of the tele-communications package), better use of spacing and headings to improve readability, more use of type faces, italics, and the like to make the online version more closely resemble the aesthetics of the print version.[9]

END USERS AND FULL TEXT

The studies described above had a professional searcher develop search strategies and search the database. As with most studies that use this methodology, dynamic modifications depending on search results were not made. End users were not involved in any stages of the search process (and were not even aware that their questions were being searched online). Since the main target audience for full text databases such as Magazine ASAP and Trade & Industry ASAP is end users, another, larger study looked at the MASAP database again, but this time with end users selecting the topics and the strategies to be searched.

When end users are involved, several interesting questions arise about full text magazine databases.[10] These include: (1) for what purposes will end users use the databases? (2) what search strategies will they use? (3) what relationships are there between purpose and successful search strategy? (4) what measures and relevance judgments are appropriate for end user searching of full text database?

The study was conducted in 1988–1989 at the University of Hawaii at Manoa School of Library and Information Studies under a grant from the Council on Library Resources. Eleven subjects participated, including undergraduates, graduate students, and faculty, mostly from social science

Table 7–7
Characteristics of End User Searchers

ACADEMIC LEVEL*	DEPARTMENT	Micros	CD-ROM	OPAC	Full Text	Intermediary Search
f	Educational Technology	y	ERIC	no	no	yes
f	Dance	y	INFOTRAC	yes	no	yes
f	Travel Industry	y	INFOTRAC	yes	no	yes
f	Communications	y	no	yes	no	yes
g	English as Second Language	y	no	yes	no	no
g	Dance	y	no	yes	no	no
g	Geography	y	no	yes	no	no
g	Communication Information Sciences	y	no	yes	no	no
u	Physical therapy	y	INFOTRAC	yes	no	no
u	Psychology	y	INFOTRAC	yes	no	no
u	Psychology	y	no	yes	no	no

(The two header rows: "ACADEMIC LEVEL* DEPARTMENT" and "EXPERIENCE WITH DATABASES"; sub-columns: Micros, CD-ROM, OPAC, Full Text, Intermediary Search)

* f: faculty; g: graduate student; u: undergraduate

or humanities fields. They all had experience with microcomputers and all but one had used the university library's online public access catalog. Some had either had an intermediary conduct an online search for them in the past or had used the library's CD-ROM databases. Table 7–7 summarizes the characteristics of the subjects.

Each subject was given approximately two hours of training on how to search MASAP on DIALOG. Enough basic DIALOG commands were taught so that they could search, retrieve, and view articles or portions of articles. Table 7–8 shows the DIALOG commands and features that were part of the initial training session. In addition, each subject was given a handout explaining other commands, search features, and MASAP fields to study before their first search session.

Actual search sessions were scheduled at each subject's convenience throughout the fall 1988 semester. A lab monitor was always present to take care of the setup and logging on process. Lab monitors were graduate students in the School of Library and Information Studies who all had at least two semester-long courses in online searching. They were instructed to help with search strategy only when asked and then mainly to show additional commands as requested by the user. We tried to minimize the role of the monitor, but some influence in search strategy was impossible to avoid. At times a close searcher-monitor partnership seemed to develop.

Data were recorded in two ways. First, all searches were downloaded (and printed out later for easier analysis). The downloaded searches can

Table 7–8
DIALOG Commands and Features Used in Training of End Users

SEARCHING:

select	Retrieve set of records containing term(s)
display sets	List all sets formed since begun
and	Boolean AND (logical intersection)
o r	Boolean OR (logical union)
(w)	terms must be adjacent and in specified order
(s)	terms must be in the same paragraph
(n N)	terms must be within n words, in either order
?	truncate with any number of characters after stem
p y =	search for articles with a specified date
j n =	search for a specified journal
a t =	search for a specified kind of article

VIEWING RECORDS:

type	show records on screen (download simultaneously)
t 3, kwic	display citation and key words in context
t ti	display titles
t 9	display full text

be used to analyze search strategy, search style, and causes of false drops. The second way to record data involved audiotaping all searches. Searchers were trained to think aloud as they searched. They explained as they went along what they were searching (and why), talked through their search strategy, and reacted to all parts of the search and each document retrieved. They were asked to make comments on three main areas: (1) relevance (Why is this item of interest to you? Why is this item of no interest to you? Why are you happy or surprised to see this item?); (2) rationale (Why are you using this command or option? What particular piece of information is important? How might you use this particular piece of information?); and (3) location (What set number are you commenting on? What item number are you commenting on?).

The think-aloud technique allowed us to get searchers' spontaneous reactions as well as their more reasoned relevance judgments as they searched. The think-aloud approach yields information that is different from interviews. According to Ericsson and Simon, who pioneered the development of this approach and its theoretical justification in cognitive science, interviews rely on expectations or retrospective recall, both of which are incomplete or inaccurate at times.[11] By comparison, concurrent verbalizations are self-witnessing accounts. They are objective descriptions of what one perceives oneself to be doing while engaged in a problem solving activity. The accuracy improves with training. Recently, Belkin

Table 7–9
Types of Uses by End Users of MASAP

USE	EXAMPLE
document location (online)	find and download articles about Chinese dance
document location (print)	find citations for relevant articles that the library has
browsing for background information	read or scan articles or portions of articles about telecommunications
browsing through a journal	scan articles from Science issues from last year
fact retrieval	What was the date and time of the Challenger explosion?
find peripheral mention of something or someone	find all mentions of Ellison Onizuka or a certain court case
word finding	locate articles that use a set of vocabulary words for students to read in an English as a Second Language class
special features	find articles about "computer use with physical therapy" that have photographs or pictures in the print version so I can show them in a class report
specific items	find recipes with certain ingredients or for quiche

Source: Produced from "Magazines Online: Users and Uses of Full Text," by Carol Tenopir, Diane Nahl-Jakobovbits, Dara Lee Howard, *Proceedings of the ASIS Annual Meeting,* 26 (1989) by permission of Learned Information, Inc., 143 Old Marlton Pike, Medford, NJ 08055.

reported using concurrent verbalizations of database searchers to develop software for human-computer interaction in end user information retrieval systems.[12]

The downloaded searches, audiotapes with think-aloud protocols, and pre- and post-interviews together give us a multidimensional view of the search process. The following categories of information were identified: search strategies used and how these were modified; error types (failure analysis) generated by both the searcher and the system; how the three domains of human behavior (affective, cognitive, and sensorimotor) interact in online searching; and searchers' intended uses of the retrieved information.

One of our main objectives was to discover what kinds of uses end users would make of full text magazines if they were given unrestricted and free use of the database. We wanted to lift the inhibiting factor of cost and not prejudice users toward any particular kind of use. Table 7–9 shows a categorization of types of uses.[13] Some searchers used the database in only one of these ways, others had several different uses. The most common use by all was to locate articles that were fully on a given topic, just as they would use a bibliographic database. Relevance judgments in these cases were often based on full document relevance—if the search words only occurred once or twice in a given document, some searchers learned to reject that article immediately as not relevant. DIALOG does not have any word frequency features, but any such features clearly would have been useful to these searchers for full document retrieval.

Once a document was identified as relevant or potentially relevant through viewing citations and KWIC portions or the beginning of the full text, most users when looking for fully relevant documents chose to download the entire article. They usually did not want to read the electronic version on the screen (except to judge relevance), but instead they elected to download and print out full texts to be read on paper at their leisure. This may have been influenced by the presence of a lab monitor and by the fact that searching was not being done in their own home or office. In a postsearch interview about subsequent use of the printout, the most frequent response (four searchers) was to use the printout to get copies of the printed magazine versions of relevant articles. In these cases the downloaded electronic version was not a substitute for print, just a convenient way to locate valuable print articles.

Another popular use of the database was to browse through articles to get background information on a topic. Our subjects made repeated use of DIALOGLINK's scrolling capabilities and the KWIC feature to scan retrieved articles. In these cases they did read on screen, sometimes just enough to get an overview of a topic. More flexibility in browsing would have helped this use; the DIALOG viewing features are not really set up for dynamic viewing. A display command is entered and it cannot be changed without interrupting the viewing process. Users would have liked to move around in documents easily, skipping some paragraphs or KWIC sections, moving on to others at will, enlarging the KWIC window while they were reading a particular section, reading more of one document than others, and so on.

Browsing and downloading entire articles are both cost-sensitive uses of full text and undoubtedly would not be so appealing if the user was paying for connect time. Search sessions were typically one to two hours in a database that normally costs $96 per hour plus $1.00 per full article typed online. In a postsearch interview, subjects were asked under what circumstances they would spend either $5-$20 per search or more than $20 per search of their own money. Some indicated they would never spend more than $20, most indicated they would spend up to $50 or so only for work-related information that could not be found by other means or when time was an important factor.[14] Clearly database producers and/or libraries will need to deal with the cost issue if they hope to exploit these important and appealing uses of full text. Full text on CD-ROM is one solution.

Some of the other uses took more advantage of the unique advantages offered by having the full text online and searchable. Fact retrieval (for example, What was the date and time of the *Challenger* explosion?) is a use mentioned frequently in the ACS/BRS studies of chemical journals. This was not so common in our study, perhaps because of the general nature of the database, but was used occasionally. In these cases, viewing the citation and KWIC online was usually sufficient. (In a mixed magazine database it is important to view the citation so that the credibility of the "fact" can be judged.) Sometimes relevant facts were retrieved when the searcher was really looking for entire documents on an article. A single relevant paragraph was at times a pleasant surprise to the user, answering an unarticulated question that was a facet of a broader topic. (If searchers had used word-frequency data to judge relevance, they would have missed these paragraphs.)

Finding peripheral mention of something or someone is a similar partial-document retrieval use. Again sometimes this was planned ("I don't expect there to be an entire article on this person, but any mention would be valuable"); other times it was an unexpected benefit of searching the entire text. Word frequency criteria for relevance judging is clearly inappropriate for this use.

The additional index value added fields in MASAP were more important to end users than we had anticipated. One undergraduate searcher used the "Special Features" field (SF =) to locate only those articles with photographs on her topic. (The ability to search captions was useful for this as well.) Standard Industrial Classification (SIC) codes were used by a faculty searcher from the School of Travel Industry Management to restrict her search to selected industries. Article Type (AT =) was used to eliminate reviews. More than one user searched for recipes, using the indexer-added word "recipe" in the title.

The search strategies used by the searchers are probably more influenced by the training session and the lab monitors than any other factor. Still, monitors tried to limit their participation to showing a searcher how to use a particular DIALOG command or feature to accomplish a strategy or goal only after it had been articulated by the searcher. The searcher had to know that linking concepts with a Boolean AND will retrieve more documents than with the (S) paragraph operator or (nN) operator, but when to use each and when to broaden or narrow a search was left to the searcher's discretion. Searchers were given a summary sheet of DIALOG commands plus the blue sheet for MASAP that lists all of the fields available for searching or displaying. Lab monitors helped searchers use any of these commands or fields only if they were asked specifically.

Among the main search strategies used by our users, linking concepts with (S) was the most frequent initial strategy, because that is the method recommended in the MASAP and DIALOG manuals and one of the methods that we taught. It is interesting to see the variations in strategy and approach after an initial failure (due to either too many or too few documents being retrieved).

In cases where there were zero documents retrieved after using (S) to link concepts, some users just assumed there were no documents and went on to another topic. Others were more tenacious and tried a variety of modifications until they got something. Although we did not study personality, our impression was that the number of modifications or tries to get something told us more about the searcher's basic personality than anything else. One particularly negative and pessimistic searcher almost always gave up if her initial strategy retrieved nothing (and rarely asked the lab monitor for help, usually not following the advice even when she did ask). Other, more positive personality types figured there must be something in the database if they would only find the right combination of commands and strategies.

Even when searchers went through many modifications of strategy to broaden their search statements, almost no one thought to add synonyms or change their initial search words. They did make liberal use of truncation to find variations in word stems, but they did not often OR together synonyms from different parts of the alphabet. DIALOG has no automatic synonym features, which might have been very useful for end users who think of a concept in the words they use, not in the variety of words that different authors of the articles might use.

Sometimes searchers vaguely expressed an expected hit rate ("there won't be much on this topic," "I'll be surprised if I find anything"), but no one expressed what "too many" documents would be. Still, almost everyone seemed to have his or her own notion of what constitutes too many and narrowed a search if the number retrieved was above this. Another reason for narrowing strategy was to improve precision after judging many of the articles retrieved to be false drops. Search strategy modifications to restrict retrieval at first often followed the pattern shown in the initial training session. After trying (S), they tried (10N), and finally a smaller N (e.g., 5 or 3N). After exhausting all the free text possibilities, some searchers looked for other effective ways to improve precision, most often settling on the use of value-added fields such as descriptors or SIC codes.

Restricting terms to the descriptor field (/DE) ended up being a fairly frequent tactic that surprised us. As mentioned above, searchers usually did this after an initial free text strategy retrieved many false drops. They noticed the descriptor field and asked about how to search it. Only after they asked did the monitors show a user the MASAP printed thesaurus and how to restrict a term to descriptors. Some users input thesaurus terms, but more often they free text searched the descriptor field to improve precision. After the initial use of this tactic, searchers started subsequent searches restricting to descriptors or codes. For example, after repeated false drops from searching the word "dance" in the text within the same paragraph or within N words of another concept, one user restricted the dance concept to danc?/de for each subsequent search on dances in many different countries.

In many cases there was a clear correlation between successful search strategy and purpose of the search. Attempting to retrieve full documents on a topic was most efficient when using descriptors for at least one of the topics. Interestingly, most searchers did not restrict their narrower concept (e.g., India) to descriptors, only their broader concept (e.g., dance). Even so, some relevant documents were missed by this technique. When one researcher discovered missed documents by other search techniques, she attributed this to indexer error.

What descriptor searching left out in more cases was partially relevant documents—those articles with a section, several paragraphs, or just a line or two of relevant information. Once a user latched on to the descriptor technique, he or she failed to see that it was less appropriate for other types of information needs. Since indexing is usually at the level of specificity of the document, an article about fine arts in India would correctly be indexed under fine arts, not under specific types of fine arts such as dance. Thus articles with extremely relevant portions are missed if the relevant portion is a part of a larger whole. In most of today's online systems it is expected that the user understand indexing policy and adjust search strategy according to results or need. We suspect that is asking too much of many end users (or many intermediaries). An end user should not be expected to think of all alternative search techniques when the system could point out possibilities or suggest alternatives.

Successful search strategies for partial document retrieval or fact retrieval should not rely on descriptors, but may very well make use of other value added fields if they describe parts of a document rather than only the document as a whole. For example, as mentioned above, one of our searchers used the Special Features (SF=) that indicate what types of graphics are included combined with a subject in a caption (/cp) when a single photograph is desired.

More likely, partial document retrieval relies on free text searching of the text. As mentioned earlier, a full range of proximity operators is necessary to adjust search results (although the system could be more helpful in suggesting broader or narrower strategies after an initial strategy fails).

Failure analysis, or examination of all of the false drops to see what is causing them, helps to provide insights into the unique characteristics of general literature full text databases that may adversely affect precision. False drops in many different questions occurred for some of the same basic reasons. Major causes of false drops are categorized in Table 7–10.

As expected, the peculiarities of the English language caused the most false drops. Many of these are due to word stems and might be solved if

Table 7–10
Causes of False Drops in MASAP

REASON	EXAMPLE
Word stems	fund? retrieved fundamental, fundamentalists, in addition to fund, funds, and funding
Figurative speech	dance retrieved "dance to the tune of"
Poetic language	Japanese(5N)danc? retrieved "leaves dancing and Japanese lanterns swaying"
Common noncontent words in a concept	grant got relevant documents, it also got Cary Grant
Unsolvable multi-meanings	Indians (American or Eastern), Aborigines (any native or Australian)
Inappropriate document types	Retrieving fiction when the purpose was fact retrieval or research
Inappropriate journals	Retrieving articles from Rolling Stone and Playboy when purpose was research, "right-wing" or other suspect sources for term papers or fact retrieval

the searchers had used the specified length-stemming options available on most online systems. These searchers used only the variable length truncation symbol (? on DIALOG.) One search that was looking for sources of funds, fund, or funding retrieved false drops with variations of the word fundamental.

The most common causes for false drops are uniquely attributable to the type of articles in MASAP. Articles are written in casual styles, almost all are nonscholarly, many are casual philosophizing, and even fiction is included. Figurative speech, idioms, and "poetic" language makes precision very difficult in full text databases. The Japanese forced to "dance to the tune of" retrieved many articles when searching for dance in Japan or Japanese dance. The poetic image of leaves dancing while Japanese lanterns swayed was another false drop. Inappropriate types of articles and inappropriate journal titles seemed to predict false drops. These are occupational hazards of searching such a database, but many could be eliminated with value-added categories either automatically invoked or invoked at the user's initiation. In addition word frequency algorithms as discussed in Chapter 6 would eliminate many of the figurative language problems.

Often the causes of false drops in magazine literature are unsolvable problems in today's information retrieval systems. Some unsolvable multi-meaning words encountered by our searchers were Indians (meaning American Indians and eastern Indians) and Aborigines used loosely to describe any native person but also used more correctly to mean natives of Australia (without necessarily also using Australia). If a misleading multi-meaning word is dropped to improve precision, recall would be adversely affected. If word frequency algorithms are used, partially relevant documents or relevant facts will be eliminated. Restricting a search to controlled vocabulary descriptors does not help for partial document retrieval, so the benefits of controlling language are not available for many valuable uses of full text. A detailed treatment of linguistic aspects of text retrieval or natural language processing are outside the scope of this book, but they offer insights into the ambiguities of language in automated systems.

As found in the other study on MASAP, grammar and punctuation are often predictors of false drops. DIALOG uses only the paragraph and BRS also recognizes the grammatical sentence, but most commercial online systems go no further in their use of punctuation for searching. Lists of words in a string separated by commas were found to be rarely related. Word frequency algorithms that take into account unique occurrences of words may help partial document retrieval.

In both pre- and post-interviews we asked all participants to tell us about their views of databases and the importance they felt information from databases had in their lives. What is particularly interesting about the results is that exposure to a full text database did not change their perceptions much, except in some cases to heighten their recognition that all electronic information is not equal. Especially for the faculty users, MASAP was not perceived as very useful. Faculty members wanted to use full text for their research interests, not so much for their personal needs. Full text of subject-specific, research-level materials would, of course, be of much more interest to them. In a sense it was heartening to see that the myth of the magic machine may no longer be valid. The content of the database was recognized as much more important than the technology that allowed it to be searched. Of course, academic faculty members are not the typical end users of a database such as MASAP, and they may have a more sophisticated view of information content versus information access systems than the typical user of general interest magazines.

Analysis of the three domains (affective, cognitive, sensorimotor) of human behavior shows an interplay of all three in the online search process. The interaction of the lab monitor and searcher played a significant role in this part of the experiment because the degree of inclusion or exclusion by the monitor when explaining or confirming a strategy is an index of affective communication.

Table 7–11 is a transcript of a portion of one search and shows the interaction between lab monitor and searcher as well as between the searcher and the system. All three behaviors are present. There is a fair amount of affective behavior in the form of stress in the search process. Most of it is generated by frustration of trying to remember commands,

Table 7-11
Search Transcript and Modes of Behavior

U: user; M: monitor	A:	affective behavior;
	C:	cognitive behavior;
	S:	sensorimotor
U: O.K That's good enough.	A:	satisfaction with hits
Allright then.	A:	orienting reflex
I want to print set 11 then set 12 with the words around it.	C:	states goal
and we'll take 50 words, huh?	C/A:	states strategy, request confirmation
(heavy sigh).. Is that good enough?	A/C:	stress, repeats confirmation request
Can we do that?	A:	repeats confirmation request
M: Yeah.	A:	confirmation
U: Well, this comes, it comes standard with 30 [words in a KWIC display] but I want to expand it a little bit.	C:	states strategic reasoning
M: Yeah.	A:	confirmation
(long pause)		
This one I'm looking up.	C:	offers command help
Try set.	C/S:	suggests command
Try type in the word set space.	C/S:	restates command
U: S-E-T space?	C/S:	requests confirmation, performs keying
M: Mm-hmm	A:	confirmation
K-W-I-C space.	C/S:	further states command
U: K? W?	A/C/S:	repeats command, requests confirmation, stress
M: I-C.	S:	restates command
U: K?W?I? space	S/C:	repeats command incorrectly, requests confirmation
M: "C" after the "I".	S:	re-phrases command
U: Hmm?	A/C:	vocal stress, confusion
M: Can you, can you add the C after I? Try C space.	C/S:	restates command
U: (Heavy sigh)	A:	vocal stress
M: And add C after I, see its KWIC.	S/C:	restates command
U: (Giddy voice) After I, let's try again.	A:	flood out
M: Let me do it. I'm not supposed to be doing it anyway, but I'm lazy.	A:	flood out, takes over keyboard.

Table 7–11 continued

U: (Laughing) Oh C! C! A little longer e!	A/C:	relief, insight
M: I set KWIC, so it should be typed with a C.	C:	states rationale
U: Oh, it is? O.K. cause she gave me, that's what she told me, was the K.	C:	justifying error
Oh, I see "K" is, contains one word is 30 just the K.		
But I put KWIC?	C:	requests clarification
M: Um.	A:	confirmation
U: Or, in other words, I don't understand what you're . . .	C:	repeats confirmation request, stress
M: What it means is that the K is going to give you 50 words cause I've changed it.	C:	states rationale
U: You've changed it. O.K.	A/C:	insight, relief

followed by an inability to get anticipated results, and for this user it is often directed at the lab monitor in the form of impatience. Reactions vary of course from searcher to searcher, but we found that searching is not just a logical, cognitive process implemented by sensorimotor skills of keyboarding. The affective reactions led to changes in strategies and, we suspect, satisfaction. Easy-to-remember commands, clear error messages or directions, and simplified keyboarding would help reduce the negative affective behavior and thus possibly increase one dimension of search satisfaction.

SUMMARY

Multititle magazine full text databases pose especially challenging problems. The writing style, length, and intended audience for the articles varies. Although no one search strategy is best for all questions, search results can be improved if users have a full range of search options. Categories for type of magazine, ability to use grammatical structure in searching, a variety of proximity operators, and value-added fields such as document type, descriptors, and so on are all useful for some searches. When each is appropriate depends in part on the purpose of the search: whether an end user is looking for a particular fact, a group of articles on a topic, or parts of documents.

In studying the behavior of end users as they search, it was found that end users exhibit a wide range of behaviors when searching and searching is not just a sensorimotor and logical cognitive process. Emotional, affective behavior interacts with the other domains. All these factors warrant further study for ways in which, this information can be incorporated into system design.

NOTES

1. Carol Tenopir and Man Evena Shu, "Magazines in Full Text: Uses and Search Strategies," *Online Review* 13, No. 2. (1989): 107–118; and C. Tenopir, "Users and Uses of Full Text Databases," *Proceedings of the International Online Meeting, December 1988, London, England* (Oxford: Learned Information, 1988), pp. 263–270.

2. R. Pagell, "Searching Full-Text Periodicals: How Full Is Full?" *Database* 10 (October 1987): 33–38.

3. Carol Tenopir, "Search Strategies for Full Text Databases," *Proceedings of the American Society for Information Science Annual Meeting, October 1988, Atlanta, Georgia* (Medford, N.J.: Learned Information, 1988), pp. 80–86.

4. F. W. Lancaster, *Information Retrieval Systems: Characteristics, Testing and Evaluation*, 2d ed. (New York: John Wiley and Sons, 1979).

5. C. Tenopir, "Search Strategies for Full Text Databases," p. 85.

6. For more information see A. Bookstein, "Probabilistic Retrieval and Fuzzy Sets," (review), *Annual Review of Information Science and Technology* 20 (1985).

7. Carol Tenopir and Man Evena Shu, "Magazines in Full Text: Uses and Search Strategies," *Online Review* 13, No. 2 (1989): 107–118.

8. Pagell, "Searching Full Text Databases."

9. Ibid.

10. C. Tenopir, D. Nahl-Jakobovits, and D. L. Howard, "Magazines Online: An Investigation of Users and Uses of Full Text," in *Proceedings of the Annual Meeting of the American Society for Information Science, November 1989, Washington, D.C.* (Medford, N.J.: Learned Information, 1989), 172–176.

11. K. Anders Ericsson and Herbert A. Simon, *Protocol Analysis: Verbal Reports as Data* (Cambridge, Mass.: MIT Press, 1984).

12. Nicholas J. Belkin, "Discourse Analysis of Human Information Interaction for Specification of Human-Computer Information Interaction," *The Canadian Journal of Information Science* 12, No. 3/4 (1987): 31–42.

13. Tenopir and Shu, "Magazines in Full Text."

14. Tenopir, Nahl-Jakobovits, and Howard, "Magazines Online."

8

Implications of Research for Searchers

Most of the research projects described in Chapters 4, 5, 6, and 7 were conducted on real databases loaded on actual online systems. Studying a real database on an existing system has the advantage of allowing researchers to formulate immediate practical suggestions for online searchers, for database producers, and for online system vendors. Suggestions for the first group, online searchers, are covered in this chapter; the next two groups are addressed in Chapter 9.

Using actual databases and systems has some disadvantages, however. In an experimental environment it is easier to control and alter system design features to test them as variables in retrieval performance. The researcher has more control over extraneous variables and is not as bound by system constraints imposed by tradition, hardware, or software. With real system studies it is more difficult to generalize findings from one database or one system to other databases or systems. All the conclusions and recommendations of this and the next chapter come from the practical research arena and attempt to cover common generalizable ground. Sometimes results of studies disagree, perhaps because of inevitable variations due to different types of full text documents.

Suggestions for strategies that are generally useful for full text searching fit into the following four categories: (1) proximity and logical operators, (2) word forms and synonyms, (3) field specification (including controlled vocabulary searching), and (4) display of search results.

PROXIMITY AND LOGICAL OPERATORS

Even though many of the user manuals for full text searching recommend always using the "same paragraph" operator to link concepts (rather than the Boolean AND), research suggests that there is probably no one best search method for all purposes. Tenopir concluded that same paragraph (or within approximately twenty to forty words on systems that do not recognize grammatical paragraphs) probably offers the best overall balance between recall and precision in many searches, but other methods are useful as well.[1] In *Harvard Business Review* SAME offered a high recall, low precision search method.[2] Love and Garson found that the same paragraph could yield high precision searches in chemical journals if strategies and word choice are carefully planned in advance.[3]

Searchers should be prepared to use the full range of proximity operators available on a system in order to impose some control over recall and precision. Shu found that the more restrictive "within the same sentence" or within ten words provided better precision, but lower recall than the same paragraph operator.[4] If a few highly relevant documents are sought, the more restrictive operators can be helpful. However, Abbott and Smith suggest not becoming too restrictive.[5] They found that over 50 percent of the relevant documents retrieved using the SAME operator were lost when the search was reexecuted using the WITH operator. Shu also found that the operators that use the grammatical structure of sentences (e.g., the BRS WITH for sentences) result in higher precision than operators that simply specify a certain number of intervening words (e.g., the DIALOG (nN) operator or LEXIS/NEXIS w/n operator).

Even the intuitive relationship between narrower operator and higher precision is not infallible, however. Tenopir found that for some questions in Magazine ASAP (5N) actually had lower precision than (10N) or (S) because relevant documents were eliminated while false drops were retained.[6] News stories or newswires seem to pose special problems because unrelated ideas are strung together in close proximity. Experience in a particular database or type of literature will help identify good strategies for that file.

Although many searchers have recommended using the Boolean AND rarely and only with caution, it has been found to be a useful strategy in some cases. Tenopir found it often retrieved partially relevant documents that were not retrieved by other methods because major concepts of a magazine article are not necessarily repeated in every paragraph.[7] This might suggest that when one search concept is expected to be much broader than another, the AND operator may be helpful. Blair and Maron found that AND yielded acceptable precision levels when many different concepts were linked together and when a conservative approach is applied to synonym development.[8] It doesn't make sense to use a highly restrictive operator such as "within N words" or "within a sentence" if several concepts are linked.

Whatever operator is used to link concepts in a full text search, the many research studies imply that a searcher should be ready to change methods interactively as needed. If too many documents are retrieved by AND or by the SAME paragraph operator, than a narrower strategy should be used. Conversely, if too few documents are retrieved by "within 10 or under words" or "within the same sentence," a broader method should be tried. Systems that allow previously created set numbers to be relinked with new connectors are especially useful for this. Searchers should be prepared to use a highly interactive approach to full text searching because there are so many variables in length of documents, length of paragraphs, writing style, word use, and so on. Perhaps even more than with bibliographic searching, users cannot expect 100 percent recall or 100 percent precision with any search method in full text searching. Full text online searching is not an exact science, especially if the full text contains documents from a variety of sources. Results can be improved (or made worse) but only rarely can they be made perfect.

WORD FORMS AND SYNONYMS

The power of free text searching is offset by the need to anticipate all possible word forms or synonyms that may be used by authors to describe a concept. One of the simplest ways to improve retrieval with natural language searching is always to remember to search for variant word endings such as singulars and plurals.[9] Unfortunately only a few systems help the searcher with even this simple form of word control. If you are searching most systems, it is up to you to remember to use that system's truncation character. Specified length truncation will allow you to retrieve singulars and plurals without retrieving a lot of additional unanticipated words and should be used as much as possible in full text.

Searching for all possible synonyms that different authors may use is more difficult, as found by Blair and Maron, and Klinkroth.[10] Free text equivalency dictionaries for subject-content words are not common in today's online systems, so the burden falls on the searcher. The use of printed vocabulary aids such as a general thesaurus and dictionaries before going online will help a searcher prepare. Pressure on database producers or online system vendors to develop better automatically invoked aids may ultimately result in online systems that help a searcher more, but for now vocabulary development is almost totally your responsibility. The one exception is automatic equivalencies for spelling variations, common abbreviations, and dates offered by NEXIS and LEXIS (and to a lesser degree by BRS). (These were described in Chapter 3.)

Several studies commented on the typographical or spelling errors found in full text databases.[11] This adds another dimension to word-form control because not even the most conscientious searcher can anticipate all misspelled words in a database. When you use the Boolean AND operator, misspellings usually won't make too much difference to your search results because the word may be spelled correctly elsewhere in the text, but if you are searching for several concepts within the same paragraph, sentence, or within N words, the misspelling may eliminate relevant or partially relevant documents. In the few systems that offer word-occurrence data, misspellings will adversely affect the utility of those features. There is no one solution to errors in a database. As a searcher you may choose to use a command to view words in the inverted index if such a feature is available, you may try several different approaches to the same problem if you are trying to retrieve more documents, or you may choose not to reuse databases that seem of particularly low quality.

FIELD SPECIFICATION

Many full text databases do not offer any choice in search method except free text searching of the text. Others allow segment searching, so that you can specify fields such as titles, citations, and perhaps abstracts. Still others provide controlled vocabulary descriptors as an alternative search technique. Searchers must know before going online what fields are available and how the system will allow them to search these fields. The more options available, the more control the searcher has over the search process and resultant success (but also the more confusing the development of strategy becomes).

The Cleveland, Cleveland, and Wise study found that search results were better for both recall and precision when searching on words from titles, abstracts, and references than when searching on texts.[12] Most other researchers recommend searching full texts in a free text mode when looking for narrow or specific concepts, or for new concepts, jargon, or fads, but relying on other fields such as title, abstract, and descriptors (if available) for broader concepts.[13] The utility of titles varies with the type of literature and subject area.[14]

The relative value of controlled vocabulary descriptors formed the basis for many of the research projects described in this book and is a large part of Chapter 5. Consensus of recent studies seems to be that a combination of controlled vocabulary and free text searching on texts provides the most satisfactory results in the greatest number of searches.[15] A searcher may choose to use a controlled term if available to describe a broad concept and link it with a free text search of a more restrictive concept. Controlled vocabulary might be used to improve precision if an initial strategy is yielding too many false drops from the text, such as happens when a word has several different meanings. Searchers are recommended to use appropriate vocabulary aids such as thesauri for the databases they search regularly.[16]

DISPLAY OF SEARCH RESULTS

Perhaps more than any other type of searching, your choice of display format with full text is an integral part of the search strategy process. Few searchers want to read online every word of any document retrieved, and there is usually a cost associated with full document display. Searchers need to be able to judge relevance quickly and efficiently.

Many of the studies reported in this book mentioned the necessity of some kind of key-word-in-context (KWIC) viewing feature. In many cases only those portions of the document that have the search words need to be displayed for a searcher to judge relevance. KWIC displays are approached differently on different systems, from full paragraph display to a certain number of words surrounding the text, but all are useful. KWIC generally does not work if you have linked concepts with the Boolean AND, so that an alternative display format may be needed. Tenopir, Nahl-Jakobovits, and Howard found that better, more flexible KWIC features are needed, but within the constraints of today's online systems, viewing a combination of the appropriate KWIC format in the system and title or title and citation makes sense both for relevance judging of whole or partial documents and for fact retrieval.[17]

Communications software that allows you to scroll backwards in text is particularly important to full text searching. Most systems do not let you change your viewing option or move forward and back dynamically in documents, thus making reading or browsing online difficult. The scrolling capabilities offered by many communications software packages allow you to get around some of the built-in viewing limitations of the online systems.

Only a few online systems allow you to use word occurrence information, but such features are especially useful. Ro and others discussed the value of such information, and called for more systems to add occurrence features.[18] If you are searching on BRS, for example, you may ask to view an occurrence table of search words to help you to judge relevance without even looking at the texts you searched.[19] You can then print HITS (the BRS KWIC format) to narrow down relevance assessment further. (Be careful, because the BRS occurrence table does not work if you used the Boolean AND to link concepts in the text.) VU/TEXT will order document displays by occurrence information, thus saving the extra step.

When a KWIC feature is not available or if you used a strategy with the Boolean AND that negated its utility, viewing an abstract, if available, can help you to judge relevance at a lower cost than browsing complete texts. Unfortunately, some database producers overlook this use of abstracts when they decide to eliminate them from full text files.

SUMMARY

The most generalizable advice about full text searching is to be prepared to vary your approach and strategy depending on the purpose of your search, the database you are searching, and your initial success or failure. Beginning with a middle-ground strategy such as same paragraph may offer the best balance between recall and precision, but a narrower proximity operator can usually be used to improve precision or the Boolean AND to increase recall when the concepts are of unequal weight.

Full text requires using all word enhancement features available to you, including truncation, synonym development with Boolean ORs, viewing inverted indexes online, and others. Searching on value-added fields can provide a cost-effective way to retrieve some documents.

Document display should be approached flexibly as well, viewing search words in context in conjunction with titles or citations and using communications software that allows scrolling as necessary. Although most of today's online systems are not designed as well as they could be for full text search and display, and much of the problem of coping with variations in language and texts will fall on the searcher, the searcher who uses all the tools available online and varies the approach dynamically will achieve good search results in today's full text systems.

NOTES

1. Carol Tenopir, "Search Strategies for Full Text Databases," in *Proceedings of the Annual Meeting of the American Society for Information Science, Atlanta, Ga., November 1988* (Medford, N.J.: Learned Information, 1988), pp. 80–86.

2. Carol Tenopir, "Retrieval Performance in a Full Text Journal Article Database" (Ph.D. dissertation, University of Illinois, 1984).

3. Richard A. Love and Lorrin R. Garson, "Precision in Searching the Full-Text Database—ACS Journals Online," in *Proceedings of the 6th National Online Meeting, New York, May 1985* (Medford, N.J.: Learned Information, 1985), pp. 273–282.

4. Carol Tenopir and Man Evena Shu, "Magazines in Full Text: Uses and Search Strategies," *Online Review* 13, No. 2 (1989): 107–118.

5. John P. Abbott and Charles R. Smith, "Full-Text and Bibliographic ACS Databases: Rivals or Companions?" *Proceedings of the 6th National Online Meeting, New York, May 1985* (Medford, N.J.: Learned Information, 1985), pp. 5–9.

6. Carol Tenopir, "Search Strategies for Full Text Databases."

7. Ibid.

8. David C. Blair and M. E. Maron, "An Evaluation of Retrieval Effectiveness for a Full-Text Document-Retrieval System," *Communication of the ACM* 28, No. 3 (1985): 289–299.

9. C. W. Cleverdon, J. Mills, and E. M. Keen, *Factors Determining the Performance of Indexing Systems*, 2 vols. (Cranfield, England: College of Aeronautics, 1966); J. E. Parker, "Preliminary Assessment of the Comparative Efficiencies of

an SDI System Using Controlled or Natural Language for Retrieval," *Program* 5 (1979): 26–34; and T. M. Aitchison et al., *Comparative Evaluation of Index Language. Part II: Results* (London, England: The Institutions of Electrical Engineers, 1970).

10. Blair and Maron, "Evaluation of Retrieval Effectiveness"; and Margaret Klinkroth, "Full-Text Databases in the Health Sciences," *Medical Reference Services Quarterly* 5, No. 3 (1986): 1–15.

11. For example see Blair and Maron, "Evaluation of Retrieval Effectiveness."

12. Donald B. Cleveland, Ana D. Cleveland, and Olga B. Wise, "Less Than Full Text Indexing Using a Non-Boolean Searching Model," *Journal of the American Society for Information Science* 35 (January/February 1984): 19–28.

13. Klinkroth, "Full-Text Databases"; and Dolores P. Huth, "ASAP—Index Access to Full Text," in *Proceedings of the 6th National Online Meeting, New York, May 1985* (Medford, N.J.: Learned Information, 1985), pp. 227–232.

14. Tenopir, "Retrieval Performance in a Full Text Journal Article Database."

15. Pauline Duckitt, "The Value of Controlled Indexing Systems in Online Full Text Databases," in *Proceedings of the 5th International Online Information Meeting, London, December 1981* (Oxford, England: Learned Information, Ltd., 1981), pp. 447–453; Ernest Perez, "Text Enhancement: Controlled Vocabulary vs. Free Text," *Special Libraries* 73, No. 3 (July 1982): 183–192; and James A. Sprowl, "WESTLAW vs LEXIS: Computer Assisted Legal Research Comes of Age," *Program* 15, No. 3 (July 1981): 132–141.

16. Don Swanson, "Searching Natural Language Text by Computer," *Science* 132 (October 1960): 1099–1104.

17. Carol Tenopir, Diane Nahl-Jakobovits, and Dara Lee Howard, "Magazines Online." An Investigation of Users and Uses of Full Text, in *Proceedings of the Annual Meeting of the American Society for Information Science, Washington, D.C., November 1989* (Medford, N.J.: Learned Information, 1989), pp. 172–176.

18. Jung Soon Ro, "An Evaluation of the Applicability of Ranking Algorithms to Improving the Effectiveness of Full Text Retrieval." (Ph.D. dissertation, Indiana University, 1985).

19. Klinkroth, "Full Text Databases."

9

Implications of Research for Database Producers and Online Vendors

The results of the many research projects on full text databases reported in this book suggest ways that database producers and system vendors can improve their products for full text retrieval. Many of these improvements will not be costly or involve drastic changes; yet, they will allow more satisfactory use of online full text. Others are more profound given the design constraints of today's major commercial online systems.

Some of the recommendations discussed in this chapter apply to database producers, some to system vendors, and some to both. Since the separation between producers and vendors is not always clear (and they may indeed be the same organization), all suggestions will be discussed together. Ultimately it is the complete product that is of interest to the user—that is the synergistic relationship between the text and the software that allows it to be accessed. Suggestions fit into the following nine categories: (1) free text proximity operators, (2) value-added fields, (3) ranking and word occurrence, (4) automatic language enhancement, (5) parsing rules, (6) quality control, (7) database content, (8) display features, and (9) user training and help.

FREE TEXT PROXIMITY OPERATORS

The possibility of searching every word in a complete text is the distinguishing power of full text searching. It means that partial documents or peripheral material in a larger document is now available to users, where once only subjects describing a document as a whole were retrievable. This could mean increased use of a database producer's product. Free text searching on full texts is only as good as the range of operators allowed by the online system, however. With so many words available as retrieval points, reliance on the Boolean AND operator to link concepts often causes an unacceptable number of false drops. Several of the studies described in this book show that good full text searching must make use of a variety of other proximity operators.

An operator to specify adjacency is common in commercial online systems and was assumed to be necessary in almost all the studies reported here. Concepts in the English language cannot all be described by uniterms, so that adjacency operators are an essential part of specifying multiword concepts. Most of the studies that have examined proximity operators have done so to determine how best to link separate concepts, comparing retrieval performance of a variety of operators.

As Zuga pointed out, a full range of proximity operators is necessary to allow users to take complete advantage of full text searching.[1] Online systems must allow choices and allow users to broaden or narrow their searches at will by exploiting various characteristics of full text documents. These include specifying terms within a specified number of words, within a sentence, within a paragraph, within a section or chapter, within a subsection, within a field, and within a subfield. Tenopir tested and found valuable the ability to choose between same paragraph and within N word operators.[2] No one method is always best. Shu compared searching different methods and found the ability to use the grammatical structure of a document (paragraphs and sentences) valuable.[3] Having a full range of Boolean and proximity operators, including many that exploit text structure, is the key to maximizing success by the greatest number of searchers.

Additional operators that use a document's natural structure should be added to systems. Within the same section, subsection, or chapter would be a natural extension of paragraph and sentence searching. Within a user-specified number of paragraphs or user-specified number of sentences or within a specified section such as introduction, conclusions or methodology would allow users to take advantage of writing style and document format.

A necessary component of this variety of proximity operators is the ability to build sets and modify previously created sets. A user who is not satisfied with the results of linking words within the same sentence, for example, should be able to reuse set numbers and modify the connecting operator without reentering all search terms. Flexibility, a wide range of options, and ease for users to modify and remodify are essential components for success in the highly interactive process of full text searching.[4]

VALUE-ADDED FIELDS

Value-added fields are any fields added to a text beyond the bibliographic citation. They usually involve some intellectual processing and serve to describe various components of what the document is about or other characteristics of the document. The most common subject-related value added fields are controlled vocabulary descriptors, enriched titles, abstracts, or classification codes. Other types of value added fields might categorize the type of document, intellectual level of a document, quality of the information in a document and other assessments. Standardization of information is a part of the value-added process, but intellectual analysis is important to the definition as well.

Value added fields add expense for the database producer and/or the system vendor and create a time lag before the materials are available to users. Many producers and vendors believe that full text databases are better searched free text and that value added fields are unnecessary when a full text is searchable. Several of the studies reported in this book examined the relative contribution of free text searching and searching subject-related value added fields. Others monitored the use of free text and value-added fields as end users searched databases. Together they make a strong case for the importance in many instances of some kind of intellectual analysis in addition to free text searching of full texts.

Subject-Related Value-Added

Markey, Atherton, and Newton, and Calkins, and Tenopir all found that free text searching of full texts was better for higher recall searches, but controlled vocabulary yielded higher precision on the average.[5] A combination of controlled vocabulary and free text was often best, or at least the ability to choose and use different methods for different situations is desirable. Controlled vocabulary searching can provide a cost-effective search when a user wants a few highly relevant documents, and it often contributes some unique documents not retrieved in a full text search.

Tenopir, Nahl-Jakobovits, and Howard discovered that end users used descriptor searching to modify search strategy when they were trying to eliminate false drops.[6] Descriptors are of greatest use when the purpose of a search is to retrieve a set of complete articles on a topic, since descriptors describe the document as a whole. Users liked the ability to control the search and use descriptors for some concepts, and free text for others. They not only were able to eliminate the frustrations of an unacceptable number of false drops that sometimes occurs in full text searching, but they also felt more in control of the search process and better about the results. Users need various options to allow them to control and choose the best search method appropriate to their search purpose.

Full text searching is good for retrieving specific concepts within broader documents. Lancaster and Perez thus suggest adding controlled terms from a broad controlled vocabulary language to complement specific concepts better retrieved by free text searching of full texts.[7] The hierarchical concept code system is another broad subject indexing approach used in full text drug databases.[8]

Although they provide a less obvious benefit than descriptors, other subject-related value added fields were found to be useful in some of the studies described here. Cleveland, Cleveland, and Wise found searching from words in titles, abstracts, and references together gave better recall and precision than full text searching.[9] Stein and associates pointed out the value of searching summaries and descriptions.[10] Zuga recommends abstracts and controlled vocabulary searching as filters for effective searching for major concepts.[11] Abstracts are also useful for relevance judgment. Tenopir observed the value of title enrichment in nontechnical magazine articles (see Chapters 5 and 7). End users also used Standard Industrial Classification (SIC) codes available for some business sources.

Other such subject-related fields, if available, would undoubtedly be used by searchers to enhance the process of searching. They all provide options to searchers to allow strategy to be modified for the best results. Full text alone does not provide the best strategy for every purpose or comprehensive retrieval. The database producer must weigh the benefits to the user and higher level of user satisfaction with the high cost and possible time-lag from adding such fields.

Nonsubject Value-Added

Fields that categorize and describe characteristics of documents were found to be of use or potential use in several studies. Tenopir noted the value of type-of-article and type-of-magazine categories in a mixed-title database.[12] These categories should be preset options for users to select, but users should be able to designate their own categories as well. In another study, Tenopir, Nahl-Jakobovits, and Howard found the "special features" field of Magazine ASAP to be useful to users who wanted to locate something specific like a photograph or chart.[13] Such fields allow a variety of uses of full text online and increase the potential of the file. All value-added fields add options for users and increased chances of success for a wider variety of purposes.

RANKING AND WORD OCCURRENCE

According to Tenopir, if a search word occurs ten times or more in a document, that document is three times more likely to be relevant than would be expected by the average precision for all documents retrieved.[14] If a search term or phrase occurs in four or more textual paragraphs, that document is slightly more than four times as likely to be relevant than is a document in which the phrase occurs only once. These findings support the suggestion by Weinberg and Cunningham that word occurrence patterns such as the number of times words occur and where they occur do assist precision.[15] These relevance-judging aids should be available as a minimum on all online systems that offer full text. They can be included as an occurrence table like BRS, but that is cumbersome and costly for the user. Better yet is a rank ordering such as that available on VU/TEXT. Word occurrences are not infallible guides to relevance, however. Additional automatic precision aids need to be developed and added to commercial systems as the full text databases get bigger. Relevance feedback as offered on Dowquest may improve performance.

The application of ranking algorithms originally suggested for automatic indexing was reported by Ro to increase the retrieval effectiveness of full text databases.[16] The effectiveness of ranking algorithms examined varied with similarity measures and document-term weighting algorithms. In Ro's study, the use of ranking algorithms achieved significantly higher levels of precision than full text searching without the use of such algorithms. The use of such algorithms in commercial online systems could improve the low precision of Boolean AND searching to equal or surpass the precision resulting from same paragraph searching and achieve a corresponding increase in recall.

Adding a single algorithm may be a simple solution but will not achieve the best results. Ro found that the relative performance of different algorithms depended on the level of recall and on the search strategy. Database vendors need to work to find the most appropriate algorithms to particular databases, search purposes, and search strategies.

AUTOMATIC LANGUAGE ENHANCEMENT

Almost all the studies reported here found full text searching offers advantages in comprehensive retrieval and retrieves documents or parts of documents that could not be retrieved by any other method. One of the biggest problems with natural language searching, however, is the inconsistencies of word use and word forms in the English language. Controlled vocabulary descriptors offer some control of both, but only at the complete document level. Research shows that online systems with full texts must offer automatic language consistency and enhancements for words throughout texts as well.

Even in early studies such as the second Cranfield study, Parker, and Aitchison and associates found that natural language searching performs best when some level of elementary control, such as consistent word endings of singulars and plurals, is imposed on words.[17] LEXIS and NEXIS both offer such a feature as described in Chapter 3, but even such a simple automatic aid is not common on other systems. Truncation is common on all systems and full control over truncation is an essential minimum requirement as Jackson pointed out, but on most of today's systems truncation must be invoked by a user.[18] Using automatic singulars and plurals puts the responsibility on the system instead. For maximum flexibility users should be able to turn off any automatic features if they desire.

Another automatic language enhancement offered by LEXIS, NEXIS, and BRS (to a lesser degree) is a variant spelling capability. Automatic searching of abbreviations/acronyms, British/American spelling variations, or variations in transliteration seems an obvious full text search feature but is not yet widely available. One of the studies by Tenopir discussed in Chapter 7 found that end users do not routinely think of word variants; they think of a concept by the terms they use and do not try to second guess authors by stringing together lots of variants with the Boolean OR. A user-invoked (or automatic until a user turns it off) spelling equivalency feature would probably make same sentence or within N word searching more successful.

A more difficult automatic word enhancement feature suggested by the research reported here is automatic synonym development. The Tenopir study cited above found that synonyms were not often used by end users unless they were prompted to think of other terms. Blair and Maron described the difficulty of thinking of all terms or phrases useful for designating a concept in legal texts.[19] Jackson suggests a minimum capability of viewing synonyms online, with automatic searching of synonyms desirable.[20]

Synonym searching would require a fairly labor-intensive startup and maintenance by database producers and online systems. It would mean linking general thesauri or dictionaries to online files and would require some system capabilities to allow user override if retrieval was too large or if multiple meanings caused false drops. It is an area that, except at the fairly trivial word-equivalency level offered by LEXIS, NEXIS, and BRS, has not been fully explored in online systems.

PARSING RULES

How words or phrases are extracted by an online system's program for machine indexing (parsing) was found in several studies to impact full text searching success. Ro found that the parsing rule for stopwords on BRS increased the number of nonrelevant documents retrieved, especially for word adjacency.[21] On BRS stopwords are not counted when other words are assigned a sequential placement number during preparation of the inverted index. Because of this rule, documents with sentences such as "... executives hard at work," "... if you try hard and work diligently," or "... is hard at work" were retrieved with the search term "hard adj work."

Parsing rules for punctuation also impact retrieval. Shu compared the impact on BRS and DIALOG and found that parsing rules and search features such as truncation go hand-in-hand.[22] Searchers must remember to use truncation to retrieve possessives if apostrophes are ignored in parsing as they are in BRS. If they are treated as blanks, as they are by DIALOG, nonsensical entries in the inverted index (e.g., s) will result. Ro found that when punctuation is ignored, false drops can occur in full text (i.e., "us" retrieves "U.S." and "us"). On the other hand, selective text editing of punctuation as done by BRS results in Oahu's being parsed as Oahus, instead of Oahu and S as happens on DIALOG. Ignoring hyphens adversely impacts searching molecular formulas as well.[23]

Typically online systems ignore most punctuation when word-parsing free text fields such as full texts. In most instances this is what is wanted, but Tenopir found that punctuation can sometimes be an important clue to false drops.[24] Concepts separated by a string of commas, for example, are often unrelated topics discussed in a news summary story. Allowing selective use of punctuation and grammar is not an easy feature to implement within the design of today's online systems, but it could be an important user-option relevance device.

QUALITY CONTROL

Not surprisingly, several studies commented on the typographical errors found in some full texts. Several end users in the Tenopir, Nahl-Jakobovits, and Howard study commented in passing on the poor quality of input, but didn't notice if it had an impact on retrieval.[25] Such errors are not only unsightly, but they affect retrieval. Blair and Maron noted that relevant documents were not retrieved because of typographical errors within the database.[26] They identified certain categories of misspellings, such as letter transpositions, that could be easily cleaned up by system vendors. Spelling check programs are commonplace these days and could catch most of the typographical errors in new input at either the database producer end or online vendor. Ro's study showed that exact spelling is required not only to locate the word or document containing the word, but also to weight the significance of the word as a content word in application of ranking algorithms.[27]

DATABASE CONTENT

The content of a database is typically the responsibility of the database producer, but it may also be influenced by the online vendor. As Pagell and Shu both found, the same database on two or three different online systems may contain different journals and/or a different number of articles.[28] At a minimum this should be conveyed clearly to users. Contents of multititle databases should be easy to find online and in printed documentation, including editorial policies that exclude or include certain parts of printed equivalents.

User studies consistently show the desire for more titles and more articles online. Abbott and Smith found that users wanted more years of coverage online, suggesting that database producers should reassess the value of retrospective information.[29] They also found that users wanted a greater variety of document types mixed together in full text online. Instead of having an online database correspond to a journal or a set of journals, more multitype products should be developed to meet full research needs. This practice has long been common in bibliographic databases where references to articles, dissertations, research reports, and the like are mixed together. More imaginative creation of combination full text databases is called for.

Multipublisher databases may also be an alternative to control the limited coverage of full text databases. ACS journals was moved from BRS to STN International with a new name (Chemical Journals of the ACS) and became a member of the multipublisher database, Chemical Journals Online described in Chapter 2.[30]

Users also consistently complain about what is not included in full text databases. The lack of graphics has been a continuing concern, including charts, tables, photographs, and other illustrative material.[31] Some of these are not difficult to convert and load online, and more database producers should make the effort to add tabular material. The inclusion of illustrations such as photographs that are constrained by hardware and transmission speeds may need to be offered first on optical disk products. Several database producers have already developed their first CD-ROM texts with graphics, a trend that must take high priority for user satisfaction.

DISPLAY FEATURES

Appropriate and flexible display features are as important to successful full text searching as good search and retrieval features. Even within the constraints of limited graphics capability, relatively slow online transmission speeds, and limited quality hardware at the searcher's end, online systems can provide a range of display options that will enhance the full text experience. Zuga points out that these aesthetic considerations can make the difference in user acceptance.[32]

The ability to view search words in context (key-words-in-context) is a minimum function required with full text searching. Search terms should be highlighted as well. Shu compared the key-word-in-context features of BRS and DIALOG.[33] She found BRS's display of full paragraphs to be easier to use for relevance judgment and more aesthetically pleasing. One study reported in Chapter 7 found that end users changed the window on DIALOG's KWIC but still wanted to view additional words or partial paragraphs at times. Dynamic KWIC features were recommended, specifically the ability to change the amount of text viewed within a certain document at will without interrupting the viewing process. Users had a variety of individual viewing needs and desires that were not fully met with existing search system software.

Zuga, Shu, and Brunelle taken together offer a shopping list of display features that can be implemented even within the constraints of online technology.[34] These include special treatment of headings and subheadings, blank lines between paragraphs, highlighted key words, clearly labeled fields, and other features. CD-ROM technology offers more opportunities for enhanced display features if full texts are designed from the beginning to emphasize the aesthetic aspects. Aesthetic considerations are noticed by end users and may play a role in acceptance of full text products.

USER TRAINING AND HELP

One aspect of user training is the friendliness and appropriateness of the system interface and whether an online system should be query driven or menu driven. Full text databases are most often marketed to the end user who may not be accustomed to the query language of any online system. On the other hand, they may soon find restriction to menu options too confusing, especially in full text searching. Research by Watters and associates, and Geller and Lesk suggests that a combination system may be best, and searchers should be allowed to choose their desired method of interaction.[35]

Another aspect of user training is the database documentation provided by either the database producer, the online system, or both. User manuals should stress the importance of using a variety of synonyms and search strategies depending on the search purpose. Users should be encouraged to alter search strategy interactively as needed. Recommending a single preferred method for linking concepts (i.e., same paragraph) does not provide a user with all of the information needed to achieve success in searching. Proximity operators could be presented as a continuum with emphasis on selecting a narrower or broader connector as needed to modify results. This continuum and choice could be offered online as well as presented in written documentation.

Many of the studies reported here have emphasized the need for varying search strategy according to purpose, topic, or type of literature. Other studies demonstrated the value of interactive modification as needed. End users cannot be expected to exploit these capabilities fully without some online guidance. Database producers and online vendors must work together to develop expert-like systems that will prompt or initiate modifications in search strategy based on user feedback.

User training and online help ultimately do not mean training the user to cope with all of the limitations and negatives of a database or online system. Unfortunately, that is what happens most often. Only highly motivated users (such as legal experts and information intermediaries) can be expected to put up with unfriendly systems and all the burden of search strategy development. Better, more helpful full text systems can be developed because a growing body of research is now available to guide database producers and online vendors. The results should be increased use of the products, greater satisfaction with the results, and more time spent online.

COSTS

A final word to database producers and online system vendors concerns costs of full text databases. User studies by Durkin and associates, Tenopir and associates and others have found that many users or potential users are inhibited by connect-time pricing algorithms and costs that are perceived to be too high.[36] Costs approaching $100 per hour were cited in several studies as restricting some potential types of use for full texts online, such as browsing. Others said they would not pay those kinds of costs unless they could not get the information any other way (and sometimes not even then).

Clearly a database producer and online vendor must make adequate revenues with their full text databases. Sometimes the costs are borne by information facilitators, sometimes by ultimate consumers of research. Willingness of institutions such as libraries to subsidize the costs is an important part of the growing number of CD-ROM products. The widespread use of certain types of full text, notably legal materials, shows that if there is strong motivation to use the texts together with an opportunity to pass on research costs to clients, use is less cost-sensitive.

Many more full text databases are not yet being used to their full potential, however, at least in part due to costs. The primary target audience of full texts online are end users in their offices or in their homes. Often they must bear the cost of database searching. Database producers and online vendors would do well to consider offering different pricing algorithms and lower overall costs to attract more members of this essential user group.

NOTES

1. Connie Zuga, "Full Text Databases: Design Considerations for the Database Vendor," in *Proceedings of the 7th International Online Information Meeting, 1983* (Oxford, England: Learned Information, Ltd., 1983), pp. 427–434.

2. Carol Tenopir, "Search Strategies for Full Text Databases," in *Proceedings of the Annual Meeting of the American Society for Information Science, 1988, Atlanta, GA* (Medford, N.J.: Learned Information, 1988), pp. 80–86.

3. Carol Tenopir and Man Evena Shu, "Magazines in Full Text: Uses and Search Strategies," *Online Review* 13, No. 2, (1989): 107–118.

4. Gary Marchionini, "Information-Seeking Strategies of Novices Using a Full-Text Electronic Encyclopedia," *Journal of the American Society for Information Science* 40, No. 1 (1989): 54–66.

5. Karen Markey, Pauline Atherton, and Claudia Newton, "An Analysis of Controlled Vocabulary and Free Text Search Statements in Online Searches," *Online Review* 4, No. 3 (1982): 225–236; Mary L. Calkins, "Free Text or Controlled Vocabulary? A Case History Step-by-Step Analysis . . . Plus Other Aspects of Search Strategy," *Database* 3 (1980): 53–67; and Carol Tenopir, "Retrieval Performance in a Full Text Journal Article Database" (Ph.D. dissertation, University of Illinois, 1984).

6. Carol Tenopir, Diane Nahl-Jakobovits, and Dara Lee Howard, "Magazines Online: An Investigation of Users and Uses of Full Text," in *Proceedings of the Annual Meeting of the American Society for Information Science, 1989* (Medford, N.J.: Learned Information, 1989), pp. 172–76.

7. F. Wilfred Lancaster, *Information Retrieval Systems: Characteristics, Testing and Evaluation*, 2d ed. (New York: John Wiley and Sons, 1979), p. 287; and Ernest Perez, "Text Enhancement: Controlled Vocabulary vs. Free Text," *Special Libraries* 73, No. 3 (July 1982): 183–192.

8. Dwight R. Tousignaut, "Indexing: Old Methods, New Concepts," *The Indexer* 15, No. 4 (1987): 197–204.

9. Donald B. Cleveland, Ana D. Cleveland, and Olga B. Wise, "Less Than Full Text Indexing Using a Non-Boolean Searching Model," *Journal of the American Society for Information Science* 35 (January/February 1984): 19–28.

10. D. Stein et al., "Full Text Online Patent Searching: Results of a USPTO Experiment," in *Proceedings of the Online '82 Conference, Atlanta, November 1982* (Weston, Conn.: Online Inc., 1982), pp. 289–294.

11. Zuga, "Full Text Databases."

12. Carol Tenopir, "Search Strategies for Full Text Databases," in *Proceedings of the 51st Annual Meeting of the American Society for Information Science, Atlanta, October 1988* (Medford, N.J.: Learned Information, 1988), pp. 80–86.

13. Tenopir, Nahl-Jakobovits, and Howard, "Magazines Online."

14. Tenopir, "Retrieval Performance in a Full Text Journal Article Database."

15. Bella Hass Weinberg and Julia A. Cunningham, "Word Frequency Data in Full Text Database Searching," in *Proceedings of the 5th National Online Meeting: New York, April 1984* (Medford, N.J.: Learned Information, 1984), pp. 425–432.

16. Jung Soon Ro, "An Evaluation of the Applicability of Ranking Algorithms to Improving the Effectiveness of Full Text Retrieval" (Ph.D. dissertation, Indiana University, 1985).

17. C. W. Cleverdon, J. Mills, and E. M. Keen, *Factors Determining the Performance of Indexing Systems*, 2 vols. (Cranfield, England: College of Aeronautics, 1966); J. E. Parker, " Preliminary Assessment of the Comparative Efficiencies of an SDI System Using Controlled or Natural Language for Retrieval," *Program* 5 (1979): 26–34; and T. M. Aitchison et al., *Comparative Evaluation of Index Language. Part II: Results* (London, England: The Institutions of Electrical Engineers, 1970).

18. Lydia Jackson, "Searching Full-Text Databases," in *Proceedings of the 7th International Online Information Meeting, London, December 1983* (Oxford, England: Learned Information, Ltd., 1983), pp. 419–425.

19. D. C. Blair and M. E. Maron, "An Evaluation of Retrieval Effectiveness for a Full-Text Document-Retrieval System," *Communications of the ACM* 28, No. 3 (1985): 289–299.

20. Jackson, "Searching Full Text Databases."

21. Ro, "Evaluation of Applicability."

22. Shu, "Retrieval Performance."

23. Richard A. Love and Lorrin R. Garson, "Precision in Searching the Full-Text Database-ACS Journals Online," in *Proceedings of the 6th National Online Meeting, 1985* (Medford, N.J.: Learned Information, Inc., 1985), pp. 273–282.

24. Tenopir, "Search Strategy for Full Texts."

25. Tenopir, Nahl-Jakobovits, and Howard, "Magazines Online."

26. Blair and Maron, "An Evaluation of Retrieval Effectiveness."

27. Ro, "Evaluation of Applicability."

28. Ruth Pagell, "Searching Full-Text Periodicals: How Full Is Full?" *Database* 10 (October 1987): 33–36; and Tenopir and Shu, "Magazines in Full Text."

29. John P. Abbott and Charles R. Smith, "Full-Text and Bibliographic ACS Databases: Rivals or Companions?" in *Proceedings of the 6th National Online Meeting, New York, May 1985* (Medford, N.J.: Learned Information, 1985), pp. 5–9.

30. John A. Hearty and Richard A. Love, "Online Full-Text Information: Experience Is the Best Guide," in *Proceedings of the 8th National Online Meeting, New York, May 1987* (Medford, N.J.: Learned Information, 1987), pp. 161–168.

31. Ibid.

32. Zuga, "Full Text Databases."

33. Tenopir and Shu, "Magazines in Full Text."

34. Bette S. Brunell, "The Production of a Full-Text Database," in *Proceedings of the 6th National Online Meeting, New York, May 1985* (Medford, N.J.: Learned Information, 1985), pp. 71–78.

35. C. R. Watters et al., "Integration of Menu Retrieval and Boolean Retrieval from a Full-Text Database," *Online Review* 9, No. 5 (1985): 391–401; and V. J. Geller and M. E. Lesk, "User Interfaces to Information Systems: Choice vs. Commands," in *Proceedings of the 6th Annual International ACM SIGIR Conference on Research and Development in Information Retrieval* (1983), pp. 130–135.

36. Kay Durkin et al. "An Experiment to Study the Online User of a Full Text Primary Journal Database," in *Proceedings of the 4th International Online Information Meeting, London, December 1980* (Oxford, England: Learned Information, Ltd., 1980), pp. 53–56; and Tenopir, Nahl-Jakobovits, and Howard, "Magazines Online."

10

Future Research Needs and Directions

Since the introduction of online full text databases, there has been a great increase in the number of databases, search services, and software. Publicly available machine-readable full text databases increased to 34 percent of the 4,062 in 1989.[1] Compared to the 18 percent of 2,453 online databases in 1983, in actual numbers, online full text databases more than tripled in this period. Searching of full text databases is provided on most online bibliographic systems or on other systems that also use standard search features such as Boolean logic and word proximity searching. DIALOG's president Roger Summit has publicly stated that one of DIALOG's major goals for the 1990s is to increase the number of full text databases. There are more than fifty text-retrieval software packages containing search facilities for full text retrieval.[2] In addition, many full text databases are now offered on CD-ROM for searching in-house.

Inverted indexes have been the standard file structure for databases for over three decades. Only textual or numeric information has been typically included; graphics have not yet become a common part of online vendors' systems. However, some recent developments in computer architecture and file structures may allow full text searching to go beyond the traditional software and systems. The increase in the number of full text databases, hardware approaches to search and retrieval, artificial intelligence techniques, and videodisc attachments promise new direction for full text databases.

Scientific research is defined as systematic, controlled, empirical, and critical investigation of hypothetical propositions about the presumed relations among natural phenomena, where a phenomenon is the relationship between variables.[3] In order to study and develop full text retrieval as a science, we could describe and explain the phenomena, state retrieval theories based on explained phenomena, and then predict and effectively control a given phenomenon in full text retrieval. To study phenomena means to study variables related to a given phenomenon and to study the relationship between the variables.

Fidel described the various roles that variables play in a research study and presented a conceptual framework for the organization of factors (independent variables) affecting online bibliographic retrieval.[4] All elements making up operating online full text retrieval systems could be investigated as variables. Among them, research is needed on the variables of database, search system, request, searcher, and search process.

THE DATABASE

The variable of database is related to full text retrieval performance. The retrieval effectiveness of a full text database may be affected by the database size, the subject matter, the writing style and language, and the form of the document collection in the full text database.

As the size of databases increases, it is assumed that full text retrieval will result in higher recall but lower precision compared with other retrieval methods.[5] Blair and Maron, however, reported high precision and low recall of a large full text database.[6] They assumed that this was the result of users narrowing their search formulations by adding intersecting terms because of their belief that a large collection results in a large size of output. This assumption was disputed by Salton.[7] The contradictory findings need to be validated by further research on large full text databases in different disciplines.

Subject matter of full text databases may affect not only the effectiveness of full text retrieval but also that of weighting algorithms useful in improving full text retrieval. It is generally accepted that subject access in the humanities and social sciences is more difficult than that in the natural and technical sciences and that differences in word frequency distributions exist between the social sciences and natural sciences.[8] It has yet to be tested with full text online searching.

The forms of the document collection may also affect the retrieval effectiveness of full text databases. Newspapers, journals, encyclopedias, books, and legal literature have different characteristics, different document length, and different degrees of vocabulary homogeneity and readability. Word frequency distribution may also be different. The different forms of document collections may require different search strategies, ranking algorithms, search systems, display format, and other features. Subject specificity of documents and generality of document collections may affect not only retrieval effectiveness of full text databases but also search strategies and search systems.[9]

Research on retrieval effectiveness of full text databases needs much testing to compare texts in different disciplines, of different sizes, different length, and different degrees of vocabulary homogeneity. Research may also focus on the relationship between the variable of database and other variables. Variant texts may require variant search systems, variant search strategies, and variant automatic language enhancements for the best performance.

THE SEARCH SYSTEM

Most commercial online retrieval systems for full text databases have standard search features such as Boolean logic and word proximity searching on an inverted index file. How files are structured, what software and search facilities are used for retrieval, and how the contents of the databases are displayed can make a significant difference.

Inverted indexes with conventional serial computers are the standard file structure for full text databases as they are for bibliographic databases. Recently there has been increased interest in the development of hardware alternatives to conventional computer architecture. Hollaar has examined unconventional hardware organization to enhance text retrieval.[10] Stanfill and Kahle reported that the new implementation of free text searching using a new parallel computer, the Connection Machine (CM), makes possible the application of exhaustive methods not previously feasible for large databases.[11]

In testing parallel CM methodology compared with the vector processing system in a conventional computer, Salton and Buckley suggested that parallel methods do not provide large-scale gains in either retrieval effectiveness or efficiency.[12] The method of implementation was the important thing, and parallelism did not in itself improve search and retrieval output. Since the two tests were conducted with different document surrogates of different databases, parallel methods need tests on full text databases, especially on large databases. Research is also needed on other computer architectures and file structures.

Searching capabilities influence the structure of search statements and performance of full text searches. More research is needed on how search capabilities affect the performance of full text retrieval and what capabilities could be designed especially for the retrieval improvement of full text databases. Users may need more proximity operators than are usually available on most systems—not only document, field, subfield, and word operators, but operators to search a specified section or chapter of text, a subsection, a paragraph, a sentence, and within a user-defined segment of N words. Proximity operators and the Boolean AND operator have each been shown to have a role in full text search strategy.[13] Other existing or potential proximity operators should be studied and evaluated in other to reveal how the proximity operators affect retrieval performance and when or how full text databases might best be searched using these operators.

There will be increased interest in automated language enhancements to improve full text retrieval. Automated language enhancements implemented to date include truncation that allows automatic searching for different form of words; string searching to retrieve variant spellings; the ability to view a list of synonyms or even to search automatically for synonyms; ranking, weighting, or document clustering based on word occurrences; and artificial intelligence techniques for natural language query and search strategy formation.[14]

Automatic language enhancement on full text databases is still in the experimental stage. Some similarity measures and a few weighting algorithms for single terms occurrence in documents, have been applied and tested to improve full text retrieval. Other document-term weighting algorithms, query-term weighting algorithms, and similarity measure algorithms should be applied. Additionally linguistic and semantic algorithms should be tested to improve the full text retrieval in various kinds of subject matter and forms of documents. Relevance feedback searching may also be tested with Boolean systems, extended Boolean systems, and parallel methods for full text databases.

Ranking algorithms used to improve the effectiveness of full text searching rank documents or paragraphs containing query terms based on the occurrence frequency of the query term in the documents or the paragraphs. In most ranking algorithms, however, the occurrence frequency of a term usually excludes the occurrence frequency of anaphoric terms like pronouns and auxiliary verbs that function as substitutes for the term. Liddy and associates compiled and tested rules for distinguishing anaphoric functioning of terms in abstracts and adding the occurrence frequency of the anaphoric terms to the occurrence frequency of the term for which the anaphoric terms function as substitutes.[15] Results of the rule testing indicate high feasibility of future algorithmic recognition of anaphoric uses of terms in full texts. The algorithm for anaphoric terms may make a difference to the relative value of ranking or weighting algorithms.

Some artificial intelligence systems demonstrate the techniques that have been suggested for implementing document retrieval systems in the future. A prototype system named INSTRUCT has facilities for natural language query processing, including the use of a stopword list, stemming algorithms and a fuzzy-matching routine that allows the automatic identification of a range of word variants. INSTRUCT also has the provision of ranked output using automatic term weighting and a nearest-neighbor searching procedure and automatic relevance feedback using probabilistic relevance weights.[16] The system PLEXUS has knowledge-based expert system techniques to improve access to a conventional Boolean text retrieval system including understanding users' queries, formulating question statement and search strategy statement, and executing searches.[17] One research study compared the retrieval effectiveness of these two systems and reported that INSTRUCT performs best if it is based on all the terms that PLEXUS introduced to the same query during the Boolean reformulations at search time.[18]

These kinds of intelligent systems may be replicated in full text databases to assist end users. The studies described in Chapter 7 suggest ways expert systems could be tested for full text retrieval. Replication of the human search modification process using variant full text strategies based on purpose of the search, type of literature, or initial success or failure could be incorporated for testing into a full text expert system.

Field design for the distinguishable parts of the text affects search strategies and search performance. The value of controlled vocabulary descriptors, meaningful titles, and abstracts was suggested in research described in Chapters 5, 6, and 7. Full text might also be separated into fields for chapter, section heading, or graphics. Previous research revealed that free text searching of full texts has both positives and negatives when compared with searching methods using other fields. Based on their experience searchers argue for the use of controlled indexing systems to enhance free text searching of full texts.[19] More research is needed to determine if controlled vocabulary indexing has a place in all full text databases because writing style and the nature of language may result in different values for different subjects. Related to this is the need for research on how to structure the vocabularies appropriate to the subject matter of documents. There is also increased interest in how to combine these techniques to improve performance of full text databases.

One characteristic of full text databases that affects online searching is the parsing rules used by the search service to construct the inverted index file. The effects of parsing rules for stopwords and punctuation has been reported.[20] Parsing rules for other aspects or on other vendors' systems may also be investigated for the improvement of full text retrieval. Optimal parsing rules may be devised.

Systems have different output format capabilities, screen displays, and viewing procedures. Full text databases require extra considerations and options beyond what database vendors have needed in the past with bibliographic files. Special emphasis may be given to the readability of the text based on its appearance on the printed page and to a capability for browsing through an article for particular phrases or sections. Plenty of white space (i.e., margins, indentions, and blank lines), highlighted search terms, boldface type and underlining for emphasis, multiple type fonts or shading for differentiating kinds of material, and special treatment of headings are considered essential to the readability of full text.[21] Special attention needs to be paid to the browsing capability provided in vendors' search

software. How large should the "window" be? In other words, when showing the selected term, how much text is needed to give a meaning context?
Should the browsing command work with the text only or with other fields
as well? How do searchers stop the scan of windows, go back to the
beginning of the particular section, and display it in full? Research on these
questions may help designers of systems for full text retrieval create the
most effective and efficient systems.

Some services provide videodisc attachments allowing localized access
to the photographs, illustrations, and other graphics that are not available
online. With a videodisc enhancement, text is searched and displayed online through the system's computer, but when an illustration accompanies
the text, the videodisc enhancement feature displays corresponding illustrations on a user's locally held videodisc player. Function keys allow users
to go back and forth between the videodisc illustration and the online text.
Significant enhancement in this area should come with developments of
videodisc technology. More research is needed on how users view text and
graphics, the impact of screen layout and graphics quality on user satisfaction, and appropriate links or retrieval aids for graphics.

THE REQUEST, THE SEARCHER, AND THE SEARCH PROCESS

Full text searching, like bibliographic searching, could be affected by
the characteristics of requests submitted or stated by users. Blair and Maron
assumed that users narrowed search formulations by adding intersecting
terms because they expected a large size of output.[22] Wagers investigated
the relationship between queries and documents in terms of the specificity
and depth of the topics as a factor affecting decisions to use text as a
searchable field in full text databases.[23] Further studies are needed on how
the user's anticipation of output affects search strategy, the degree of
request specificity or difficulty of requests, the degree to which the query
could be translated into a Boolean expression, and the extent to which the
concepts used could be translated into the system vocabulary.

With bibliographic databases, characteristics of searchers such as cost-
consciousness, personality traits, cognitive factors, demographic variables,
education, online experience, and training are widely described in literature
on online retrieval. Full text databases require extra considerations because
they are almost always marketed to the end user. More research is needed
on why and how end users will use full text databases with special emphasis
given to the system and database knowledge of the users. It is reported
that verbs are extremely useful when searching full text databases and the
words to choose depend on a time factor as the story develops, especially
when searching a news wire database.[24] Effective retrieval may be possible
only when one knows the subject of the database. A knowledge of the
structure of databases also is useful. Blair and Maron reported some im-

provement (but not statistically significant) in resulting recall from paralegals to lawyers.[25] Stein and associates reported no significant difference in training durations for full text database end users.[26] All these characteristics of users could be tested under carefully designed experiments.

Full text databases are of particular interest to the end user, and full text system developers are recognizing that the end user will be their primary user. Thus developments in user-friendly search protocols, enhanced graphics capability, and ease of use will be necessary. Future research should also take into consideration the different possible uses of full text, including browsing, fact retrieval, and finding articles on a given topic. Users with different types of needs may have different requirements for search and display features.

Most user studies have gathered reactions to a full text database on an existing search system with search capabilities. Research is needed to examine what search or display capabilities are desired and needed by users. Additional user studies are needed that will reveal how potential users would most like to use full text databases if they are not restricted by current system constraints, including search capabilities, display, and cost.

Study on information-seeking and search behavior of online searchers is necessary in the design and implementation of user-friendly systems. This is an area of much potential research for full text databases as has been done in bibliographic databases. Marchionini listed some questions which bear study: "What mental models do people have for search systems? How do mental models for search systems change as electronic information systems are experienced? What conceptual models are best devised to help users build appropriate mental models for these systems and improve their information-seeking strategies?"[27]

CONCLUSIONS

Experimental, observational, or survey studies try to investigate the relationships between variables to understand, predict, and then affectively control the relationships between the variables. As we have noted, the number of full text databases has increased and will continue to increase with various subject matter, database sizes, and document forms. There is increased interest in the characteristics of search systems such as file structure, search and display capabilities, effective user interfaces based on artificial intelligence technology, and automated language enhancement to improve full text retrieval. Full text databases are expected to be of particular interest to the end user. Significant developments in this area may come in the near future with the increased development of alternative computer architecture and technology. Research will reveal how users perceive, use, and search full text online databases. Designers of systems for full text retrieval and database producers must heed the results of this research to create the most effective and efficient systems. Studies on the interrelationship between every element of the full text retrieval process and the relationship between each element and retrieval performance may at last provide a link between theory and practice in full text database development.

NOTES

1. *Directory of Online Databases* 10, No. 1 (January 1989) (New York: Cuadra/Elsevier, 1989).

2. Robert Kimberly, *Text Retrieval: A Directory of Software* (Aldershot, Brookfield, Vt.: Gower, 1987).

3. Fred N. Kerlinger, *Foundations of Behavioral Research*, 2d ed. (New York: Holt, Rinehart and Winston, 1973), p. 11.

4. Raya Fidel and Dagobert Soergel, "Factors Affecting Online Bibliographic Retrieval: A Conceptual Framework for Research," *Journal of the American Society for Information Science* 34, No. 3 (1983): 163–180.

5. Carol Tenopir, "Retrieval Performance in a Full Text Journal Article Database" (Ph.D. dissertation, University of Illinois, 1984).

6. D. C. Blair and M. E. Maron, "An Evaluation of Retrieval Effectiveness for a Full-Text Document-Retrieval System," *Communications of the ACM* 28, No. 3 (1985): 289–299.

7. Gerard Salton, "Another Look at Automatic Text-Retrieval Systems," *Communications of the ACM* 29, No. 7 (July 1986): 648–656.

8. Pierce Butler, "The Research Worker's Approach to Books—The Humanist," in *The Acquisition and Cataloging of Books*, ed. William M. Randall (Chicago: University of Chicago Press, 1940); D. W. Langridge, *Classification and Indexing in the Humanities* (London: Butterworth, 1976); Walter S. Achtert, "Abstracting and Bibliographical Control in the Modern Languages and Literature," in *Access to the Literature of the Social Sciences and Humanities*, ed. Robert A. Colby and Morris A. Gelfand (Flushing, N.Y.: Queens College Press, 1974); D. J. Foskett, "Problems of Indexing and Classification in the Social Sciences," *International Social Science Journal* 23, No. 2 (1971): 244–255; Maurice B. Line, "Concluding Considerations," in *Access to the Literature of the Social Sciences and Humanities* (Flushing, N.Y.: Queens College Press, 1974); Stephen E. Wiberley, "Subject Access in the Humanities and the Precision of the Humanist's Vocabulary," *Library Quarterly* 53 (1983): 420–433; and Mary E. Rowbottom and Peter Willett, "The Effect of Subject Matter on the Automatic Indexing of Full Text," *Journal of the American Society for Information Science* 33 (1982): 139–141.

9. R. Wagers, "The Decision to Search Databases Full Text," in *Proceedings of 10th International Online Information Meeting, London, December 1986* (Oxford, England: Learned Information, Ltd., 1986), pp. 93–107.

10. Lee A. Hollaar, "Unconventional Computer Architectures for Information Retrieval," *Annual Review of Information Science and Technology* 14 (1979): 129–151; and Idem., "The Utah Text Retrieval Project," *Information Technology: Research and Development* 2 (1983): 155–168.

11. C. Stanfill and B. Kahle, "Parallel Free-Text Search on the Connection

Machine System," *Communication of the ACM* 29, No. 12 (December 1986): 1229–1239.

12. Gerard Salton and Chris Buckley, "Parallel Text Search Methods," *Communication of the ACM* 31, No. 2 (February 1988): 202–215.

13. Jung Soon Ro, "An Evaluation of the Applicability of Ranking Algorithms to Improving the Effectiveness of Full Text Retrieval" (Ph.D. dissertation, Indiana University, 1985); Carol Tenopir, "Search Strategies for Full Text Databases," in *Proceedings of the 51st Annual Meeting of the American Society for Information Science, Atlanta, October 1988* (Medford, N.J.: Learned Information, 1988), pp. 80–86.

14. Lydia Jackson, "Searching Full-Text Databases," in *Proceedings of the 7th International Online Information Meeting, December 1983, London* (Oxford, England: Learned Information, Ltd., 1983), pp. 419–425.

15. Elizabeth Liddy et al., "A Study of Discourse Anaphora in Scientific Abstracts," *Journal of the American Society for Information Science* 38, No. 4 (1987): 255–261.

16. Jan G. Hendry, Peter Willett, and Frances E. Wood, "INSTRUCT: A Teaching Package for Experimental Methods in Information Retrieval. Part I. The Users' View," *Program* 29, No. 3 (July 1986): 245–263; and Idem., "INSTRUCT: A Teaching Package for Experimental Methods in Information Retrieval. Part II. Computational Aspects," *Program* 20, No. 4 (October 1986): 382–393.

17. Alina Vickery, Helen Brooks, and Bruce Rovinson, "A Reference and Referral System using Expert System Techniques," *Journal of Documentation* 43, No. 1 (March 1987): 1–23.

18. Stephen Wade et al., "A Comparison of Knowledge-Based and Statistically-Based Techniques for Reference Retrieval," *Online Review* 12, No. 2 (1988): 91–108.

19. Pauline Duckitt, "The Value of Controlled Indexing Systems in Online Full Text Databases," in *Proceedings of the 5th International Online Information Meeting, London, December 1981* (Oxford, England: Learned Information, Ltd., 1981), pp. 447–453; and Ernest Perez, "Text Enhancement: Controlled Vocabulary vs. Free Text," *Special Libraries* 73, No. 3 (July 1982): 49–59.

20. Ro, "An Evaluation"; and Carol Tenopir and Man Evena Shu, "Magazines in Full Text: Uses and Search Strategies," *Online Review* 13, No. 2, (1989): 107–118.

21. Connie Zuga, "Full Text Databases: Design Considerations for the Database Vendor," in *Proceedings of the 7th International Online Information Meeting, London, December 1983* (Oxford, England: Learned Information, Ltd, 1983), pp. 427–434.

22. Blair and Maron, "An Evaluation."

23. Wagers, "The Decision."

24. Jackson, "Searching," p. 420.

25. Blair and Maron, "An Evaluation."

26. D. Stein et al., "Full Text Online Patent Searching: Results of a USPTO Experiment," in *Proceedings of the Online '82 Conference, Atlanta, GA, November 1982* (Weston, Conn.: Online Inc., 1982) pp. 289–294.

27. Gary Marchionini, "Information-Seeking Strategies of Novices Using a Full-Text Electronic Encyclopedia," *Journal of the American Society for Information Science* 40, No. 1 (1989): 65.

Bibliography

Abbott, John P., and Smith, Charles R. "Full-text and Bibliographic ACS Databases: Rivals or Companions?" In *Proceedings of the 6th National Online
Meeting, 1985*, pp. 5–9. Medford, N.J.: Learned Information, Inc., 1985.

Achtert, Walter S. "Abstracting and Bibliographical Control in the Humanities."
In *Access to the Literature of the Social Sciences and Humanities*, pp. 55–
60. Edited by Robert A. Colby and Morris A. Gelfand. Flushing, N.Y.:
Queens College Press, 1974.

Aitchison, T. M., Hall, A. M., Lavelle, K. H., and Tracey, J. M. *Comparative
Evaluation of Index Languages. Part II: Results*. London, England: The
Institution of Electrical Engineers, 1970.

Angell, R. C., Freund, G. E., and Willett, P. "Automatic Spelling Correction
Using a Trigram Similarity Measure," *Information Processing and Management* 19, no. 4 (1983): 255–261.

Angione, Pauline V. "On the Equivalence of Boolean and Weighted Searching
Based on the Convertability of Query Forms," *Journal of the American
Society for Information Science* 26 (March/April 1975): 112–224.

Artandi, S. "Computer Indexing of Medical Articles," *Journal of Documentation*
25 (1969): 214–223.

Artandi, S., and Wolf, E. H. "The Effectiveness of Automatically Generated
Weights and Links in Mechanical Indexing," *American Documentation* 20
(1969): 198–201.

Attar, Rony, and Fraenkel, Aviezri S. "Experiments in Local Metrical Feedback
in Full Text Retrieval Systems," *Information Processing and Management*
17, no. 3 (1981): 115–126.

Bar-Hillel, Y. "The Mechanization of Literature Searching." In *Mechanization of
Thought Processes*, vol. 2, pp. 4–8. Symposium No. 10. National Physical
Laboratory. England, 1959.

Batty, C. D. "Automatic Generation of Index Language," *Journal of Documentation* 25 (1969): 142–151.

Baxendale, P. B. "Machine-Made Index for Technical Literature—An Experiment," *I.B.M. Journal of Research and Development* 2 (1958): 354–361.

Beard, Joseph J. "Information Systems Application in Law," *Annual Review of Information Science and Technology* 6 (1971): 369–396.

Belzer, J. "Justification for Automatic Indexing by Frequency Distribution of Words," *Journal of the American Society for Information Science* 22 (1971): 226.

Bender, Avi. "Application of a Full-Text Storage and Retrieval System for Records Management," *Journal of Information and Image Management* (April 1986): 19–24, 36, 54.

Benjamin, William A., Jamieson, Kathleen C., and Rutt, James P. "The Design of a Full-Text Company Information Database for Multi-Vendor Delivery." In *Proceedings of the 4th National Online Meeting, New York, April 1983*, pp. 33–37. Edited by Martha E. Williams and Thomas H. Hogan. Medford, N.J.: Learned Information, Inc., 1983.

Benson, Dennis A., Standing, Roy A., and Goldstein, Charles M. "A Microprocessor-Based System for the Delivery of Full-Text, Encyclopedic Information." In *The Information Community: An Alliance for Progress: Proceedings of the American Society for Information Science (ASIS) 44th Annual Meeting, Washington, D.C., October 1981*, pp. 256–259. Washington, D.C.: ASIS, 1981.

Bernstein, L. M., and Williamson, R. E. "The Effect of Subject Matter on the Automatic Indexing of Full Text," *Journal of the American Society for Information Science* 33, no. 3 (1983): 139–141.

Bhattacharyya, K. "The Effectiveness of Natural Language in Science Indexing and Retrieval," *Journal of Documentation* 30 (September 1974): 235–254.

Bing, Jon. "Performance of Legal Text Retrieval Systems: The Curse of Boole." *Law Library Journal* 79, no. 2 (Spring 1987): 187–202.

———. "Text Retrieval in Norway." *Program* 15, no. 3 (July 1981): 150–162.

Bing, Jon, and Harvold, Trygue. *Legal Decisions and Information*. Oslo, Norway: Universitetsforlaget, 1977.

Bing, Jon, and Selmer, Knut S. *A Decade of Computer and Law*. Oslo, Norway: Norwegian University Press, 1980.

Bird, R. M. "Associative File Processor, A Special Purpose Hardware System For Text Search and Retrieval." In *Institution of Electrical and Electronic Engineers (IEEE) Proceedings of the National Aerospace and Electronics Conference, Dayton, Ohio, May 1979*, pp. 433–449. New York: IEEE, 1979.

Blaine, William L. "Computers and Legal Research," *California State Bar Journal* 50, no. 2 (March/April 1975): 100–102, 104.

Blair, David C. "Full Text Retrieval: Evaluation and Implications." *International Classification* 13, no. 1 (1986): 18–23.

Blair, D. C., and Maron, M. E. "An Evaluation of Retrieval Effectiveness for a Full-Text Document-Retrieval System," *Communications of the ACM* 28, no. 3 (1985): 289–299.

Bochmann, G. V., Gecsei, J., and Lin, E. "Keyword Access in Telidon—An Experiment." In *Videotex 82: International Conference and Exhibition on*

Videotex, Viewdata and Teletext, pp. 345–357. Northwood Hills, England: Online Conferences, 1982.

Bonwit, K., and Aste-Tonsmann, J. "Negative Dictionaries," *Information Storage and Retrieval* (ISR–XIII). Ithaca, N.Y.: Cornell University, 1970.

Bonzi, Susan. "Terminological Consistency in Abstract and Concrete Disciplines." Ph.D. dissertation, University of Illinois, 1983.

Bookstein, Abraham. "Perils of Merging Boolean and Weighted Retrieval Systems," *Journal of the American Society for Information Science* 29, no. 3 (May 1978): 156–157.

———. " Probability and Fuzzy-Set Application to Information Retrieval," *Annual Report of Information Science and Technology* 20 (1985): 117–151.

Bookstein, Abraham, and Swanson, Don R. "Probabilistic Models for Automatic Indexing," *Journal of the American Society for Information Science* 25, no. 5 (September/ October 1975):312–318.

Bowers, Richard, ed. *Optical Publishing Directory, 1988*. Medford, N.J.: Learned Information, Inc., 1988.

Brunelle, Bette S. "The Production of a Full-Text Database." In *Proceedings of the 6th National Online Meeting, 1985*, pp. 71–78. Medford, N.J.: Learned Information, Inc., 1985.

Buckingham, M. C. S., Franklin, J., and Westwater, J. "IRCS On-Line: Experiences with the First Electronic Biomedical Journal." In *Proceedings of the 7th International Online Information Meeting, London, December 1983*, pp. 105–109. Oxford, England: Learned Information, Ltd., 1983.

Bull, Gillian. "A Brief Survey of Developments in Computerized Legal Information Retrieval," *Program* 15, no. 3 (1981): 109–119.

Burson, Scott F. "A Reconstruction of Thamus: Comments on the Evaluation of Legal Information Retrieval Systems," *Law Library Journal* 79, no. 1 (Winter 1987): 133–143.

Burton, Barbara. "The New York Times and the Wall Street Journal Online: A Friendly Dialogue." In *Proceedings of the 8th National Online Meeting, New York, May 1987*, pp. 137–140. Medford, N.J.: Learned Information, Inc., 1987.

Butler, Brett. "Economics of Full-Text Information." In *Proceedings of the 6th National Online Meetings, 1985*, pp. 79–84. Medford, N.J.: Learned Information, Inc., 1985.

Butler, Pierce. "The Research Worker's Approach to Books—The Humanist." In *The Acquisition and Cataloging of Books*, pp. 270–283. Edited by William M. Rabdall. Chicago: University of Chicago Press, 1940.

Byrne, Jerry R. "Relative Effectiveness of Titles, Abstracts, and Subject Headings for Machine Retrieval from the COMPENDEX Services," *Journal of the American Society for Information Science* 26 (July/August 1975): 223–229.

Calkins, Mary L. "Free Text or Controlled Vocabulary?" *Database* 3 (June 1980): 53–60.

Carroll, John M., and deBruyn, J. G. "On the Importance of Root-Stem Truncation in Word-Frequency Analysis," *Journal of the American Society for Information Science* 21, no. 5 (September–October 1970): 368–369.

Carroll, John M., and Roeloffs, Robert. "Computer Selection of Keywords Using

Word-Frequency Analysis." *American Documentation* 20 (July 1969): 227–233.

Carroll, John M., and Roeloffs, Robert. "Computer Selection of Keywords Using Word-Frequency Analysis." *American Documentation* 20 (July 1969): 227–233.

Carrow, Deborah, and Nugent, Joan. "Comparison of Free-Text and Index Search Abilities in an Operating Information System." In *Information Management in the 1980s: Proceedings of the American Society for Information Science 40th Annual Meeting, September 1977*, pp. 131–138. White Plains, N.Y.: Knowledge Industry Publications, 1981.

Charton, Barbara. "Searching the Literature for Concepts," *Journal of Chemical Information and Computer Science* 17 (1977): 45–46.

Choueka, Yaacov. "Computerized Full-Text Retrieval Systems and Research in the Humanities: The Responsa Project," *Computers and the Humanities* 14 (1980): 153–169.

Cleveland, Donald B., Cleveland, Ana D., and Wise, Olga B. "Less Than Full-Text Indexing Using a Non-Boolean Searching Model," *Journal of the American Society for Information Science* 35, no. 1 (January 1984): 19–28.

Cleverdon, C. W. *A Comparative Evaluation of Searching by Controlled Language and Natural Language in an Experimental NASA Data Base*. Washington, D.C.: National Technical Information Service, 1977.

———. "The Cranfield Tests on Index Language Devices." *Aslib Proceedings (U.K.)* 19, no. 6 (June 1967): 173–194.

———. *Report on the Testing and Analysis of an Investigation into the Comparative Efficiency of Indexing Systems*. Cranfield, England: College of Aeronautics, 1962.

Cleverdon, C. W., Mills, J., and Keen, E. M. *Factors Determining the Performance of Indexing Systems*, 2 vols. Cranfield, England: College of Aeronautics, 1966.

Coco, Al. "Full-Text vs. Full-Text Plus Editorial Additions: Comparative Retrieval Effectiveness of the LEXIS and Westlaw Systems," *Law Library Journal* 4, no. 2 (Summer 1984): 27–37.

Cohen, S. M., Schermer, C. A., and Garson, L. R. "Experimental Program for Online Access for ACS Primary Documents," *Journal of Chemical Information and Computer Science* 20 (1980): 247–252.

Collen, Morris F. "Full-Text Medical Literature Retrieval by Computer," *Journal of the American Medical Association* 254, no. 19 (November 15, 1985): 2768–2774.

Conger, Lucinda D. "1983 Database Review: Current Affairs, Government Affairs, Public Affairs, and Legal Affairs." In *Proceedings of the Online '83 Conference, Chicago, October 1983*, pp. 15–20. Weston, Conn.: Online Inc., 1983.

Corbett, Lindsay. "Controlled versus Natural Language: A Report on the Great Debate," *Information Scientist* 5 (September 1971): 114–120.

Cotton, R. L. "Where Full-Text Is Viable," *Online Review* 11, no. 2 (1987): 87–93.

Craig, Gary R. *HBR/Online: User Guide*. New York: John Wiley and Sons, Inc., Electronic Publishing Division, 1983.

Dabney, Daniel P. "The Curse of Thamus: An Analysis of Full-Text Legal Document Retrieval," *Law Library Journal* 78, no. 1 (Winter 1986): 5–40.

Damerau, Fred J. "An Experiment in Automatic Indexing." *American Documentation* 16, no. 4 (October 1965): 283–289.

Davis, Richard P. "The LITE System," *Judge Advocate General Law Review* 8, no. 6 (November/December 1966): 6–10.

Dehncke, Nancy. "Full-Text Business News: Panacea or Problem." In *Proceedings of the 8th National Online Meeting, New York, May 1987*, pp. 87–103. Medford, N.J.: Learned Information, Inc., 1987.

Dennis, S. F. "The Construction of a Thesaurus Automatically from a Sample of Text." In *Statistic Association Methods for Mechanized Documentation*, pp. 61–148. Edited by Mary E. Stevens. Washington, D.C.: National Bureau of Standards Miscellaneous Publications, 1965.

———. "The Design and Testing of a Fully Automated Indexing—Searching System for Documents Consisting of Expository Test." In *Information Retrieval—A Critical View*, pp. 67–94. Edited by G. Schechter. Washington, D.C.: Thompson, 1967.

Detemple, W. "Future Enhancements for Full-Text—Graphics, Expert Systems and Front-End Software." In *Proceedings of the 12th International Online Information Meeting, London, December 1988*, pp. 271–278. Oxford, England: Learned Information, Inc., 1988.

Dialog Information Services, Inc. *ASAP: Full-text Files—Coming Soon*, 12, no. 4 (1984).

Directory of Online Databases. 10, no. 1. New York: Cuadra/Elsevier, 1989.

Duckitt, Pauline. "The Value of Controlled Indexing Systems in Online Full Text Databases." In *Proceedings of the 5th International Online Information Meeting, London, December 1981*, pp. 447–453. Oxford, England: Learned Information, Ltd., 1981.

Durkin, Kay, Egeland, Janet, Garson, Lorrin R., and Terrant, Seldon W. "An Experiment to Study the Online Use of a Full Text Primary Journal Database." In *Proceedings of the 4th International Online Information Meeting, London, December 1980*, pp. 53–56. Oxford, England: Learned Information, Ltd., 1980.

Eaton, Edward Arthur, III. "The Retrieval of Answers to Natural Language Questions from Text." Ph.D. dissertation, University of Texas at Austin, 1978.

Edmondson, H. P. "New Methods in Automatic Extracting," *Journal of Association Computing Machinery* 16 (1969): 165–185.

Edmondson, H. P., and Wyllys, R. E. "Automatic Abstracting and Indexing— Survey and Recommendation," *Communication of the Association for Computing Machinery* 4 (1961): 226–234.

Eldridge, W. B. "An Appraisal of a Case Law Retrieval Project." In *Proceedings of the Computers and the Law Conference—1968*, pp. 36–61. Edited by David Johnston. Kingston, Ontario, 1968.

Fels, Eberhard M. "Evaluation of the Performance of an Information Retrieval System by Modified Mooers Plan," *American Documentation* 14, no. 1 (January 1963): 28–34.

Fidel, Raya, and Soergel, Dagobert. "Factors Affecting Online Bibliographic Retrieval: A Conceptual Framework for Research." *Journal of the American Society of Information Science* 34, no. 3 (May 1983): 163–180.

Foskett, D. J. "Problems of Indexing and Classification in the Social Sciences," *International Social Science Journal* 23, no. 2 (1971): 144–155.

Frakes, William B., Katzer, Jeffrey, McGill, Michael, Tessier, Judith A., and Dasgupta, Padmini. "A Study of the Impact of Representations in Information Retrieval Systems." In *Information Community: Proceedings of the 44th Annual Meeting of the American Society for Information Science, Washington, D.C., October 1981*, pp. 301–303. Washington, D.C.: ASIS, 1981.

Franklin, J., and Buckingham, M.C.S. "The Simultaneous Publication of a Primary Biomedical Journal in Electronic and Paper Formats." In *Proceedings of the Computer Applications in Medical Care 6th Annual Symposium, Washington, D.C., October 1982*, pp. 1055–1056. New York: IEEE, 1982.

Franklin, J., Buckingham, M. C., and Westwater, J. "Biomedical Journals in an Online Full Text Database: A Review of Reaction to ESPL." In *Proceedings of the 7th International Online Information Meeting, London, December 1983*, pp. 407–410. Oxford, England: Learned Information, Ltd., 1983.

Freund, G. E., and Willett, P. "Online Identification of Word Variants and Arbitrary Truncation Searching Using a String Similarity Measure," *Information Technology: Research and Development* 1, no. 3 (July 1982): 177–187.

Garson, Lorrin R., and Cohen, Stanley M. *Users' Manual, Primary Journal Database ACS Full-Text File*. Revised May 1983. Washington, D.C.: American Chemical Society (ACS), 1983.

Geller, V. J., and Lesk, M. E. "User Interfaces to Information Systems: Choice vs. Commands." In *Proceedings of the 6th Annual International ACM SIGIR Conference on Research and Development in Information Retrieval*, pp. 130–135. 1983.

Gilbert, H., and Sparck Jones, K. *Statistical Bases of Relevance Assessment for the "Ideal" Information Retrieval Test Collection*. Chicago: University of Chicago, 1979.

Goffman, W. "A General Theory of Communication." In *Introduction to Information Science*, pp. 726–747. Edited by T. Saracevic. New York: Bowker, 1970.

———. "An Indirect Method of Information Retrieval," *Information Storage and Retrieval* 4 (December 1968): 361–373.

Goldsmith, N. "An Appraisal of Factors Affecting the Performance of Text Retrieval Systems," *Information Technology: Research and Development* 1, no. 1 (January 1982): 41–53.

Gordon, Helen. "Full-Text Newspapers Online." *Databases* (August 1986): 98–111.

Griffith, William G. "Advances in Merging Full Text and Video-text Features for Information Retrieval." In *Proceedings of the 3rd National Online Meeting, New York, March 30–April 1, 1982*, pp. 159–161. Medford, N.J.: Learned Information, Inc., 1982.

Harrington, William G. "A Brief History of Computer-Assisted Legal Research," *Law Library Journal* 77, no. 3 (1984–1985): 543–556.

Harrington, W. G., Wilson, H. D., and Bennett, R. L. "The Mead Data Central System of Computerized Legal Research," *Law Library Journal* 64 (May 1971): 185–189.

Harter, Stephen P. "A Probabilistic Approach to Automatic Keyword Indexing." Ph.D. dissertation, University of Chicago, 1974.

—————. "A Probabilistic Approach to Automatic Keyword Indexing. Part 1. On the Distribution of Specialty Words in a Technical Literature." *Journal of the American Society for Information Science* 26 (July/August 1975): 197–206.

—————. "A Probabilistic Approach to Automatic Keyword Indexing. Part 2. An Algorithm for Probabilistic Indexing." *Journal of the American Society for Information Science* 26 (September/October 1975): 280–289.

—————. "Statistical Approaches to Automatic Indexing," *Drexel Library Quarterly* 14 (April 1978): 57–74.

Haskin, Roger L., and Hollaar, Lee A. "Operational Characteristics of a Hardware-Based Pattern Matcher," *ACM Transactions on Data Base Systems* 8, no. 1 (March 1983): 15–40.

Hawkins, Donald T. *On-Line Information Retrieval Bibliography, 1964–1979.* Medford, N.J.: Learned Information, Inc., 1980.

—————. "Online Information Retrieval Bibliography. 6th Update." *Online Review* 7, no. 2 (April 1983): 127–187.

HBR/Online: User Guide. New York: John Wiley & Sons, Inc., Electronic Publishing Division, 1983.

Heaps, H. S. *Information Retrieval: Computational and Theoretical Aspects.* New York: Academic Press, 1978.

Hearty, John A., and Love, Richard A. "Online Full-Text Information: Experience Is the Best Guide." In *Proceedings of the 8th National Online Meeting, New York, May 1987*, pp. 161–168. Medford, N.J.: Learned Information, Inc., 1987.

Hearty, John A., and Smith, Cynthia G. "Marketing Strategies for Promoting Online Full-Text Primary Information." In *Proceedings of the Ninth National Online Meeting, New York, May 1988*, pp. 91–97. Medford, N.J.: Learned Information, Inc., 1988.

Hendry, Jan, Willett, Peter, and Wood, Frances E. "INSTRUCT: A Teaching Package for Experimental Methods in Information Retrieval. Part I. The Users' View," *Program* 29, no. 3 (1986): 245–263.

—————. "INSTRUCT: A Teaching Package for Experimental Methods in Information Retrieval. Part II. Computational Aspects," *Program* 20, no. 4 (1986): 382–393.

Hersey, David F., Foster, Willis R., Stalder, Ernest W., and Carlson, William T. "Comparison of On-Line Retrieval Using Free Text Words and Scientist Indexing." In *The Information Conscious Society: Proceedings of the 33rd Annual Meeting of the American Society for Information Science, Philadelphia, October 1970*, pp. 265–268. Washington, D.C.: ASIS, 1970.

—————. "Free Text Word Retrieval and Scientist Indexing: Performance Profiles and Costs," *Journal of Documentation* 27 (September 1971): 167–183.

Hjerppe, Roland. "Electronic Publishing: Writing Machines and Machine Writing," *Annual Review of Information Science and Technology* 21 (1986): 123–166.

Hollaar, Lee A. "Hardware Systems for Text Information Retrieval." In *Proceedings of the International Association for Computing Machinery SIGIR*

6th Annual Conference on Research and Development in Information Retrieval, Bethesda, Md., June 1983, vol. 17, pp. 3–9. Baltimore, Md.: ACM, 1983.

———. "Text Retrieval Computers," *Computer* 12, no. 3 (March 1979): 40–50.

———. "Unconventional Computer Architectures for Information Retrieval," *Annual Review of Information Science and Technology* 14 (1979): 129–151.

———. "The Utah Text Retrieval Project," *Information Technology: Research and Development* 2 (1983): 155–168.

Holland, Maurita P. "ZyINDEX; Full Text Retrieval Power," *Online* (July 1985): 38–42.

Holsti, R. *Content Analysis for the Social Sciences and Humanities.* Reading, Mass.: Addison-Wesley, 1969.

Horty, J. F. "Experience with the Application of Electronic Data Processing Systems in General Law," *Modern Uses of Logic in Law* 60D (1960): 158–168.

———. "Electronic Data Retrieval of Law," *Current Business Studies* 36 (1961): 35–46.

Huth, Dolores P. "ASAP—Index Access to Full Text." In *Proceedings of the 6th National Online Meeting, 1985*, pp. 227–232. Medford, N.J.: Learned Information, Inc., 1985.

International Research Communication System (IRCS). Medical Science. "IRCS Speeds Publication in Powerful Database Link," *IRCS Medical Science* 11 (1983): 189–192.

Jackson, Lydia. "Searching Full-Text Databases." In *Proceedings of the 7th International Online Information Meeting, London, December 1983*, pp. 419–425. Oxford, England: Learned Information, Ltd., 1983.

Jennings, E. Judson. "Sam, You Made the Window too Small." In *Proceedings of the 8th National Online Meeting, New York, May 1987*, pp. 197–203. Medford, N.J.: Learned Information, Inc., 1987.

Johnson, Eric William. "Full Text vs. Abstracts." *NFAIS News-letter* 25, no. 5 (October 1983): 3–4.

Katzer, Jeffrey, McGill, Michael J., Tessier, Judith A., Frankes, William, and Dasgupta, Padmini. "A Study of the Overlap Among Document Representations," *Information Technology: Research and Development* 1, no. 4 (October 1982): 261–274.

Katzer, Jeffrey, Tessier, Judith A., Frakes, William, and Dasgupta, Padmini. *A Study of the Impact of Representations in Information Retrieval Systems.* Syracuse, N.Y.: School of Information Studies, Syracuse University, 1982.

Kaufmann, Arnold. *Introduction to the Theory of Fuzzy-Subsets.* New York: Academic Press, 1975.

Keen, E. Michael. "The Aberystwyth Index Language Test," *Journal of Documentation* 29, no. 1 (March 1973): 1–35.

Kehl, W. B. "Communication between Computer and User in Information Searching." In *Information Retrieval Management*, pp. 83–91. Edited by L. H. Hattery and E. M. McCormick. Detroit, Mich.: American Data Processing, 1962.

———. "An Information Retrieval Language for Legal Studies." *Communication of the Association for Computing Machinery* 4 (1961): 380–389.

Kilgour, Frederick G. "Online Electronic Delivery of Published Information." In

Proceedings of the 8th National Online Meeting, New York, May 1987, pp. 223–227. Medford, N.J.: Learned Information, Inc., 1987.

Kimberley, Robert. *Text Retrieval: A Directory of Software*. Aldershot, Brookfield, Vt.: Gower, 1987.

King, D. W., and Bryant, E. C. *The Evaluation of Information Services and Products*. Washington, D.C.: Information Resources Press, 1971.

King, Donald W., Neel, Peggy W., and Wood, Barbara L. *Comparative Evaluation of the Retrieval Effectiveness of Descriptor and Free-Text Search Systems Using CIRCOL (Central Information Reference and Control On-Line)*. Rockville, Md.: Westat Research, Inc., 1972.

Klinkroth, Margaret M. "Full-Text Databases in the Health Sciences," *Medical Reference Services Quarterly* 5, no. 3 (1986): 1–15.

Kucera, H., and Francis, W. N. *Computational Analysis of Present-day American English*. Providence, R. I. Brown University Press, 1967.

Lancaster, F. W. "The Cost-Effectiveness Analysis of Information Retrieval and Dissemination Systems," *Journal of the American Society for Information Science* 22, no. 1 (1971): 12–27.

———. "Electronic Publishing: Its Impact on the Distribution of Information," *National Forum* (Summer 1983): 3–5.

———. "Evaluation within the Environment of an Operating Information Service." In *Information Retrieval Experiment*, pp. 105–127. Edited by Karen Sparck Jones. London: Butterworth, 1981.

———. *Information Retrieval Systems: Characteristics, Testing and Evaluation*, 2d ed. New York: John Wiley and Sons, 1979.

———. "MEDLARS: Report on the Evaluation of its Operating Efficiency," *American Documentation* 20 (April 1969): 119–142.

———. *Vocabulary Control for Information Retrieval*. Washington, D.C.: Information Resources Press, 1972.

Lancaster, F. W., Rapport, R. L., and Penry, J. K. "Evaluating the Effectiveness of an On-Line, Natural Language Retrieval System," *Information Storage and Retrieval* 8 (1972): 222–245.

Langridge, D. W. *Classification and Indexing in the Humanities*. London: Butterworth, 1976.

Larson, Signe E., and Williams, Martha E. "Computer Assisted Legal Research," *Annual Review of Information Science and Technology* 15 (1980): 251–286.

Lerner, Rita G., Metaxas, Ted, Scott, John T., Adams, Peter D., and Judd, Peggy. "Primary Publication Systems and Scientific Text Processing," *Annual Review of Information Science and Technology* 18 (1983): 127–149.

Lesk, M. E., and Salton, G. "Relevance Assessments and Retrieval System Evaluation," *Information Storage and Retrieval* 4 (1968): 343–359.

Lindeman, Martha J., Bonneau, John R., and Pocius, Kym E. "A Task Analysis for a Hypermedia System," presented at the Midyear Meeting of the American Society for Information Science, May 1989.

Line, Maurice B. "Concluding Considerations." In *Access to the Literature of the Social Sciences and Humanities*. Flushing, N.Y.: Queens College Press, 1974.

Love, Richard A., and Garson, Lorrin R. "Precision in Searching the Full-Text Database—ACS Journals Online." In *Proceedings of the 6th National Online*

Meeting, 1985, pp. 273–282. Medford, N.J.: Learned Information, Inc., 1985.

Love, Richard A., Martinsen, D. P., and Garson, L. R. "Multiple Use of Primary Full-Text Information—A Publisher's Perspective." In *Proceedings of the 12th International Online Information Meeting, London, December 1988*, pp. 249–254. Oxford, England: Learned Information, Ltd., 1988.

Luhn, H. P. "Auto-Encoding of Documents for Information Retrieval Systems." In *Modern Trends in Documentation*, pp. 45–58. Edited by M. Boaz. London, Pergamon Press, 1959.

————. "The Automatic Creation of Literature Abstracts," *IBM Journal of Research and Development* 2 (April 1958): 159–165, 317.

————. "A Statistical Approach to Mechanized Encoding and Searching of Literary Information," *IBM Journal of Research and Development* 1 (October 1957): 309–317.

Madelung, Hans-ole. "Subject Indexing in the Social Science: A Comparison of PRECIS and KWIC Index to Newspaper Articles," *Journal of Librarianship* 14 (January 1981): 45–58.

Marchionini, Gary. "Information-Seeking Strategies of Novices Using a Full-Text Electronic Encyclopedia," *Journal of the American Society for Information Science* 40, No. 1 (1989): 54–66.

Markey, Karen, Atherton, Pauline, and Newton, Claudia. "An Analysis of Controlled Vocabulary and Free Text Search Statements in Online Searches," *Online Review* 4, no. 3 (1980): 225–236.

May, R. A. *Automated Law Research*. Chicago: American Bar Association, 1973.

McCarthy, W. E. "LITE (Legal Information Thru' Electronics): Progress Report," *Law Library Journal* 64 (May 1971): 193–197.

McDermott, Jo. "Another Analysis of Full-Text Legal Document Retrieval," *Law Library Journal* 78, no. 2 (Spring 1986): 337–343.

McGill, M. J., Koll, M., and Noreault, Terry. *An Evaluation of Factors Affecting Document Ranking by Information Retrieval Systems*. Syracuse, N.Y.: Syracuse University, 1979.

McGonigal, Richard M. "Implementation and Cost Effectiveness of Computerized Legal Research—LEXIS and WESTLAW Compared for Your Evaluation." *Computer/Law Journal* 1, no. 2 (Fall 1978): 359–378.

Milstead, Jessica. "Indexing the News." In *Communicating Information: Proceedings of the ASIS 43rd Annual Meeting, Anaheim, Calif., October 1980*, pp. 149–151. White Plains, N.Y.: Knowledge Industry Publications, Inc., for ASIS, 1980.

Morris, David A. "General Electric's Word and Information Scanner: The Hardware Solution to the Information Explosion." In *Communicating Information: Proceedings of the ASIS 43rd Annual Meeting, Anaheim, Calif. October 1980*, pp. 338–341. White Plains, N.Y.: Knowledge Industry Publications, Inc., for ASIS, 1980.

————. "Processor Matches Text at High Speeds," *Mini-Micro Systems* 16, no. 7 (June 1983): 227–228, 230, 232, 235.

Moulton, James C. "Dow Jones News/Retrieval." *Database* 2, no. 1 (March 1979): 54–64.

Myers, J. M. "Computers and the Searching of Law Texts in England and North

America: A Review of the State-of-the Art," *Journal of Documentation* 29, no. 2 (June 1973): 212–228.

————. "The Impact of LEXIS on the Law Firm Library: A Survey," *Law Library Journal* 71, no. 1 (February 1978): 158–169.

Newcy, Julie M., and Lancaster, F. W. "The Correlation Between Pertinence and Rate of Citation Duplication in Multidatabase Searches," *Journal of the American Society for Information Science* 34, no. 4 (1983): 292–293.

Noreault, Terry, McGill, M., and Koll, M. "Automatic Ranked Output from Boolean Searches in SIRE," *Journal of the American Society for Information Science* 28 (1977): 333–341.

————. "A Performance Evaluation of Similarity Measures, Document Term Weighting Schemes and Representation in a Boolean Environment." In *Information Retrieval Research*, pp. 57–76. Edited by R. N. Oddy. London: Butterworth, 1981.

O'Connor, John. "Answer-Passage Retrieval by Text Searching," *Journal of the American Society for Information Science* 31, no. 4 (July 1980): 227–239.

————. "Data Retrieval by Text Searching," *Journal of Chemical Information and Computer Science* 17 (1977): 181–186.

————. "Mechanized Indexing Methods and Their Testing," *Journal of Association for Computing Machinery* 11 (1964): 437–449.

————. "Retrieval of Answer-Sentences and Answer-Figures from Papers by Text Searching," *Information Processing and Management* 11, nos. 5/7 (1975): 155–164.

————. "Some Remarks on Mechanized Indexing and Some Small-Scale Experimental Results." In *Machine Indexing: Progress and Problems*, pp. 266–279. Washington, D.C.: American University, 1971.

————. "Text Searching Retrieval of Answer-Sentences and Other Answer-Passages," *Journal of the American Society for Information Science* 24 (November/December 1973): 445–460.

Oddy, R. N., ed. *Information Retrieval Research*. London: Butterworth, 1981.

Olive, G., Terry, J. E., and Datta, S. "Studies to Compare Retrieval Using Titles with That Using Index Terms," *Journal of Documentation* 29, no. 2 (June 1973): 108–191.

Orenstein, Ruth M., ed. *Fulltext Sources Online: For Periodicals, Newspapers, Newsletters and Newswires*. Needham Heights, Mass.: Bibliodata, 1989.

Overhage, Carl F., and Reintjes, J. Francis. "Project INTREX: A General Review," *Information Storage and Retrieval* 10, nos. 5–6 (May–June 1974): 157–188.

Pagell, Ruth A. "Primary Full-Text Information: Databases for the End-User." In *Proceedings of the 12th International Online Information Meeting, London, December 1988*, pp. 255–262. Oxford: Learned Information, Ltd., 1988.

————. "Searching Full-Text Periodicals: How Full Is Full?" *Database* 10 (October 1987): 33–38.

————. "Searching IAC's Full-Text Files: It's Awfully Confusing," *Database* 10 (October 1987): 39–47.

Pao, Miranda Lee. "Automatic Text Analysis Based on Transition Phenomena of

Word Occurrences," *Journal of the American Society for Information Science* 29, no. 3 (May 1978): 121–124.

Parker, J. E. "Preliminary Assessment of the Comparative Efficiencies of an SDI System Using Controlled or Natural Language for Retrieval," *Program* 5 (1979): 26–34.

Perez, Ernest. "Text Enhancement: Controlled Vocabulary vs. Free Text," *Special Libraries* 73 (July 1982): 182–192.

Piternick, Anne B. "Requirements for the Scholarly Journal in Transition," *Scholarly Publishing* (October 1982): 49–59.

Prabha, Chandra, and Rice, Duane. "Assumptions About Information-Seeking Behavior in Nonfiction Books: Their Importance to Full Text Systems." In *Proceedings of the 51st Annual Meeting of the American Society for Information Science, Atlanta, Ga., October 1988*, pp. 147–151. Medford, N.J.: Learned Information, Inc., 1988.

Preston, J. F. "OBAR and the Mead Data Central System," *Law Library Journal* 64 (May 1971): 190–192.

Provenzano, Dominic. "NEXIS," *Database* 4 (December 1981): 30–41.

Quigley, Edward J. "MEDIS: Full-Text Medical Information Retrieval Service." *Database* (June 1986): 112–117.

Quint, Barbara. "Newsbanks and News Data Bases." In *Online Search Strategies*, pp. 279–304. Edited by Ryan E. Hoover. White Plains, N.Y.: Knowledge Industry Publication, 1982.

Rayfield, Robert Emmett. "Two Experiments in Computer Analysis of Newspaper Prose: Readability, Assessment and Automatic Indexing." Ph.D. dissertation, University of Texas, 1977.

Rees, A. M., and Schultz, D. G. *A Field Experimental Approach to the Study of Relevance Assessments in Relation to Document Searching*, 2 vols. Cleveland, Ohio: Center for Documentation and Communication Research, Case Western Reserve University, 1967.

Regazzi, John J. "Evaluating Indexing Systems: A Review After Cranfield," *The Indexer* 12 (April 1980): 14–21.

Resnick, A. "Relative Effectiveness of Document Titles and Abstracts for Determining Relevance of Documents," *Science* 134, no. 3484 (October 6, 1961): 1004–1006.

Rinewalt, J. R. "Evaluation of Selected Features of the EUREKA Full Text Information Retrieval System." Ph.D. dissertation, University of Illinois, 1976.

———. "Feature Evaluation of a Full Text Information Retrieval System," *Online Review* 1 (January 1977): 43–51.

Ro, Jung Soon. "An Evaluation of the Applicability of Ranking Algorithms to Improving the Effectiveness of Full Text Retrieval." Ph.D. dissertation, Indiana University, 1985.

———. "An Evaluation of the Applicability of Ranking Algorithms to Improve the Effectiveness of Full-Text Retrieval. I. On the Effectiveness of Full-Text Retrieval," *Journal of the American Society for Information Science* 39, no. 2 (1988): 73–78.

———. "An Evaluation of The Applicability of Ranking Algorithms to Improve the Effectiveness of Full-Text Retrieval. II. On the Effectiveness of Ranking

Algorithms on Full-Text Retrieval," *Journal of the American Society for Information Science* 39, no. 3 (1988): 147–160.

Robertson, S. E. "The Parametric Description of Retrieval Tests." *Journal of Documentation* 25, no. 1 (March 1969): 1–27.

——. "The Parametric Description of Retrieval Tests. Part 2," *Journal of Documentation* 25, no. 2 (June 1969): 93–107.

——. "Progress in Documentation: Theories and Models in Information Retrieval," *Journal of Documentation* 33 (June 1977): 126–148.

Robertson, S. E., van Rijsbergan, C. J., and Porter, M. F. "Probabilistic Models of Indexing and Searching." In *Information Retrieval Research*, pp. 35–56. Edited by R. N. Oddy. London: Butterworth, 1981.

Rosenberg, V. "A Study of Statistical Measures for Predicting Terms Used to Index Documents," *Journal of the American Society for Information Science* 22, no. 1 (January 1977): 41–51.

Ross, Nina M. "Newspaper Databases." In *Proceedings of the 2nd National Online Meeting, New York, March 1981*, pp. 415–421. Medford, N.J.: Learned Information, Inc., 1981.

——. "Newspaper Database Update, 1982." In *Proceedings of the 4th National Online Meeting, New York, April 1983*, pp. 463–473. Medford, N.J.: Learned Information, Inc., 1983.

Rothenburg, Douglas H. "An Efficiency Model and a Performance Function for an Information Retrieval System," *Information Storage and Retrieval*, 5, no. 3 (October 1969): 109–122.

Rowbottom, Marry E., and Willett, Peter. "The Effect of Subject Matter on the Automatic Indexing of Full Text," *Journal of the American Society for Information Science* 33 (May 1983): 139–141.

Rowlett, Russell J., Jr. "Keywords vs. Index Terms," *Journal of Chemical Information and Computer Science* 17 (1977): 192–193.

Runde, Craig E., and Lindberg, William H. "The Curse of Thamus: A Response," *Law Library Journal* 78, no. 2 (Spring 1986): 345–347.

Sager, Naomi. "Natural Language Information Formatting: The Automatic Conversion of Texts to a Structured Database." In *Advances in Computers*, vol. 17, pp. 89–162. New York: Academic Press, 1978.

Sager, W. K. H., and Lockemann, P. C. "Classification of Ranking Algorithms," *International Forum on Information and Documentation* 1, no. 4 (1976): 12–25.

Salton, Gerard. "Another Look at Automatic Text-Retrieval Systems," *Communications of the ACM* 29, no. 7 (1986): 648–656.

——. "Automated Language Processing," *Annual Review of Information Science and Technology* 3 (1968): 169–199.

——. "Automatic Text Analysis," *Science* 169 (April 1970): 335–343.

——. "A New Comparison Between Conventional Indexing (MEDLARS) and Automatic Text Processing (SMART)," *Journal of the American Society for Information Science* 23 (1973): 75–84.

——. *The SMART Retrieval System: Experiments in Automatic Document Processing*. Englewood Cliffs, N.J.: Prentice-Hall, 1971.

Salton, G., and Buckley, Chris. "Parallel Text Search Methods," *Communications of the ACM* 31, no. 2 (1988): 202–215.

Salton, G., and Lesk, M. E. "Computer Evaluation of Indexing and Text Processing," *Journal of Association Computer Machinery* 25 (January 1968): 8–36.

Salton, G., and McGill, Michael J. *Introduction to Modern Information Retrieval.* New York: McGraw-Hill, 1981.

Salton, G., Wu, H., and Yu, C. T. "The Measurement of Term Importance in Automatic Indexing," *Journal of the American Society for Information Science* 32 (May 1981): 175–186.

Salton, G., and Yang, C. S. "On the Specification of Term Values in Automatic Indexing," *Journal of Documentation* 29 (December 1973): 351–372.

Saracevic, Tefko. "Comparative Effects of Titles, Abstracts and Full Texts on Relevance Judgments." In *Cooperating Information Societies: Proceedings of the American Society for Information Science (ASIS) 32nd Annual Meeting, San Francisco, Calif. October 1969*, pp. 293–299. Westport, Conn.: Greenwood Press, 1969.

————. "The Concept of 'Relevance.' In "Information Science: a Historical Review." In *Introduction to Information Science*, pp. 111–151. Edited by Tefko Saracevic. New York: R. R. Bowker, 1970.

————. "RELEVANCE: A Review of and a Framework for the Thinking on the Notion in Information Science," *Journal of the American Society for Information Science* 26 (November/December 1975): 321–343.

Schipma, P. B., and Becker, D. S. "Text Storage and Display via Videodisc or 'Someday My Prints Will Come.' " In *Proceedings of the 2nd National Online Meeting, New York, March 1981*, pp. 427–431. Medford, N.J.: Learned Information, Inc., 1981.

Schreiber, Aaron M. "Computer Storage and Retrieval of Case Law Without Indexing: The Hebrew Responsa Project," *Law and Computer Technology* 2 (November 1969): 14–21.

Schuegraf, Ernst J. "Associative Processors: Have They Finally Arrived?" In *Communicating Information: Proceedings of the American Society for Information Science 43rd Annual Meeting, Anaheim, Calif., October 1988*, pp. 329–331. White Plains, N.Y.: Knowledge Industry Publications, Inc., 1980.

Scott, William A. "Reliability of Content Analysis: The Case of Nominal Scale Coding," *Public Opinion Quarterly* 19 (1955): 321–325.

Senko, M. E. "Information Retrieval and Application Areas: Impact and Feedback." In *Proceedings of the Fourth Annual National Colloquium on Information Retrieval*, pp. 177–184. Edited by A. B. Tonik. Philadelphia: International Information Incorporated, 1967.

Shannon, Claude E., and Warren Weaver. *The Mathematical Theory of Communication.* Urbana: University of Illinois Press, 1967.

Sievert, MaryEllen, Mckinin, Jean, and Slough, Mariene. "A Comparison of Indexing and Full-Text for the Retrieval of Clinical Medical Literature." In *Proceedings of the 51st Annual Meeting of the American Society for Information Science, Atlanta, GA, October 1988*, pp. 143–146. Medford, N.J.: Learned Information, Inc., 1988.

Silbergeld, Israel, and Reginiano-Peterson, Naomi. "Full Text Information Retrieval Software for Use in Government Administration (A Selection Procedure and Process)," *Online Review* 11, no. 2 (1987): 107–117.

Smith, Linda C. "Selected Artificial Intelligence Techniques in Information Retrieval Systems Research." Ph.D. dissertation, Syracuse University, 1979.

Sparck Jones, Karen. "Automatic Indexing," *Journal of Documentation* 30 (1974): 393–432.

———. "Index Term Weighting," *Information Storage and Retrieval* 9 (November 1973): 619–633.

———. "Performance Averaging for Recall and Precision," *Journal of Informatics* 2 (1978): 95–105.

———. "Progress in Documentation: Automatic Indexing," *Journal of Documentation* 30, no. 4 (December 1974): 393–432.

———. "Retrieval System Tests 1958–1978." In *Information Retrieval Experiment*, pp. 213–255. Edited by K. Sparck Jones. London: Butterworth, 1981.

———. "A Statistical Interpretation of Term Specificity and Its Application in Retrieval," *Journal of Documentation* 28, no. 1 (March 1972): 11–21.

———, ed. *Information Retrieval Experiment*. London: Butterworth, 1981.

Spencer, Mima, and Rothenber, Diane. "Building an Online Full-Text Files: A Case Study of the ERIC Digest File." In *Proceedings of the 6th National Online Meeting: 1985*, pp. 439–444. Medford, N.J.: Learned Information, Inc., 1985.

———. "ERIC Digests Online: Developing a New Full Text File." In *Proceedings of the 9th International Online Information Meeting, London, December 1986*, pp. 85–94. Oxford, England: Learned Information, Ltd., 1986.

Spigai, Fran, and Somer, Peter. *Guide to Electronic Publishing*. White Plains, N.Y.: Knowledge Industry Publications, Inc., 1982.

Sprowl, James A. "WESTLAW vs. LEXIS: Computer Assisted Legal Research Comes of Age," *Program* 15, no. 3 (1981): 132–141.

Stein, D., Parker, W., Hollan, C., and Kiron, A. "Full Text Online Patent Searching: Results of a USPTO Experiment." In *Proceedings of the Online '82 Conference, Atlanta, GA. November 1982*, pp. 289–294. Weston, Conn.: Online Inc., 1982.

Steinacker, I. "Indexing and Automatic Significance Analysis," *Journal of the American Society for Information Science* 25, no. 4 (July-August 1974): 237–241.

Stanfill, Craig, and Kahle, Brewster. "Parallel Free-Text Search on the Connection Machine System," *Communications of the ACM* 29, no. 12 (1986): 1229–1239.

Stevens, M. E. *Automatic Indexing: A State-of-the-Art Report*. Washington, D.C.: National Bureau of Standards, 1970.

Stone, Don C., and Rubinoff, Morris. "Statistical Generation of a Technical Vocabulary," *American Documentation* 19, no. 4 (October 1968): 411–412.

Suchman, E. A. *Evaluative Research, Principles and Practices in Public Service and Social Action Programs*. New York: Russell Sage Foundation, 1967.

Svenonius, Elaine. "Directions for Research in Indexing, Classification and Cataloging," *Library Resources and Technical Services* 25 (January/March 1981): 88–103.

———. "An Experiment in Index Term Frequency," *Journal of the American Society for Information Science* 23 (1972): 109–121.

Swanson, Don R. "Searching Natural Language Text by Computer," *Science* 132 (October 1960): 1099–1104.

Swanson, Rowena Weiss. "Performing Evaluation Studies in Information Science,"

Journal of the American Society for Information Science 26 (May/June 1975): 140–156.

Tague, Jean M. "The Pragmatics of Information Retrieval Experimentation." In *Information Retrieval Experiment*, pp. 59–102. Edited by Karen Sparck Jones. London: Butterworth, 1981.

Tague, Jean M., and Farradune, J. "Estimation and Reliability of Retrieval Effectiveness Measures," *Information Processing and Management* 14, no. 1 (1978): 1–16.

Tapper, Colin. *Computer and the Law*. London: Weidenfield and Nicolson, 1973.

Tenopir, Carol. "Contributions of Value Added Fields and Full-Text Searching in Full-Text Databases." In *Proceedings of the 6th National Online Meeting, 1985*, pp. 463–470. Medford, N.J.: Learned Information, Inc., 1985.

———. "Full Text Databases," *Annual Review of Information Science and Technology* 19 (1984): 215–246.

———. "Full Text Databases Retrieval Performance," *Online Review* 9 (1985): 149–164.

———. "Newspapers Online," *Library Journal* 109, no. 4 (March 1, 1984): 452–453.

———. "Online '83 in Chicago," *Library Journal* 108, no. 22 (December 15, 1983): 2310–2311.

———. "Online Information in the Health Sciences," *Library Journal* 108, no. 18 (October 15 1983): 1932–1933.

———. "Retrieval Performance in a Full Text Journal Article Database." Ph.D. dissertation, University of Illinois, 1984.

———. "Search Strategies for Full Text Databases." In *Proceedings of the 51st Annual Meeting of the American Society for Information Science, Atlanta, October 1988*, pp. 80–86. Medford, N.J.: Learned Information, Inc., 1988.

———. "Users and Uses of Full Text Databases." In *Proceedings of the International Online Meeting, London, December 1988*, pp. 263–270. Oxford, England: Learned Information, Ltd., 1988.

Tenopir, Carol, Nahl-Jakobovits, Diane, and Howard, Dara Lee. "Magazines Online: An Investigation of Users and Uses of Full Text." In *Proceedings of the 52nd Meeting of the American Society for Information Science, Washington, D.C. November 1989*. Medford, N.J.: Learned Information, Inc., 1989.

Tenopir, Carol, and Shu, Man Evena. "Magazines in Full Text: Uses and Search Strategies," *Online Review* 13, no. 2, (1989): 107–118.

Terrant, Seldon W. "The Computer and Publishing," *Annual Review of Information Science and Technology* 10 (1975): 273–301.

———. "Computers in Publishing," *Annual Review of Information Science and Technology* 15 (1980): 191–219.

———. "Special Report: Publishing Scientific Information Today . . . and Tomorrow," *Chemical and Engineering News* 61, no. 17 (April 25, 1983): 51–58.

Terrant, Seldon W., Garson, Lorrin R., and Meyers, Barbara E. "Online Searching—Full Text of American Chemical Society Primary Journals," *Journal of Chemical Information and Computer Science* 24, no. 4 (1984): 230–235.

Tousignaut, Dwight R. "Indexing: Old Methods, New Concepts," *The Indexer* 15, no. 4 (1987): 197–204.

Van Rijsbergen, Cornelis J. "Retrieval Effectiveness." In *Information Retrieval Experiment*, pp. 32–43. Edited by K. Sparck Jones. London: Butterworth, 1981.

Veith, Richard. "Videotex and Teletext," *Annual Review of Information Science and Technology* 18 (1983): 3–28.

Vickery, Alina, Brooks, Helen, and Rovinson, Bruce. "A Reference and Referral System Using Expert System Techniques," *Journal of Documentation* 43, no. 1 (1987): 1–23.

Wade, Stephen, Willett, Peter, Robinson, Bruce, Vickery, Brian, and Vickery, Alina. "A Comparison of Knowledge-Based and Statistically-Based Techniques for Reference Retrieval," *Online Review* 12, no. 2 (1988): 91–108.

Wagers, R. "The Decision to Search Databases Full Text." In *Proceedings of the 10th International Online Information Meeting, London, December 1986*, pp. 93–107. Oxford, England: Learned Information, Ltd., 1986.

Walker, Donald E. "Text Analysis: Session Introduction." In *Proceedings of the Conference on Applied Natural Language Processing*, February 1983, pp. 107–108. Santa Monica, Calif.: Association for Computational Linguistics, 1983.

Wanger, Judith, and Landau, Ruth N. "Nonbibliographic On-Line Data Base Services," *Journal of the American Society for Information Science* 31, no. 3 (May 1980): 171–180.

Wanger, Judith, McDonald, Dennis, and Berger, Mary. *Evaluation of the Online Process: Final Report*. Santa Monica, Calif.: Cuadra Associates, 1980.

Watters, C. R., Shepherd, M. A., Grundke, E. W., and Bodorik, P. "Integration of Menu Retrieval and Boolean Retrieval from a Full-Text Database," *Online Review* 9, no. 5 (1985): 391–401.

Weinberg, Bella H. "Interactions of Statistical Phenomena in Human and Automatic Indexing." In *Proceedings of the 45th ASIS Annual Meeting*, 1982, pp. 324–326. Washington, D.C.: ASIS, 1982.

———. "Multiple Sets of Human Indexing for Civil Engineering Documents: Comparison of Structure and Occurrence Rates in Full Text," *Science and Technology Libraries* 2, no. 3 (Spring 1982): 13–33.

———. "Word Frequency and Automatic Indexing." Ph.D. dissertation, Columbia University, 1981.

———. "Word Frequency Data in Full Text Data Base Searching." In *Proceedings of the 5th National Online Meeting, New York, April 1984*, pp. 425–432. Medford, N.J.: Learned Information, Inc., 1984.

Weinberg, Bella H., and Cunningham, Julie A. "Online Search Strategy and Term Frequency Statistics." In *Proceedings of the 46th ASIS Annual Meeting, 1983*, pp. 32–35. Washington, D.C.: ASIS, 1983.

Wellisch, Hans, H. *Indexing and Abstracting: An International Bibliography*. Santa Barbara, Calif.: ABC-Clio, 1980.

Wiberley, Stephen E. "Subject Access in the Humanities and the Precision of the Humanist's Vocabulary," *Library Quarterly* 53 (October 1983): 420–433.

Williams, J. H., Jr., and Perriens, M. P. "Automatic Full Text Indexing and Searching System." In *Proceedings of Information System Symposium, Washington, D.C. September 1968*, pp. 335–350. Gaithersburg, Md.: IBM, 1968.

Williams, Martha E. "Analysis of Terminology in Various CAS Data Files as Access Points for Retrieval," *Journal of Chemical Information and Computer Sciences* 17 (1977): 16–20.

Winker, Karen J. "Chemical Society Offers Full Texts of Scholarly Journals by Computer," *The Chronicle of Higher Education* 22 (June 1983): 23–24.

Winter, Don, Lindgren, Nilo, Kaye, Judy, and Stewart, Don. *System Concepts for Network Use of Full-Text Files*. Pasadena, Calif.: Xerox Electro-Optical Systems, 1977.

Zipf, G. *Human Behavior and the Principle of Least Effort*. New York: Addison-Wesley, 1949.

Zuga, Connie. "Full Text Databases: Design Considerations for the Database Vendor." In *Proceedings of the 7th International Online Information Meeting, London, December 1983*, pp. 427–434. Oxford, England: Learned Information, Ltd., 1983.

Index

Abbott, J. P.: on comparison of chemistry databases, 80; on proximity operators, 190; on retrospective information, 204

Absolute frequency theories, effectiveness of, 153–57. *See also* Frequency theories

Absolute recall, defined, 77

Abstracts, anaphoric terms in, 212; compared to full text retrieval, 113–14; and controlled vocabulary searching, 112, 126; increased precision, 122; jargon in, 127–28; and language inconsistency, 126, 127; relevance judgment, 193, 200. *See also* Value-added fields

ACS. *See* American Chemical Society

ACS Journal Online (CFTX): development online systems, 40; precision of full text (Love and Garson), 81

ACS Primary Journal Database, on BRS, 40

Additional indexes (DIALOG), creation of, 53(figure). *See also* Basic index; Inverted index

ADJ operators (BRS), 138. *See also* Adjacency operators

Adjacency operators: compared, 60–61; to specify multi-word concepts, 198. *See also* ADJ operators (BRS); Proximity operators

Adonis, described, 16–17

Aesthetics of system display: considerations, 204; hardware dependence, 4; highlighting of search terms, 176; improvements, 16; recommendations, 176

Affective behavior in online searching, 179, 185–87

Agora databases, 34

Aitchison, T. M.: on automatic language enhancement, 201; on retrieval performance, 70

All England Law Reports, 75–76

American Bar Foundation and International Business Machines Project, 76

American Chemical Society (ACS): comparison of databases, 80–81; full text retrieval testing, 40; user studies, 71–73

American Documentation Institute (ADI): comparison of full text and abstracts, 78

Anaphoric terms: in abstracts, 212–13; defined, 212

About the Authors

CAROL TENOPIR is Associate Professor in the School of Library and Information Studies at the University of Hawaii. Her areas of interest are database searching, full text databases, and database design. She is the author or coauthor of several books and has published extensively in the technical literature.

JUNG SOON RO is Associate Professor in the Department of Library Science at Hannam University in Korea. Her present area of interest is information storage and retrieval.